Vocational Instruction

VOCATIONAL INSTRUCTION

Edited by
Aleene A. Cross

American Vocational Association

Staff Editor: Toni H. Lydecker

ISBN: 0-89514-007-1

Published 1979 by
The American Vocational Association, Inc.
2020 North Fourteenth Street
Arlington, Virginia 22201

Printed in the United States of America

INTRODUCTION

Vocational Instruction is a book about the teaching and learning process, about teachers and students. The authors have written about unique programs and adaptations of accepted principles, concepts and methods to vocational education. Readers may discover new ideas, find reinforcement for their own practices or recognize the philosophical base for decisions they and other educators make every day.

This book deals with six major areas related to instruction: foundations of instruction, curriculum planning and development, instructional strategies, instruction for students with special needs, student organizations as an integral part of instruction and the appraisal of the instructional process.

Effective instruction has a base in the foundations of learning. This section contains three chapters that emphasize humanistic and affective education. The other chapters give attention to the role of leadership and supervision in improving instruction.

The curriculum section includes a chapter on the principles of curriculum planning, as well as chapters on competency-based programs. Expectations and standards are discussed in another chapter. The use of research data and employer needs as bases for instruction are the topics of the last two chapters.

The first two chapters in the instructional strategies section focus on individualized instruction. The third chapter explores several uses of materials and techniques appropriate for vocational education. There are also chapters on career development, the use of military curriculum materials and the importance of instructional media.

Students with handicaps and other special needs pose challenges for vocational instruction and administration. It is hoped that this section will provide new ideas, as well as a comprehensive summary of instruction for a variety of special needs students. Two chapters discuss special instructional techniques for mentally handicapped and minority students. Others give suggestions for curriculum modification and classroom management for students with special needs.

Student organizations provide a unique contribution to the vocational education instructional process when they are an integral part of the curriculum and when their activities are used to make instruction relevant to the daily lives of students. Three of the student organizations are used as examples: Future Farmers of America, Future Homemakers of America, and Distributive Education Clubs of America.

Appraisal of the outcomes of instruction provides feedback to students, parents, administrators and possible employers, as well as to the teacher. One of the two chapters in the final section of this book focuses on assessment as a base for instructional evaluation and the other deals with appraisal techniques.

Vocational Instruction is designed for secondary and post-secondary teachers, administrators, supervisors and teacher educators. The authors have addressed several of the major concerns of educators in all occupational specialties. The content is appropriate for a college text and as a practical reference for classroom instructors.

Effective teachers are also learners—they never cease to be students. They learn from their own students, from their experiences in directing learning, from life's experiences and from inquiry. I hope this yearbook will enhance the effectiveness of all vocational educators who read it.

A.A.C.
Athens, Georgia
July 1979

CONTENTS

Introduction

I. The Foundations of Learning

II. Planning and Developing the Curriculum

III. Instructional Strategies

IV. Instruction for Students with Special Needs

V. Student Organizations: An Integral Part of Instruction

VI. The Appraisal of Instruction

Yearbook Authors

THE FOUNDATIONS OF LEARNING

1.
THE BASIS FOR HUMANISTIC EDUCATION

Morrell J. Clute

Crimes against people are increasing in society as a whole. In particular, violence in schools and among youth is staggering. Significantly, police departments report that more than 75 percent of homicides are committed by people who know their victims. Violence, brutality, alienation and feelings of worthlessness have come to be prominent characteristics of our society.

School administrators often say that "hoodlums" outside the school are causing the trouble in the schools. The tragedy of that response is that usually those hoodlums were once students in the school.

Violent behavior is an outward expression of violent feelings within. We are facing a tremendous challenge to identify those forces that contribute to students' feelings of defeat, anger, hostility and worthlessness.

ANSWERING HUMAN GROWTH NEEDS

Though schools have not caused the increase in violence and crime, they have major responsibility for the healthy growth of children and youth. Therefore, we must do all that is possible to reduce the development of feelings that are destructive to positive growth. We must be as adamant in identifying the negative side effects of educational practices that may increase a student's feelings of hostility toward himself or herself and society as we are in requiring that the pharmaceutical industry determine accurately what the side effects of a drug may be before it is released on the market.

A careful examination of all educational theory, organization and practice can determine the long-range positive or negative effects they may have on basic human growth needs. We must eliminate all conditions in our educational institutions that cause students to feel helpless, fearful, hostile or worthless. How an individual feels about himself or herself is often more important in determining behavior than what he or she knows.

Organized education can help students to become more competent, independent and cooperative, and to understand and accept themselves and others. This humanistic need must be the all-encompassing concern of education.

PERCEPTIONS DEPEND ON PAST EXPERIENCE

Dr. Adelbert Ames, Jr., who did research in visual perception at Hanover, New Hampshire, from 1938 to 1948, was among the first to show the relationship between past experiences and human uniqueness. He demonstrated that what we see, hear, taste, smell or feel is dependent for its selection and its meaning upon past experience. This means that what is stored in the brain from experience is all any of us has with which to make meaning from our perceptions. A person who has limited or narrow experience derives limited meanings and narrow selections from the environment.

The personal meaning we find in each clue or situation is limited or modified by our own purposes and experiences. As we change or add to our experiences, we increase our potential for learning. One of the most significant breakthroughs in the last 20 years is the recognition that intelligence is as alterable as other human talents. Research with the federally funded Headstart programs has provided sound evidence, for example, that intelligence can be altered by broadening experience. To gain some understanding of the importance of past experience and its relationship to classroom practice, we need to understand the significance of human uniqueness.

Human Uniqueness

To demonstrate the miracle of uniqueness, I ask my graduate students to look at all the faces in the room. I then ask them to marvel at how different each person looks from every other. Moreover, there are approximately four billion people on earth and no person is exactly like another. In other words, each person is unique.

Every human being has the potential for creation, production and service, and no one has the ability to predict for another individual what that person can achieve. There is no limit to human potential.

People from all periods of time, all geographic areas, all cultures have contributed concepts, insights and understanding that have made possible the tremendous social and technological changes of today. It appears that the strengths of our society come from our differences.

We have thus reached the greatest stage of world interdependence ever known. Our existence depends upon worldwide cooperation. The challenge for education, then, is to nurture the value of differences in societies, cultures and individuals.

Implications of Uniqueness for Schools

Perhaps the greatest violation by schools of the concept of uniqueness has been the inability to value the range of differences in human abilities. Think of all the different kinds of work that have to be done in order for a community to survive. *The Dictionary of Occupational Titles* (U.S. Department of Labor, 1977) lists over 25,000 job titles that require specific talents.

When so many different kinds of human talent are necessary to our survival and well-being, why is it that schools have valued so few? Schools communicate to students that the only kind of worthwhile human talent is academic. It may turn out that other skills are equally important for our success as a society.

Calvin Taylor (1968) urges schools to be talent developers as well as knowledge dispensers. He reports that of more than 135 traits of intelligence identified, 80 are measurable. If these 80 human talents were grouped into six categories—academic, decision making, creative, forecasting, planning and communications—90 percent of all students in a school system would be above average in at least one of the talent areas. Therefore, if we educators really want to help develop human potential, we must nurture the growth of a variety of human talents.

Need for Communication

Though each of us is different from every other individual, we all have a desperate need to relate to and communicate with others. Of course, our very survival in the early years of life depends upon the care of others, but perhaps more importantly, our intelligence develops only through interaction with other human beings. The cortex of the brain develops only through the stimulation of communication with others. Healthy growth depends not only upon verbal communication, but on all the other senses, particularly on the tactile communication that comes through loving care. "Dullness" is probably a learned response to a sterile environment.

Education is the process of searching for meaning, but meaning for each individual will to some degree be different. This is precisely the problem that has confounded education ever since it became an institutionalized process. Since learners have their own unique past experiences and unique patterns for growth, no one method or no resource material is adequate for all. This is why there is no research that reports that one particular method is better than another. One method will be appropriate to one student's learning style, while another may employ an entirely different style.

UNIQUENESS AND THE LEARNING ENVIRONMENT

Fortunately, we do know a great deal about conditions that facilitate an individual's learning. Learning is an individual responsibility. The belief that a teacher transfers knowledge directly to a student is nonsense. Each person gives himself or herself to learning or withholds himself or herself from it.

What teachers really do—and this is a highly developed professional skill—is to manage a learning environment. Good teachers know that "telling ain't teaching," that a classroom group is made up of individual students who learn at different rates and in different ways.

It is now possible for a teacher to determine far more precisely the cognitive style of an individual. One of the most promising concepts now in use is the process of cognitive mapping developed by Dr. Joseph Hill, president of Oakland Community College:

> Oakland Community College accepts the premise that no two students seek meaning in exactly the same manner. We believe that 90 percent of the students with normal ability can learn 90 percent of the material 90 percent of the time if the teaching methods and media are adjusted to the student's educational cognitive style. The College maps the cognitive style of each student to provide a picture of the various ways in which the individual searches for meaning. Each student has a relatively unique cognitive style or way of seeking meaning or knowing.
>
> Cognitive styles are determined by the way individuals take note of their surroundings—how they seek meaning, how they become informed. Are they listeners or are they readers? Are they concerned only with their own viewpoints or are they influenced in decision making by their families or associates? Do they reason as mathematicians, or as social scientists, or as automotive mechanics?
>
> These are but a few examples of the facets of human makeup that are included in a student's cognitive style. Family background, life experiences, and personal goals make each of us unique. Each map reflects each student's cognitive style. A cognitive map provides a picture of the diverse ways in which an individual acquires meaning. It identifies cognitive strengths and weaknesses. This information can be used to build a personalized program of instruction (Hill, 1976).

Gains in Brain Research

Exciting new evidence from brain research and split brain theory explains why traditional approaches to education have been so ineffective. Leslie Hart (1978) suggests that the schools are now largely "brain antagonistic" and that much of school practice is "brain incompatible." This speaks to the need to provide for and respect individualized learning. Hart reviews five areas of findings from brain research that may explain the ineffectiveness of standard classroom teaching for large numbers of students, concluding that: "The human brain is intensely aggressive. Each brain is highly individual, unique; it seeks out, demands, and will accept only what it needs next to 'make sense' of surrounding reality."

If students are to progress in knowledge and achievement, they must be in an environment that is safe to explore and where mistakes are seen as positive indicators that learning is in progress. The obvious way to avoid mistakes is not to try. This has always been known by understanding teachers, but new brain research provides further evidence. Again, Hart reports:

> The neocortex, the newest part of the brain and in humans nearly five-sixths of the whole, does not function well under pressure, or what in Proster Theory is called "threat." It cuts short its elaborate, relatively slow processing, and "downshifts," so that the much older limbic system has more influence. When students see classroom activities as threatening, the learning that should occur in the neocortex is inhibited.

The Teacher Is Crucial

The teacher is crucial to the classroom climate. The teacher's self-concept has much to do with how he or she functions in a classroom. How teachers use their own uniqueness will be a measure of their effectiveness. It is precisely this uniqueness in teachers that makes it possible for a school to facilitate the learning of a large number of students. What students don't find in one teacher, they may find in another.

How a teacher feels about his or her students is an extremely important aspect of a learning environment attuned to student achievement. The teacher's expectations and values, the congruence between speech and action, and his or her willingness to listen and understand are now known to be essential to student achievement.

Some of the most significant research of this century was done by Aspy and Roebuck (1976), who measured the correlation between student achievement and the humane characteristics of a teacher in a learning environment.

The mass of evidence collected by the National Consortium for Humanizing Education from research sponsored in forty-two states and seven foreign countries provides conclusive evidence that students in classrooms where teachers are operating with high levels of empathy, congruence and positive regard achieve significantly more than do students in classrooms where these conditions do not exist. When these conditions are lacking, discipline problems and negative attitudes toward school are likely to arise.

We can no longer afford the ineffectiveness of non-humanistic approaches to learning. Research has supplied overwhelming evidence that people develop to their full potential only when their experiences nurture feelings of worth and adequacy. Doing the wrong thing harder will not help.

A NEW NEED FOR BALANCE IN THE CURRICULUM

Educators have long advocated balance in the curriculum, meaning that there should be a variety of offerings to meet the large variety of student needs. This type of curriculum is now receiving significant support based on a new source of evidence. Split-brain theory and research is providing substantial data showing the different functioning of the right hemisphere of the brain compared with the functioning of the left side.

Most instruction in schools is oriented to the left brain functions—reading, writing, arithmetic. The right side has more to do with qualitative intelligence or experiential learning such as music, art, imagery, intuition. Interestingly, we are finding more and more evidence that experiences affecting the right side are preconditional to the development of cognitive skills on the left side. Thus, the recent tendency to label all parts of the curriculum that do not deal with cognitive skill development as a frill is a tremendous barrier to learning. It will be pure madness if lack of school finances and the "Back to Basics Movement" cause schools to eliminate those aspects of the curriculum that stimulate right brain activity.

The appropriate concern for curriculum developers must become the balance between right brain experiences and left brain experiences. The evidence is solid that students in school programs offering a curriculum balanced between right and left hemisphere activities have produced higher test scores in the basic areas.

A Need for Humanistic Education

This chapter has focused on human uniqueness, its significance, and the problems that educators must address if optimum learning is to be provided for all youth. Feelings of hostility, anger and defeat must be reduced if the quality of life is to improve. There is a great need in America for an educational system that respects the individual and recognizes human variability. Humanistic education encompasses these major dimensions.

Humanistic education is a commitment to education and practice in which all facets of the teaching-learning process give major emphasis to the freedom, value, worth, dignity and integrity of all persons. Education models developed from this base will be distinctly different from those industrial models that consider students as products and talk about a delivery system. That very language identifies them for what they are—systems designed to produce mass conformity. Uniqueness is the most precious characteristic of humanity. When uniqueness is respected, individuals are valued. People who are treated decently achieve more than people who are not.

REFERENCES

Aspy, David, and Roebuck, Flora. *A lever long enough.* Washington, D.C.: National Consortium for Humanistic Education, Catholic University, 1976.

Cantril, Hadler. *The morning notes of Adelbert Ames, Jr.* New Brunswick, N.J.: Rutgers University Press, 1960.

Combs, Art, et al. *Humanistic education: Objectives and assessment.* Washington, D.C.: Association for Supervision and Curriculum Development, 1978.

The Basis for Humanistic Education

Grady, Michael P., and Luecke, Emily A. *Education and the brain.* Bloomington, Ind.: Phi Delta Kappa Educational Foundation, 1978.

Hart, Leslie. The new brain concept of learning. *Phi Delta Kappan,* February 1978.

Hill, Joseph E. *The educational sciences.* Bloomfield Hills, Mich.: Oakland Community College, 1976.

Taylor, Calvin. As well as knowledge dispensers. *Education Today,* December 1968.

U.S. Department of Labor. *Dictionary of occupational titles.* Washington, D.C.: U.S. Government Printing Office, 1977.

THE FOUNDATIONS OF LEARNING

2.
THE HUMANISTIC TEACHER

L. H. Newcomb

The late 1960s and early 1970s were a period of unparalleled growth for vocational education. Society wanted more and better vocational education and was willing to pay for it. As programs were conceived, planned and enacted, there was a tremendous challenge for state and local leaders to provide adequate facilities and equipment.

In initiating programs, the last consideration was an adequate cadre of competent and compassionate teachers. In fact, some would argue that because vocational teachers have often been trained with little regard for their interests and talents, they are not humanistic enough in teaching their own students. Masterful vocational teachers must be highly competent in their field of technical expertise. But they must be more than that.

Vocational teachers must possess pedagogical competence, i.e., competence in the art and science of teaching. A teacher who is highly knowledgeable and skilled in his or her technical area, but who does not possess a high level of pedagogical competence is fulfilling only part of the requisites for a good teacher. A teacher must be both technically and pedagogically competent.

It seems reasonable to insist that vocational teachers must be technically competent, skilled in the art and science of teaching, and humane. Edgar Dale (1974) defines humane as "related to man's tender and compassionate feelings." He further asks, ". . . Do we work in schools . . . to build a humanity that relates us tenderly and compassionately with other people?"

That question is the central focus of this chapter. Let us now turn our attention to the specifics of how to become a humanistic teacher.

CARING FOR THE STUDENT

Perhaps a good beginning point for a teacher who wishes to be humanistic is to realize that students are worthwhile, vulnerable people. They often become sophisticated very early in life, perhaps as a survival or coping mechanism. A part of the sophistication includes hiding behind false facades that can mislead the typical teacher.

Humanistic teachers on the other hand work at seeing behind these facades. They recognize that their students are insecure even when they act like bullies. They sense the hidden fears, hopes and dreams of those they teach and therefore they treat each student as an individual.

Humanistic teachers also realize that their students want to receive caring attention. Students in intensive vocational classes (two or more hours per day) may spend more time with their teacher than with their parents. Thus, this sense of being cared about becomes important and real to the maturing individual.

Humanistic teachers are not naive or overly idealistic. Like other teachers, they do not like everything their students do. However, humanistic teachers do not stereotype their students and they realize that poor behavior is partly the manifestation of a desire for recognition and individual attention. Though humanistic teachers must deal firmly with disruptive students, they do so in a sincere, caring manner.

Many Students Ignored

Most teachers would argue that they care about students, but sometimes they forget to show their concern. Not only do teachers sometimes deal with their students in less than humane ways, but they may also completely ignore individual students.

In a number of instances, for example, certain students in large high schools have been followed and observed daily for a week. Much to the astonishment of all concerned, many of these students were ignored totally day in and day out by both their teachers and classmates. Unless their names were called for the purpose of checking attendance, they were never acknowledged. These students were treated as though they did not exist, as though they were brooms standing against a wall. Not only did their teachers totally ignore their presence, but these students' classmates also did nothing to acknowledge their existence.

Chances are that each vocational teacher reading these words knows students who are treated in this manner. The students affected know too. What effect does such treatment have on students? One can be sure it is not a desirable effect.

Students Are Sensitive

Though students who are ignored or treated inhumanely may not protest, they still feel the effects of this treatment. They become aware of the lack of concern and caring both through what uncaring teachers say and by what they do not say.

You have undoubtedly heard the expression, "Your actions speak so loud, I can't hear a word you say." Teachers who lack humaneness often speak to students in ways that strip them of their sense of worth.

18

Perhaps even more devastating and dehumanizing to the "left out" and "put down" students are the nonverbal communiques issued by some teachers. When a teacher offers no smiles, nods or other facial evidences of trust and belief that students can perform, the students decode these nonverbal messages and decide, justifiably, that their teacher sees them as persons of little or no worth. Under these circumstances, students often begin to believe accordingly.

The important thing to remember is that students are indeed able to tell if their teacher cares about them as worthwhile human beings. Both parties have a part to play. But the teacher must assume the leadership needed for maintaining or restoring humaneness in the classroom and laboratory.

A GOOD SELF-CONCEPT

Newcomb (1977) suggests that the teacher all of us want to be has a personality that others react to positively. Such teachers are people-centered, not knowledge-centered. They are teachers of students, not teachers of subject matter. They are big enough to go around, big enough for all the students to have a part of them.

Humanistic teachers are more than purveyors of facts. They know that technology is expanding too quickly for anyone to teach or try to learn all the facts. Therefore, they work to help people learn how to solve problems rather than remember the solutions of others. They are guides, philosophers and friends to students.

Newcomb points out that we have not yet and never will fully describe the teacher. Certainly, humanistic teachers possess all the qualities outlined and many more. There are thousands of these teachers and they all appear to be different. This is true because effective teachers are individuals.

Effective Teachers Like Themselves

According to Felker (1974), "Self-concept is the sum total of the view which an individual has of himself." Effective teachers have positive self-concepts. That is, they see themselves accurately and like what they see. They know their own values, feelings, fears, hopes. They know what they have been and what they wish to become and are pleased with that knowledge. They perceive that they can be of value to others and get on with the task. They believe what they are doing is worthwhile and are glad they have decided to do it.

Moreover, they feel good about their students and know how to help them feel good about themselves. Their mission is to help others be successful rather than to be failures. When the teacher who makes a difference walks into the classroom, the nonverbal message is, as Dr. Charles Galloway of Ohio State University puts it, "I'm glad I'm here because you're here, and before today's class ends you'll be glad you're here, too." The non-humanistic teacher's body language says, on the other hand,

"I'm not glad I'm here, and before you leave today, you'll wish you weren't here, too."

How can teachers do a better job in helping their students develop positive self-concepts? Felker says, "The people who are important to him [the student] influence what he [the student] thinks of himself."

Combs (1976) says that the "notions about self-concept are probably the greatest contributions that we have from psychology. The self-concept is learned by an individual; learned over a period of time by the ways the individual is treated. Once the self-concept is developed, it is rather stable, but can be changed over time."

Unfortunately, many may feel the self-concept is a terribly mysterious psychological construct that they are not capable of handling without sophisticated training. However, this is not the case. Most teachers can help their students develop better self-concepts if they become: (1) sensitive to the notion of the self-concept, (2) committed to acting positively with regard to that sensitivity, and (3) willing to put forth the needed effort.

A Dramatic Piece of Evidence

Let me offer a dramatic piece of evidence to support the importance of the self-concept. A classic example is the work of Robert Rosenthall, who gave a standardized test to a wide range of students. The test purported to predict students who were about to experience a great spurt in academic achievement. Actually, it measured nothing. The tests were never even scored.

He then randomly selected 20 percent of the students in each class and told the teachers that these students would experience phenomenal spurts in achievement during that school year. And guess what? They did. At the end of the year, the randomly identified students had experienced significantly more academic growth than would be expected. That year, those students were treated differently by the teachers. The teachers thought the students could achieve, the students sensed that belief in them and this made a difference.

It is no wonder, then, that we can visit one classroom or laboratory and hear the teacher say, "Hey, these kids are great—I wish I had a hundred like them," while another teacher says, "I sure wish they'd send me some decent kids. How can anyone do anything with these losers?" To us as visitors, both groups of students seem similar and they are—but not to the two teachers. The first teacher will make a difference for the better in the lives of his or her students. The second teacher will add to the burdens of his or her students' existence.

SIX TYPES OF ACTIVITIES

Teachers must set conditions and create experiences that cause students to succeed rather than fail. The education students experience under our guidance must be success oriented rather than failure oriented.

Six broad categories of activities for helping students improve their self-concept are offered here. My colleagues and I have used these methods and know they produce results.

Home Visits

Home visits are a requisite to understanding each student. The best way to get to know students is to visit them and their parents at home. One must remember that the teacher does not go to the home to "snoopervise" or inspect, but to gain a better understanding of each student and to show he or she cares.

The payoff from improved understanding and appreciation is unbelievable. A teacher must experience the quality the home visit adds to his or her effectiveness with each student in order to realize the full potential of this activity. Students learn only that which personally affects them. By getting to know students personally through the home visit, teachers are able to individualize their instruction better.

My suggestion to vocational teachers is to make five home visits and if it doesn't enable them to become more humane teachers and to teach their students more effectively, forget the suggestion. If this technique does produce the desired results, all their students can profit from such visits. In the long run, the teacher is the real winner because he or she gives more to the students and in turn receives more satisfaction from teaching.

Student Organizations

Another appropriate and effective way to get to know your students better is through working with them in vocational student organizations. Many students who may not "turn on to" classroom or laboratory work may show an entirely different side of themselves as they participate in organizational activities. As teachers coach and advise students in vocational student organization activities, they will get to know the students better as individuals.

Student organization advisors must "have a genuine and sincere interest in helping [students] develop [their] abilities and interests . . ." (Bender, Hansen, Newcomb and Taylor, 1979). The well-managed student organization offers powerful avenues for motivating students as well as for recognizing them and helping them to feel accepted and liked.

Special Projects

Teachers can also get to know their students better through helping them work on special projects. A special project can be any project in which the student has a great interest and which is not required by the teacher. Such a project may be big or small, simple or complex. The important thing is that the student wishes to do it.

Perhaps the horticulture student comes to the teacher and asks to make a special flower arrangement in lab today. By helping the student complete this special project, the teacher can strengthen the bond with him or her. Their humanity will have grown together.

School-Sponsored Functions

Teachers can get to know their students better through avenues other than vocational classes. There are significant opportunities for seeing the whole individual in many school-sponsored functions.

Vocational students are very excited when teachers take time to see them participate and perhaps excel in school functions such as athletics, music, drama or student government. Students crave the personal recognition given by teachers who have personally witnessed their performance in an extracurricular activity. By seeing students as whole persons, the teacher will know them better and, I believe, teach them better as a result.

Personal Chats

Teachers should take the time to initiate personal chats with each student. Students often feel that teachers are "different" from other people. If you don't believe this, just watch what happens in the summer if a teacher goes to the local swimming pool. The kids cannot believe it. You'll hear comments such as, "Can you believe Mr. Cartney is wearing those red swimming trunks?" And if the teacher jumps in the pool, the kids will probably all bail out. They are convinced something is wrong.

Teachers create this myth, so they can remove it. The easiest way is to show personal interest in each student and take time to have a simple person-to-person visit from time to time.

Calculated Success Experiences

Finally, vocational teachers need to use "calculated success experiences" to make their teaching more humanistic. All people need to experience a feeling of success. Teachers can do much more to help meet this need. Learning experiences and assignments that are tailored for individual students must be provided, especially for those who need to have some success. When the student successfully completes the task, the teacher is able to give legitimate praise and recognition.

A PLAN FOR PROGRESS

Perhaps the easiest way for a teacher to develop a plan for progress is to begin by evaluating the need for a change in behavior. To evaluate the potential benefits of becoming more humanistic and doing a better job of helping students develop positive self-concepts, consider the following questions (Combs, 1976):

1. How can a person feel liked unless someone likes him or her?
2. How can a person feel wanted unless somebody wants him or her?

3. How can a person feel acceptable unless somewhere he or she is accepted?
4. How can a person feel he or she has dignity and integrity unless someone treats him or her accordingly?
5. How can someone feel competent unless he or she has some success?

These questions should provide the incentive for you to become a more humanistic teacher.

REFERENCES

Bender, R. E., Hansen, C., Newcomb, L. H., and Taylor R. *The FFA and you: Your guide to learning.* Danville, Ill.: The Interstate, 1979.

Combs, Arthur. Humanism and the self-concept in vocational education. Paper presented at a conference of Ohio vocational state staff leaders, Columbus, Ohio, 1976.

Dale, Edgar. *The humane leader.* Bloomington, Ind.: The Phi Delta Kappa Educational Foundation, 1974.

Felker, Donald W. *Building positive self-concepts.* Minneapolis, Minn.: Burgess, 1974.

Newcomb, L. H. It starts with the teacher. No. 1, *The heart of instruction* (a series of 13 booklets). Columbus, Ohio: Ohio Agricultural Education Curriculum Materials Service, 1977.

3.
AN EXEMPLARY MODEL FOR CHANGE

Helen A. Loftis

Vocational instructors are characteristically pragmatic in philosophy and practice. Those who wish to improve the quality of instruction devote full attention to the newest and best knowledge available, incorporating advanced technology into the development of marketable skills. The focus on doing, as opposed to an emphasis on human development, may appear contradictory. Yet the vocational instructor may find that "the way to do is to be" (Bynner, 1962). Perhaps change in vocational instruction is indicated, with a concern for human development not eliminating but taking precedence over pragmatic instructional goals.

THE SETTING FOR CHANGE

The world of the vocational instructor is complex with constantly changing demands and restraints. The classroom environment is a setting where teachers and students interact daily. A teacher brings to each encounter a unique personality with personal attitudes, values and perceptions. To this are added varying degrees of knowledge and skills in interpersonal relations.

The students, too, are highly diverse, creating a situation multiplied not only by the total number of persons, but including the interaction patterns between each individual and the group. In addition, all the teachers, administrators, students and employees within the school affect the vocational classroom. The larger community of parents and citizens must also be taken into account. Small wonder, then, that teachers need increased competence in interpersonal relationships.

The Teacher's Role

The teacher is the single most important factor in the total educational enterprise. He or she is the basic unit of the school organization and is capable of creative choices and actions if conditions that thwart these kinds of behaviors are removed and supporting conditions are developed (Chin and Benne, 1969).

When teachers achieve greater interpersonal development, they will be more effective in their professional roles and the learning enterprise will be enhanced. As Wolfe says, "Teachers teach as much of what they are as of what they know . . . The content one teaches may or may not directly affect the lives of students, but it appears certain that the perceptions which teachers and students have of one another affect the personal development of both" (1977).

Outcomes of Vocational Instruction

Like other teachers, the vocational teacher draws instructional goals from all categories of knowledge, attitudes and skills to be mastered by students. Unless affective or attitudinal goals are made explicit and become a guide for action, however, the desired learning is unlikely to occur. Although attention has been drawn to the absence of vocational education research which studies affective behavior (Travers, 1973), increasing consideration of affective learning is apparent (Murray, 1966, 1968; Wilhelm, 1968; Loftis, 1974, 1975, 1976, 1977, 1978; Stiffler, 1977).

Murray's research revealed that "self-actualizing" teachers will be perceived by their students as more concerned than non-self-actualizing teachers. Concern is the quality attributed to teachers by students who think the teacher knows, understands and helps them. In Stiffler's study, affective measures were correlated with indices of probable success in teaching. Students tested had participated in a teacher education program in which affective goals were important. Those students who completed the program scored well above the norms for college freshmen, juniors and seniors when they completed a measure of self-actualization as sophomores. The students were more highly self-actualizing than college students in general. The research conducted by Loftis at Winthrop College revealed similar outcomes for inservice teachers.

Affective learning becomes evident as the instructor and the student interact during the learning process. The teacher gains a better understanding of her or his own assets, beliefs and values and improves her or his competencies. In terms of human relationships, the teacher behaves in warm, empathetic ways, conscious and appreciative of cultural differences. Decisions concerning the instructional process tend to promote openness and critical thinking.

Will affective learning, with its long-lasting and vital outcomes, become characteristic of vocational instruction? Will gains be by design or serendipity? Vocational educators must not only draw on existing research dealing with change, but must increase their own efforts. Scott (1977) decribes the task: "We must be willing to take risks, to experiment, to learn, and to innovate in order to create growth, movement, and change in the institutions and organizational systems in which we live and work.

An Exemplary Model for Change

The focus on planned change has shifted from questions of "Should change be sought?" to "How to plan for particular changes for particular people in particular settings" (Bennis, Benne and Chin, 1969).

The Process of Change

The teacher who aspires to become a change agent must get his or her own act together. To state it another way, the change agent who would function successfully in relation to clients must be free of restrictive self-concerns. Rogers posed useful self-examination questions such as, "Can I *be* in some way which will be perceived by the other person as trustworthy, as dependable, as consistent in some deep sense? . . . Can I act with sufficient sensitivity in the relationship that my behavior will not be perceived as a threat?" (1969). Pondering such questions frees one to act toward acquiring knowledge and skills.

Teachers may begin a change process within their own classrooms. Here innovations may be tried, experimentation with different strategies risked and new personal behaviors practiced. Within this environment, the teacher can become an agent for change with the students as the benefactors.

The teacher can either influence change without official sanction or be selected by administrators or colleagues to assume the role of the change agent. The larger professional settings in organizations and the community provide opportunities for varying degrees of influence. The teacher may function in relation to a small group or committee or, indeed, may be responsible for serving an entire organization.

Knowledge and abilities required to effect change can be learned by the teacher. When vocational instructors have acquired the necessary understanding and skills, they can influence individuals, organizations and institutions. Essential to the entire enterprise is having teachers and other educational decision makers consider human factors and feelings as legitimate.

A MODEL OF INSERVICE TEACHER EDUCATION

Since 1972, the Department of Home Economics Education at Winthrop College has engaged in an innovative inservice teacher education program funded under the Education Professions Development Act (EPDA), Part F, Section 553. The model exemplifies a program in which affective concerns were primary. A series of institutes begun in June 1973 has had considerable impact on selected vocational teachers and administrators.

The change agents for the five projects were an adjunct staff fellow of the NTL Institute for Applied Behavioral Science who served as consultant and trainer and the Winthrop director who assisted with planning, logistical details and evaluation.

Descriptions and evaluation data from each project will be used to illustrate generalizations about teachers as change agents. The change agent emphasis for the teachers was made explicit only in the last project.

Vocational Instruction

The five EPDA projects conducted will be referred to as Institutes I, II, III (which was an extension of II), the Communications project and the Special Needs project.

The institutes were designed to help 48 experienced teachers (1) improve understanding, sensitivities and skills in interpersonal relationships; (2) develop clearer ideas of the consequences of personal behavior; (3) discover behavioral alternatives and decide whether to change behavior by choosing and practicing an alternative; and (4) generalize and apply learnings to back-home teaching situations. The themes of the three-week institutes were: building interpersonal trust; building subgroups and the total group into a system; interpersonal styles of behavior; feedback; group process; decision making by consensus; conflict; group decision making; involving students in decision making; and evaluation and application of learning.

The model of the third institute capitalized on the growing autonomy of the teachers. Since the teachers were able to design learning experiences for themselves, the institute was structured to facilitate group decision making. Although teachers continue to work on personal concerns, the total group activities centered on the process of group development and common needs. Among the activities designed and implemented by the teachers was a values clarification workshop. Those who had participated earlier in such a workshop were the teachers for their peers. Concepts were presented and strategies appropriate for the secondary level were introduced and practiced by the teachers. Gradually, the teachers became aware that they had experienced the process of clarifying values throughout the institutes. Another expressed need was for assertiveness training. Considerable gains in assertive behavior were observed during the remaining time.

The Laboratory Strategy

The first two institutes were planned and conducted as basic laboratory training for two groups of selected teachers. Institute III provided an advanced laboratory for the teachers who had been enrolled in Institute II. The laboratory strategy has been defined by Golembiewski and Blumberg (1970) as ". . . an educational strategy which is based primarily on the experiences generated in various social encounters *by the learners themselves,* and which aims to influence attitudes and develop competencies toward learning about human interactions. Essentially, therefore, laboratory training attempts to induce changes with regard to the learning process itself and to communicate a particular method of learning and inquiry."

Evidence of Change

The teachers provided evidence of their levels of development during the exercises, discussions and informal evaluation procedures throughout the institutes. Although informal data indicated that the desired outcomes were being met, several efforts were made to secure substantive evidence. Two instruments used were Shostrom's Personal Orientation Inventory (POI) and Rokeach's Dogmatism Scale (DS).

The POI is a comprehensive measure of values and behavior important in the development of the self-actualizing person (Shostrom, 1974). The POI was administered initially at the beginning of Institute II, before any activities had started. It was administered a second time to the same teachers at the end of Institute II. A third administration took place approximately six months following the end of Institute II. The time interval permitted practicing self-selected new behavior in back-home situations. When the three profiles of the POI subscales mean scores were examined, substantial evidence of growth was apparent. The teachers were more independent, held values of self-actualizing people, expressed feelings more easily, had greater self-esteem, saw humans as essentially good and perceived the opposites of life as meaningfully related.

In addition to the examination of the POI data, a comparison was made with a norm group of self-actualizing adults. The teachers' subscale mean scores from the third administration were compared with the subscale mean scores found in the POI manual (Shostrom, 1974).

The institute teachers were most similar to the norm group of self-actualizing adults in three areas: feeling, self-perception and interpersonal awareness concerns. The teachers differed most from the self-actualizing adults in the rigid application of values, limited capacity for intimate contact and the extent of living in the past or future rather than in the present. They appeared to be somewhat more other-directed or inner-directed than the balanced position of autonomous self-support. The subjective evidence gained through observation seemed to support the results from the POI data analyses.

The POI data suggested that behavioral changes were occurring and in the desired direction. These results led to a research effort to explore additional evidence of change. A randomly selected group of home economics teachers was identified to serve as a control group. The control and institute teachers were administered Rokeach's Dogmatism Scale (DS). The DS is designed to measure individual differences in openness and closeness of belief systems (Rokeach, 1960).

The institute teachers' DS mean score was significantly higher than the control teachers' mean score. The institute teachers were significantly less dogmatic, more open-minded than the control teachers. Although the control group may be viewed as a self-selected group, the results lend credence to the belief that the laboratory experiences did lead to change in the desired direction.

Strategies of Change

The strategies of change described by Bennis, Benne and Chin (1969) are those implemented in the institutes. Other vocational educators may find it instructive to review a summary of the salient points:

1. "Men are inherently active, in quest of impulse and need satisfaction. The relation between man and his environment is essentially transactional . . ."

The institute teachers were energetic and diligent in seeking to fulfill their own needs. In doing so, they interacted with other teachers, administrators, students and family members.

2. "Intelligence is social . . . Men are guided in their actions . . . by a normative culture. At the personal level, men are guided by internalized meanings, habits, and values."

Most institute teachers quickly adapted to the cultural norms of the institute as established by the trainer. Others found the expectations confusing. Teachers were assisted in guiding their own intellectual process. The norm of assuming personal responsibility for learning and of using one's own experience as a source of learning was communicated throughout the institutes. As Institute II progressed, the teachers so internalized the values of laboratory training that when an extension was confirmed, all agreed to attend without any explanation of the objectives and activities. Meanings, norms, habits, values gained social significance at a personal level and were internalized to guide future behavior and development.

3. "Man must participate in his own reeducation if he is to be reeducated at all."

The principle of personal responsibility was implemented through group activities and interaction. Much self-directed searching and learning was carried on by individuals, as witnessed in individual conferences with the trainer and director, through various written documents and from observation and self-report accounts of behavior changes.

4. "Only as a man finds ways of becoming aware of . . . non-conscious wellsprings of his attitudes and actions will he be able to bring them into conscious self-control . . . The collaborative relationship between change agent and client is a major tool in reeducating the client."

The trainer and teachers, within a climate of trust and openness, engaged in activities that helped teachers develop insight into their own actions, freeing them to explore, use or adapt new behaviors. Teachers reeducated themselves toward self-awareness, self-understanding and self-control. The extent and direction of individual teacher involvement was self-directed. The trainer and director were facilitators.

5. "The methods and concepts of the behavioral sciences are resources which change agent and client learn to use selectively, relevantly, and appropriately in learning to deal with the confronting problem and with problems of a similar kind in the future."

Although the needed change at times called for added knowledge, the problems dealt with were people-centered, not information-centered. The concepts of behavioral sciences were available for teachers to choose and use. The problems on which institute activities centered arose from the immediate experiences of the teachers.

The ultimate focus of all laboratory activities was the back-home situation. At times it appeared that the real-world simulation was the actual event when teachers struggled to understand and use their new behavior. The trainer and the teachers learned to provide and accept feedback in a setting of trust, openness, acceptance and support. Teachers gained communication skills, using "non-verbal exchange along with verbal dialogue in inducing personal confrontation, discovery and commitment to continuing growth" (Bennis, Benne and Chin). The long-term goal was that personal growth and reeducation would lead to changes in vocational programs as a whole. As Bennis, Benne and Chin emphasize, "People must learn to learn from their experiences if self-directed change is to be maintained and continued."

Communication Project

Persons at all levels of the vocational education organizational hierarchy, when asked, viewed improved communication skills as essential. Accordingly, the 36 persons selected for the Communications project represented all organizational levels and units and all vocational areas (agriculture, trade and industry, distributive education, home economics, office occupations, health occupations, industrial arts and prevocational education). The teachers, supervisors, consultants and administrators who participated were required to plan and carry out an individual project in which change in communication skills was the focus. On-campus sessions dealt with the specific communication problems being identified and encountered.

The final reports submitted by the participants revealed the effectiveness of experience-centered reeducation and the dissemination model used. Through group activities and individual projects, vocational educators became aware of elements of effective communication, barriers and distortions in communicating, and the potential risks of applying their knowledge in real settings. Up to 500 individuals were involved, from top administrators to elementary pupils. A network of mutual support and assistance developed among small groups within the project group. These individuals and supportive systems will continue to influence the quality of interaction and instruction in vocational education.

TEACHERS AS AGENTS FOR CHANGE

Participants for the 1977-1978 project were selected from among the teachers who had been in the first two institutes. Bice (1970) stated that in identifying opinion leaders among teachers, two particular areas needed to be considered: "These are the personal and social characteristics of individual teachers and characteristics of the school systems in which the teachers work." The teachers involved in the project had earlier exemplified their abilities as opinion leaders. They were ready to consolidate gains and undergo new experiences.

The project objectives were: (1) prepare teachers to become change agents among vocational teachers of special needs students; (2) provide specialized instruction about the nature and needs of special needs students in vocational education; and (3) provide specialized instruction in the adaptation of teaching strategies and physical settings for these students.

The conceptualization and development of the project was a cooperative enterprise involving the Department of Special Education Chairperson and faculty. The project included sessions on current legislation, learning needs of handicapped and disadvantaged pupils, and adaptations for effective instruction. Stereotypes and negative attitudes were brought into the open where they could be examined and reevaluated.

A Commitment to Mainstreaming

The focus was on helping teachers to extend their individual development and interaction skills to become effective change agents on behalf of special needs students in their programs. All teachers had made a commitment to design and carry out a plan within their own schools or districts to facilitate mainstreaming into vocational and other classes.

The project had several features in addition to the laboratory strategy common to the earlier institutes. It included a survey to determine the status of mainstreaming in vocational programs in the state, presentations and demonstrations by special education experts, videotaping of all presentations for later use by the teachers and individual planning for a self-directed application project by each teacher. Total group sessions on campus were interspersed with small group meetings held in three areas of the state. The development of a back-home support system for each teacher was an important feature.

Learning to be change agents began with the basic training the institute participants had received. Each teacher brought to this new project the knowledge and skills in interpersonal relations gained and consolidated in the intervening time.

Before the first session, the trainer or a project director visited each teacher's school to enlist the principal's support for that teacher's participation. The principal was asked to participate in one of the area meetings with other project teachers and their principals. Administrative support was essential because the change agent role would eventually involve other teachers and school personnel. Although no effort was made to measure the attitudes of the principals toward the project, all expressed interest and pledged their cooperation. Some of the principals expressed enthusiastic appreciation for the contribution of the project activities to their schools.

Major Themes

In the first session, the teachers identified and discussed their perceptions and concerns about mainstreaming. The trainer helped the group gain a sense of responsibility for mainstreaming, showing them ways to assume authority and to deal with others who had authority. Concerns about teachers' needs for self-determination were identified and examined.

Issues relating to the change agent role were discussed. The need to examine personal motivations, determine how to help others become aware of the desirability of change, diagnose situations needing modification, and guide the process of change were major themes in the first session.

Information about the status of mainstreaming in vocational programs was available from the survey of vocational teachers. Teachers were provided with survey findings on perceived needs, attitudes and preparation for working with special needs students.

Project experiences provided further opportunity for teachers to practice their roles as change agents. They met in groups to build their own learning agenda for the area meetings scheduled during the following month. The teachers identified the personal resources individuals could contribute to the group effort. The network of cooperation and mutual support was reinforced by the necessity of planning the details of the area meetings.

The teachers formed three subgroups and planned two area meetings in a convenient location. They planned the agendas, secured meeting places and made arrangements for securing resources. The school principals were involved in the second area meeting. All participated in the further development of the teachers' plans for dissemination. In addition to the lively discussion about each teacher's plan, the discussion included questions and suggestions relating to broader school concerns such as sex equity in home economics. The concensus of opinion was that the area meetings were both interesting and productive.

The last campus meeting provided the opportunity for recapitulation of the area meetings. The participants had positive feelings about the meetings and they seemed clear about their plans to be change agents during the coming year. Further training was provided in the final session for strengthening the teachers' skills in the change agent role. The themes were initiating change, involving others in setting goals and building support systems within the schools and districts. The trainer presented a lecture-discussion on the change process, including an explanation of Lewin's force-field analysis model. The teachers divided into small groups to apply the model to a problem. From the group reports, the trainer was able to clarify and provide further information.

Outcomes of the Project

A major requirement of the project was the dissemination plan. Each teacher initiated the change process in the local school and district by designing and implementing a sequence of decisions. Most of the teachers had accomplished much of their plan by the end of the semester, even though the original time projected was for the following school year. Consequently, additional activities could be held.

Each plan was unique, designed by the teacher to fit particular people and situations. The types of activities fell into the following categories:

1. Sharing materials with other groups and persons.
2. Planning, directing and participating in inservice meetings.
3. Consulting resource persons.
4. Collecting and exhibiting materials from many sources.
5. Working with school administrators.
6. Publicizing inservice activities in local newspapers.

Teachers had completed an opinion inventory before conducting any project activities. The inventory was designed to measure attitudes toward handicapped persons and their learning needs. Comparisons were made between the "before" and "after" opinion inventory mean scores of the project teachers. Although the value was not significant at the 5 percent level, it was close to the table value. When the survey teachers' scores were compared with those of the project teachers, however, the value was significant beyond the 1 percent level. The involvement of the teachers in the project clearly inflenced their attitudes.

The long-range effectiveness of the project will not be completely known for some time. However, the laboratory method—with its emphasis on individual and group development of competencies in human relations, combined with specific training in skills designed to help participants disseminate their knowledge among co-workers—seems to be an efficient and effective use of human and material resources.

REFERENCES

Bennis, W. G., Benne, K. D., and Chin, R. *The planning of change.* New York: Holt, Rinehart and Winston, 1969.

Bice, G. R. Working with opinion leaders to accelerate change in vocational-technical education. Columbus, Ohio: Center for Vocational and Technical Education, 1970. (ERIC Document Reproduction Service No. VT 011 796).

Bynner, W. (Ed.) *The way of life according to Laotzu.* New York: Putnam, 1962.

Chin, R., and Benne, K. D. General strategies for effecting changes in human systems. *The planning of change.* New York: Holt, Rinehart and Winston. 1969.

Golembiewski, R. T., and Blumber. J. A. *Sensitivity training and the laboratory approach.* Itasco, Ill.: F. E. Peacock, 1970.

Loftis, H. A. *Modification of teaching practices of home economics teachers of economically disadvantaged pupils* (Education Professions Development Act Project). Rock Hill, S.C.: Winthrop College, 1974.

Loftis, H. A. *Development of competencies in interpersonal relationships for consumer and homemaking teachers: Final report* (Education Professions Act Project). Rock Hill, S.C.: Winthrop College, 1975.

Loftis, H. A. *Development of competencies in interpersonal relationships for consumer and homemaking teachers: final report* (Education Professions Development Act Project). Rock Hill, S.C.: Winthrop College, 1976.

Loftis, H. A. *Communication skill development for vocational education personnel in South Carolina* (Education Professions Development Act Project). Rock Hill, S.C.: Winthrop College, 1977.

Loftis, H. A., and Huber, A. L. *A multidisciplinary inservice project for teachers of special needs students* (Education Professions Development Act Project). Rock Hill, S.C.: Winthrop College, 1978.

Moustakas, C. *Creativity and conformity. New York:* D. Van Nostrand, 1967.

Murray, M. E. *An exploration of the relationship of self-actualization to teacher success.* Unpublished master's thesis, Pennsylvania State University, 1966.

Murray, M. E. *Self-actualization and social values of teachers as related to students' perceptions of teachers.* Unpublished doctoral dissertation, Pennsylvania State University, 1968.

Rogers, C. R. The characteristics of a helping relationship. *The Planning of Change.* New York: Holt, Rinehart and Winston, 1969.

Rokeach, M. *The open and closed mind.* New York: Basic Books, 1960.

Scott, B. A. "Planned change: Women as change agents," *American Association of University Women Journal, 70* (6), 1977.

Shostrom, E. L. *EDITS Manual for the personal orientation inventory.* San Diego: Educational and Industrial Testing Service, 1974.

Stiffler, E. J. Variables related to probable success in teaching. *Home Economics Research Journal, 5* (3), 1977.

Travers, R. M. W. *Second handbook of research on teaching.* Chicago, Ill.: Rand McNally, 1973.

Wilhelm, W. P. *Self-actualization of teachers and students as factors in teaching effectiveness.* Unpublished master's thesis, Pennsylvania State University, 1968.

Wolfe, D. T., Jr. The scholar and the pedagogue: Different breeds of humanists. *Clearinghouse, 50, 1977.*

THE FOUNDATIONS OF LEARNING

4.
LEADERSHIP IN
VOCATIONAL INSTRUCTION

Ralph C. Wenrich

The quality of instruction in vocational education is determined largely by the kind of leadership provided by vocational educators in the management of our educational institutions. These institutions are complex social organizations that operate more effectively if persons in managerial roles can create an atmosphere in which the goals of the organization and the needs of members can be satisfied simultaneously. Organizational effectiveness has been defined as "the extent to which an organization as a social system, given certain resources and means, fulfills its objectives without incapacitating its members" (Georgopoulous and Tannenbaum, 1957).

It is sometimes assumed that managerial functions are performed only by persons in official administrative roles, but I take the position that administrative functions are widely dispersed in educational institutions so that virtually every professional employee has some of these functions to perform. The behavior of managers in administrative and supervisory roles is no more important to the successful operation of vocational programs than is the behavior of the teacher as manager of the learning environment.

It is further assumed, for the purposes of this chapter, that leadership (like managerial functions) is widely dispersed among personnel in any social organization, including educational institutions. The concept of leadership and much of the research on leader behavior is applicable in all types of social organizations and at all levels, but this chapter will attempt to relate what we know about leadership to instructional functions at the local level.

Persons in managerial positions in vocational education at the state and federal levels might also be expected to give more effective leadership in solving problems related to instruction, but educational excellence will be attained only through local leadership and not by mandates from

Washington or any state capital. The leadership of the local administrator of vocational education or community college dean of occupational education and their instructional staffs can make the difference between mediocre and outstanding instructional programs.

ORGANIZATIONAL CHARACTERISTICS AND CONCEPTS

After examining some of the more widely cited definitions of organization, the authors of *Behavior in Organizations* (Porter, Lawler and Hackman, 1975) concluded that organizations have five basic features. They are (1) composed of individuals and groups (2) in order to achieve certain goals and objectives (3) by means of differentiated functions (4) that are intended to be rationally coordinated and directed (5) through time on a continuous basis.

Organizations have goals or purposes toward which the activities of the people in them are directed. In addition, individuals within organizations are responsible for different tasks. In more permanent types of organizations, such as educational institutions, these work roles tend to remain stable, while people occupying them change, resulting in a structured social organization. Organizational structures can be defined as those patterns of behavior in the organization that are relatively stable and that change slowly.

We tend to think of organizations as more or less self-contained units, but they are usually part of a larger social system and are also made up of a number of subsystems. The school, for example, is part of the local school system, which is itself a part of the state school system. Also, the school is made up of subsystems in the form of subject-matter departments or divisions assigned certain specialized functions. Each subsystem is usually composed of small work groups or social systems. The basic unit, or subgroup, in the structure of an educational institution is a group of students in the classroom, shop or laboratory.

Individuals in the organization interact with others in their immediate group or social system, but they may also interact with persons in the larger system of which their unit is a part. Thus, the individual occupies a role (or roles) in a work group within an organization, within a culture. Griffiths illustrates the levels at which the individual may interact with others within the organization and with the supporting environment by a series of circles with one point of contact.

Organizations as Social Systems

Positions of people within organizations are arranged to define the relationships of people to each other. The hierarchy of superordinate-subordinate relationships facilitates the allocation of functions and resources for achieving the goals of the organization. Any given position is the location of one individual or class of individuals within the social system.

The way people behave in these positions depends in part on how they think they are expected to behave, but it is also influenced by the expectations of others. The interaction of roles comprises the organizational structure through which members of an organization, together with their clients outside the organization, arrive at mutual goals and ways of achieving them.

Formal and Informal Structures

Organizations have both a formal and an informal structure. The formal organization consists of roles and relationships as prescribed by top management of the organization and approved by the governing body. The formal organization for a large institution, such as a school system, can usually be presented graphically in an administrative chart, which frequently takes the form of a series of boxes arranged in a hierarchical order, each box denoting a position or role in the organization. Organizational charts tend to be more functional when each box contains a brief description of the duties, activities or functions of that particular unit or subunit.

The informal or operating structure of an organization refers to the unplanned, informal set of groups, friendships and attachments that inevitably develop when people are placed in proximity to one another—it is the human side of the enterprise. The relationships that grow out of the individual needs of members of the organization cannot be fully accounted for by the formal organization. These behaviors, attitudes, and values have no place in the formal plan—officially, they do not exist. Yet they have a significant effect on the total organizational effort. In fact, sometimes the formal structure is modified to reflect some of the informal relationships.

Management of Social Organizations

Organizations attempt to insure orderliness and predictability in several ways, one of which is a system of authority. For purposes of our discussion, authority is considered to be the right of a person to decide, determine or influence what others in the organization will do. Authority may be acquired through formal action such as laws and board policies (authority of legitimacy) or conferred by the organization through the position or office that one occupies (authority of position). Authority (or at least influence) may also be acquired through professional or technical competence or experience (authority of competence) or by personal characteristics such as seniority, popularity, knowledge of human aspects of administration, rapport with subordinates, persuasive ability and ability to mediate individual needs (authority of person). Peabody (1962) classified the first and second categories (legitimacy and position) as *formal bases of authority* and the last two (competence and person) as *functional authority*.

Authority and Power

Katz and Kahn (1966) define authority as legitimate power, that is, "power which is vested in a particular person or position, which is recognized as so vested, and which is accepted as appropriate not only by the wielder of the power, but by those over whom it is wielded and by the other members of the system." They claim that the managerial subsystem and the structure of authority are inseparable.

To understand authority and power, we must examine other terms such as *influence and control*. Katz and Kahn (1966) describe the concept of *influence* as a kind of psychological force; it includes virtually any interpersonal transaction in which one person acts in such a way as to change the behavior of another in some intended fashion. *Control* on the other hand, implies a distinction between successful and unsuccessful attempts to influence. That is, a person has control over another in some matter if his or her influence is so strong that the desired behavior will be completed and any resistance or counterinfluences will be overcome in the process. *Power* generally refers to a potential set of transactions, rather than actions actually occurring; it is the capacity to influence, but it is seldom used to refer to a single act.

Porter, Lawler and Hackman (1975) concluded that the concentration of authority at the top of an organization seems most appropriate in an organization that has a stable environment, deals with familiar and relatively simple tasks and possesses a work force in which only a small number of individuals at the top possess long experience, technical skills and a strong desire to exercise discretion in making decisions. If, on the other hand, the organization generally faces an unpredictable and constantly changing environment, involves many complex tasks, and contains a work force in which skills and experience are broadly dispersed, a system of more widely distributed authority would seem to be in order, with a greater degree of autonomy for individuals and units at lower levels in the hierarchy.

A Good Case for Decentralization

This would seem to make a good case for a decentralized system of authority for educational institutions, especially with regard to the management of vocational programs. In fact, a change in the authority bases for those who manage public institutions is now under way. The shift is from formal authority to functional authority bases in most institutions. An exception to this trend may be found in schools with strong collective bargaining contracts. As the content and structures of vocational education increase in complexity and diversity, teachers (by virtue of authority of competence and person) have assumed more responsibility for the management of their specialized areas.

Managers of vocational and technical programs are especially susceptible to this change since for many years they relied heavily upon the authority derived from federal legislation plus authority of position. But the vocational manager of the future will need to rely more on competence and person as sources of authority and power. It should be noted that functional authority is related to successful achievement of given ends—performance is the basis for allocating or removing such authority.

LEADERSHIP IN SOCIAL ORGANIZATIONS

In *The Art of Leadership* (1935), Ordway Tead says, "Leadership is the activity of influencing people toward some goal which they come to find desirable." Wenrich and Wenrich (1974) have adapted this definition to the organizational setting, and define organizatonal leadership in administrative roles as "the process of influencing an individual or a group in efforts toward the achievement of organizational goals." Katz and Kahn (1966) consider the essence of organizational leadership to be that "influential increment over and above mechanical compliance with the routine directives of the organization."

LEADERSHIP AND MANAGEMENT

Most research on organizational leadership has focused on the leadership of persons in positions that are largely administrative or supervisory and which carry with them varying degrees of authority (authority of legitimacy and of position). In fact, most of my experience in leadership development has centered on the preparation of persons for leadership roles in the administration of vocational education.

As mentioned earlier, however, leadership is not limited to persons in administrative positions, but is widely dispersed in most social organizations. Therefore, what we have to say about leadership applies to a wide range of people involved in the management of vocational education, including teachers, department heads, supervisors, coordinators, directors, principals and deans.

In an unpublished paper titled "Leadership as Viewed by a Psychologist," Kenneth Little makes a clear distinction between leadership and management:

> The leadership function requires the capacity to "live ahead" of his institution; to interpret his institution's needs to the public and the public's needs to his institution; and to conceive and implement strategies for effecting changes required for the institution to fulfill its purpose. The management function requires the capacity to arrange and operate his institution in a manner which elicits an efficient and effective effort of the total membership of his institution toward its purposes. The leadership function is a stimulating, prodding, and sometimes disruptive influence, while the management function has a smoothing and stabilizing influence.

Leadership Behavior

Research suggests that one cannot differentiate leaders from nonleaders on the basis of personality characteristics or traits. While social scientists are not in complete agreement on leadership theories, the most extensive research deals with the behavioral styles of leaders.

Landmark studies conducted at Ohio State University by Stogdill (1957) and others undertook to describe the major behavioral dimensions of leader style and then to determine how these dimensions relate to employee productivity and morale. The following dimensions that emerged:

1. *Consideration* was defined as the leader's behavior indicative of friendship, mutual trust, respect and warmth in the relationships between the leader and group members.
2. *Initiating structure* was defined as the leader's behavior in delineating the relationships between himself or herself and the members of the work group, and in establishing clear organizational goals, communication channels and procedures for accomplishing group tasks.

Other studies done at about the same time by the Survey Research Center at The University of Michigan led to similar findings. Cartwright and Zander (1960) concluded that most group objectives may be accomplished under the two headings of "goal achievement behaviors" and "group maintenance behaviors." The kinds of leadership behavior directed toward goal achievement are: The leader (1) initiates action, (2) keeps members' attention on the goal, (3) clarifies the issue, (4) develops a procedural plan, (5) evaluates the quality of work done, and (6) makes expert information available.

The types of leadership behavior that exemplify group maintenance include the following: The leader (1) keeps interpersonal relations pleasant, (2) arbitrates disputes, (3) provides encouragement, (4) gives the minority a chance to be heard, (5) stimulates self-direction, and (6) increases the interdependence among members.

Though most of the early research on leadership behavior was done in organizations other than schools, several studies using "consideration" and "initiating structure," the two dimensions of leader behavior just outlined, were done in school settings. Halpin (1960) did a study of superintendents of schools, and Everson (1959) did a study of high school principals. Both studies indicated that effective leadership was characterized by high schools on both "consideration" and "initiating structure."

Yet these two dimensions are relatively independent. The fact that a person rates high in one dimension does not necessarily mean that he or she will be high or low in the other. The behavior of a leader can be described as any mix of both dimensions.

Table 1 illustrates these relationships. The vertical axis is given the generic term "Human-Relations-Oriented Behavior," or concern for people, and the horizontal axis is called "Task-Oriented Behavior," or concern for production.

Table 1
MIX OF TWO DIMENSIONS OF LEADER BEHAVIOR

	High Consideration (Group maintenance)	High Consideration (Group maintenance)
	Low Initiating structure (Goal achievement)	High Initiating structure (Goal achievement)
	Low Consideration (Group maintenance)	High Initiating structure (Goal achievement)
	Low Initiating structure (Goal achievement)	Low Consideration (Group maintenance)

HUMAN-RELATIONS-ORIENTED BEHAVIOR "Concern for People" — High / Low

Low .... High

TASK-ORIENTED BEHAVIOR
"Concern for Production"

Leadership Is Situational

Fiedler (1967) defines leadership as a problem of "influencing and controlling others." He takes the position that different situations require different leadership behavior. He believes that both modes of leader behavior—consideration and initiating structure—have been effective in some situations and not in others.

Fiedler identifies three major situational factors that determine whether a leader will find it easy or difficult to influence a group: (1) the degree to which the group accepts and trusts its leader, (2) the leader's "position power," that is, the power the organization gives the position, and (3) the degree to which the task of the group is structured or unstructured. But these factors by themselves do not determine group performance. Just as there is no one style of leadership that is effective for all groups, so there is not one type of situation that makes an effective group. Effective group performance, then, requires the matching of leadership style with the appropriate situation. The effective leader will diagnose the situation and then modify the situation to fit his or her leadership style.

Leadership and Decision Making

A basic tenet of the democratic process is that people should have a right to participate in making decisions that directly affect their lives. In an educational organization, presumably this right would extend to faculty, staff, students and the community at large.

Decisions are inevitably made at every level of any organization by every member of the organization. Even policy decisions made at the highest executive level of an institution are modified by every employee as he or she helps (or hinders) in the implementation of decisions.

It might be useful to differentiate between *policy making* and *management decision making*. *Policy making* involves the development and formal adoption of the major overall goals of the institution, while management decision making relates to the development of intermediate objectives and means for achieving long-range goals. Though every vocational administrator should try to maximize his or her influence in the policy-making process—in the definition and formulation of overall goals and purposes of the institution—this discussion on decision making will consider the process by which intermediate objectives are determined and implemented. Decision making on this level should involve administrators, faculty, staff and students to the extent that each of these groups will be affected by the decisions and to the extent that the situation warrants it.

The leadership style adopted by a manager on any level could range from highly authoritarian to extremely democratic. The authoritarian leader tends to make decisions and then inform subordinates while the democratic manager tends to involve subordinates in the decision-making process. Tannenbaum and Schmidt (1958) put this range of behavior of managers on a continuum in which each type of action is related to the degree of authority used by the manager and to the amount of freedom available to subordinates in reaching decisions. At one extreme is the manager who maintains a high degree of control, while at the other is the manager who releases a high degree of control. They point out, "Neither extreme is absolute; authority and freedom are never without their limitations."

The position that any manager should take on this continuum of leadership behavior depends upon the personality of the manager-leader, the attitudes, needs and problems of subordinates, and the forces operating in the situation. For example, decisions would tend to be made by the manager-leader when he or she has a legal responsibility, when subordinates expect him or her to make certain decisions, or when there is insufficient knowledge or a lack of group skill in decision making. Also, sufficient time may not be available for group decision making. But when the reverse of these conditions is present, the manager-leader should tend toward what Tannenbaum and Schmidt (1958) call "subordinate centered leadership." Porter, Lawler and Hackman (1975) state that:

> . . . it ultimately is impossible to draw up a set of behavioral specifications for the "perfect" leader . . . Effective leadership, then, seems to us to be characterized mainly by (1) an *awareness* of factors which influence the interpersonal and work behavior of group members, (2) the capacity to *diagnose* with sensitivity which of those factors are impairing the effectiveness of the group at any given time—and which are waiting to be developed in furthering group goals, and (3) the willingness and the skill to *share selectively* with group members responsibility for making those decisions and performing those leadership acts which are necessary to keep the group moving toward its goals.

THE MANAGEMENT OF VOCATIONAL INSTRUCTION

Vocational instruction is provided through a variety of educational institutions—secondary and postsecondary—with a tremendous range of administrative structures and management systems. In some states vocational instruction is a function of comprehensive high schools and community colleges, while in other states specialized vocational schools and technical institutes predominate.

Each institution has a unique administrative structure designed to achieve its goals. Staff roles are delineated in many different ways and carry a variety of titles, but for our purposes, let us consider briefly three categories of personnel with management responsibilities: (1) general school administrators, (2) vocational administrators and supervisors, and (3) vocational teachers.

General School Administrators

Most school superintendents, secondary school principals and community college presidents have the responsibility for the management of both vocational and general education programs. If persons in such positions are to provide leadership for instruction in vocational education, they should understand and be able to apply the principles of effective organizational management. But they must also understand vocational education as one of the primary goals of public education. An understanding and appreciation of vocational education should be a part of preparatory programs for general school administrators. Since this occurs all too seldom, it becomes the responsibility of vocational administrators and their staffs to educate general school administrators on an inservice basis.

If any major changes in the management system are to be made in a school or a school system, the chances for success are much better if the changes are at least approved by the manager at the top level of the institution. Change is not likely to occur if the top administrator does not approve. His or her approval does not guarantee change, however, since subordinates must implement the change.

45

Vocational Instruction

Vocational education operates as a subsystem in the total educational system, and if vocational instruction is to be effective, interaction of vocational educators with other components in the system is as important as relationship within the vocational subsystem. The superintendent of schools, the community college president and the principal of a comprehensive high school should be as concerned and informed about instruction in vocational programs as they are about any other programs under their jurisdiction. This happens when vocational education is well integrated into the total system through the involvement of vocational educators in policy making and other decisions that affect the whole system.

In many school systems, the superintendent uses the group process in decision making by involving his or her immediate associates in an administrative council. The associate or assistant superintendent for vocational education (sometimes inappropriately titled director) should certainly be a member of such a decision-making work group. Similarly, community college presidents and high school principals should (and many of them do) use the group process in decision making.

In short, one or more persons representing vocational education should be included on administrative, instructional or other decision-making councils. The vocational educator serves as a communication link between general administration and others in the system.

Vocational Administrators and Supervisors

The chief vocational administrator in any local school system and his or her supervisory staff must assume the responsibility for quality instruction. They can improve the quality of instruction by securing adequate funding, providing appropriate facilities, hiring well-qualified teachers, promoting inservice training of teachers, making available suitable teaching materials, developing sound personnel policies and practices, evaluating programs and building community support for vocational education. But the diligent performance of these and other generally accepted functions of administration and supervision will not assure optimum success.

The administrator-leader who can accept and apply the results of organizational research can enhance the performance of his or her administrative unit. To the extent that he or she is able to build a sense of importance and personal worth in subordinates so that a feeling of mutual trust and confidence exists, the organization will be more effective. If the administrator-leader will ask for and use subordinates' ideas and involve them in major decisions affecting them, mutual confidence and trust will follow.

The administrator-leader can also enhance the performance of the unit by working with subordinates on a group problem-solving basis, but he or she cannot build an effective team without also developing a mutually rewarding one-to-one interaction with each subordinate. The administrator-leader will have a more effective organization to the extent that the organization has clearly defined goals to which other members of the organization are committed.

Leadership in Vocational Education

What has been said about leadership as it applies to the chief vocational administrator and staff for the entire school system applies equally to the administration of vocational education *within* the school. The administrator-leader for vocational programs in a school is the principal. In a vocational high school or an area vocational-technical center, the principal is generally a person who has specialized in the administration of vocational education, but this is seldom true of comprehensive high school principals.

As a result, vocational programs in a typical comprehensive high school are not well coordinated. There are generally separate departments of business education, industrial education and home economics, each offering several courses but with little interaction among the department members in program planning. And there is even less interaction with the academic departments such as English, math and science.

We need to reexamine the administrative structure for vocational education in the comprehensive high school, with a view toward forming work groups of teachers across departmental lines to help make decisions that will improve the quality of vocational programs. But this requires administrative leadership. In some schools, the principal can and does provide such leadership, but in larger comprehensive high schools, it might be desirable to give this responsibility to an assistant principal for vocational education. What appears to be needed is a designated leader, preferably selected by vocational teachers, who would be expected to bring together and make the most effective use of the resources—both human and physical—within the school in order to improve the quality of all vocational programs.

Vocational Teachers and Managers

The management of instruction in vocational education is a function of both administration and faculty, but the teacher and the student are the primary actors in the instructional process. Wenrich and Wenrich (1974) discuss the teacher as manager of the learning environment, pointing out that the vocational teacher has three distinct roles: (1) the key person working with a group of students in a classroom, shop or laboratory, (2) a professional working with other teachers, supervisors and administrators within the organizational structure, and (3) a liaison with employers and workers engaged in the occupation taught. Here we will consider only the role of the teacher as a manager of a group of students in a classroom, shop or laboratory.

The vocational teacher and this group of students constitute a work group. Where vocational teachers spend two or three hours each day with the group, effective leader behavior can have greater impact than in classes of shorter duration. Like managers of other work groups, the teacher represents the larger organization in which the work group operates. Also, as in other work groups, the teacher-manager has formal authority and is expected to maintain control of the group and to increase productivity (learning). To continue the analogy, the teacher, like other managers, is faced with the problem of encouraging the group to determine objectives and how they are to be achieved. Finally, the teacher and students are motivated by such extrinsic factors as salary, grades and promotions, as well as such intrinsic factors as pride in one's work (achievement of a learning task) and the satisfaction of successfully meeting one's responsibilities.

Obviously, there are also important differences between the instructional and other work environments. One is the nature of the "work," and another is that in business or industry the task often requires the cooperation of an entire work group, while in the classroom setting, the task is often more individualized. Recognizing these differences, let us consider how the teacher can effectively use some of the leadership techniques that have been tested in other work groups.

The perceptions students have of their leader, the teacher, and their relationships with him or her will affect the way they react to the teacher's leadership behavior. Three major factors involved in this relationship are: (1) the formal authority of the teacher, (2) the expertise of the teacher, and (3) the philosophy of the teacher.

The Teacher's Authority. The teacher has formal authority by virtue of the position he or she holds. How the teacher uses this formal authority is the important consideration. To the extent that vocational teachers can allow students to share in the decision-making process, the learning environment will be enhanced. Though there are times when the teacher must behave authoritatively to create a productive learning environment, teachers have often tended to use formal authority and the power derived from it when other means might have been more useful.

The effective teacher-leader will get most of his or her power by building a sense of importance and personal worth in students and by asking for and constructively using students' ideas, thereby creating an environment of mutual trust and respect. The acceptance by students of the teacher's invitation to participate in the management of the class will give the teacher personal power. The effective teacher-leader can influence the group through the judicious use of this personal power. It has been suggested that most teachers would improve their instructional leadership if they were to make more use of the behavioral skills they find useful in other interpersonal relationships.

The Teacher's Expertise. If well-qualified teachers are employed, they will be recognized as experts in their occupations by both employers and the practitioners in that occupation and by the students who are preparing to enter it. Furthermore, the vocational teacher who maintains contact with employers in the occupation will very likely be consulted when new workers are recruited. The vocational teacher who can help students find suitable employment has functional power that can be used constructively to influence student performance.

Leadership in Vocational Education

The Teacher's Philosophy. The teacher's perception of his or her role will affect relationships with students. The vocational teacher can either function primarily in an authoritarian way as the dispenser of knowledge, skills and attitudes, *or* the teacher can structure the learning environment so that the student becomes a participating member of the group and, as such, shares in the decision-making processes related to goal setting, planning learning activities and evaluating progress.

Jenkins (1960) states, "Effective leadership behavior can be developed if the teacher works diligently to develop it." He then lists a number of principles the teacher should follow to develop good working relationships with students.

SUMMARY

Teachers, supervisors and administrators should work toward the decentralization of authority through the meaningful involvement of their subordinates or work groups in decision making and policy formulation. To the extent that they do, in a sense, give away authority, they will become more powerful and more influential. This power will be derived not from the official position occupied, but from the satisfaction people get from working in an organization in which they share in determining goals and making decisions.

Vocational programs have expanded dramatically during the past decade, but the time has come when more attention must be given to the quality of instruction in these programs. Since all public education, including vocational education, is currently under public scrutiny, the future of vocational education may depend upon the kind and quality of leadership provided by vocational educators. Basically, the quality of instruction in vocational education depends upon good leadership at the local level by vocational administrators, supervisors, coordinators and teachers.

REFERENCES

Cartwright, Dorwin and Zander, Alvin (Eds.). *Group dynamics: Research and theory.* Evanston, Ill.: Row, Peterson, 1960.

Everson, Warren L. Leadership behavior of high school principals. *National Association of Secondary School Principals Bulletin,* September 1959.

Fiedler. Fred E. A theory of leadership effectiveness. New York: McGraw-Hill, 1967.

Georgopoulous, B., and Tannenbaum, Arnold S. A study of organizational effectiveness. *American Sociological Review,* October 1957.

Halpin, Andrew W. *The leadership behavior of school superintendents.* Chicago: Midwest Administrative Center, University of Chicago, 1960.

Jenkins, David H. Characteristics and functions of leadership in instructional groups. *The Fifty-Ninth Yearbook of the National Society for the Study of Education.* Chicago: NSSE, 1960.

Katz, Daniel, and Kahn, Robert. *The social psychology of organizations.* New York: John Wiley, 1966.

Vocational Instruction

Marrow, Alfred J., Bowers, David G., and Seashore, Stanley E. *Management by participation.* New York: Harper and Row, 1967.

Peabody, Robert L. Perceptions of organizational authority: a comparative analysis. *Administrative Science Quarterly,* March 1962.

Porter, Lyman W., Lawler, Edward E., III, and Hackman, J. Richard. *Behavior in organizations.* New York: McGraw-Hill, 1975.

Stogdill, Roger M., and Coons, Alvin E. (Eds). *Leader behavior: Its description and measurement.* Research Monograph, no. 88. Columbus, Ohio: Bureau of Business Research. Ohio State University, 1957.

Tannenbaum, Robert, and Schmidt, Warren H. How to choose a leader pattern. *Harvard Business Review,* March-April 1958.

Tead, Ordway. *The art of leadership.* New York: McGraw-Hill, 1935.

Wenrich, Ralph C., and Wenrich, J. William. Leadership in administration of vocational and technical education. Columbus, Ohio: Charles E. Merrill, 1974.

I

THE FOUNDATIONS OF LEARNING

5.
SUPERVISION:
A LOST ART

Gordon F. Law

The supervision of vocational education is fast becoming a lost art, and the supervisor, an endangered species. Decimated by forces of expediency, negotiated into limbo by the legalistic newspeak of contract negotiations, struck down by default in federal laws and guidelines, and caught in the coils of bureaucracy, the person directly responsible for the improvement of vocational teaching may soon be only a pleasant memory. But before this rare and valuable person fades from the scene, let us take measures to recognize his or her value and help insure that the supervisor will once again flourish as a vital ancillary to quality teaching.

This chapter will present the argument that the supervision of vocational education, especially the part concerned with the improvement of instruction, is indispensable to program quality. Also discussed are some of the conditions associated with the decline of supervision and recommendations for reversing the trend.

UNIQUE ASPECTS OF VOCATIONAL TEACHING

The teaching of vocations in the United States is unique. It differs in goals, form and methods from that of other countries and has a number of special characteristics that are not usually associated with the general school curriculum. Widely divergent forces, some in sharp conflict with others, have contributed to the shaping of vocational education in the United States (Cremen, 1968). Older traditions of apprenticeship training and home handicrafts were dramatically influenced in America by changing circumstances. New land, rapid industrial growth, waves of immigrants to port cities, the development of a national system of free education, the Morrill Act of 1862 establishing the nation's system of land-grant colleges and the Smith-Hughes Act of 1917 all helped to produce a system of vocational education that, in its several settings and forms, may be described by the following characteristics:

1. It is mainly preparatory.
2. It is free and public, mainly under the shared jurisdiction and control of federal, state and local education agencies.
3. It includes a strong general education component.
4. It is based upon the primacy of the individual.
5. It employs facilities, equipment, materials and teaching methods that are closely associated with employment practices.
6. It is individualized in terms of pace, content and specific routes to learning.
7. It makes special provisions for persons with handicaps.
8. It provides organized and systematic instruction, based on continuing study of jobs and processes.

VOCATIONAL TEACHERS ARE SPECIAL

Of all the aspects of vocational education that make it different, none is more significant than the special qualities of its teachers. The person who becomes a vocational teacher is typically making a career decision after the acquisition of substantial occupational experience. This seasoned practitioner, with firsthand knowledge of the work place, injects a special elixir of reality and immediacy into the school environment. Such experience is the lifeblood of vocational education. It makes schooling real and meaningful, practical and useful—not about life, but life itself.

But occupational skills and experiences do not themselves insure a successful transition to teaching. The transformation of a craftsperson, scientist or technician into teacher is at best a difficult process, calling for the rapid acquisition of new behavior, skills, attitudes and values. In most cases, the beginning vocational teacher needs help through supervision— for it is the supervisor, especially in a nonthreatening role of counselor, guide and exemplary master teacher, who is critically important in helping to shape the future effectiveness of this person.

THE SUPERVISOR IS A TEACHER

To insure that the supervisor carries out a supportive and teaching role with faculty members, responsibilities must be defined clearly. Otherwise, the supervisor's job could be occupied entirely with clerical and administrative chores such as budgeting, scheduling, form filling, list making and that ubiquitous mandate, teacher evaluation.

As priorities for vocational education are established in various administrative offices and collegiate think tanks across the country, it is important to remember that teaching—i.e., the cultivated talent to transmit skills and knowledge to groups and individuals—determines the quality of education. It is the final line for accountability, and no model or management system can take its place.

The teaching and helping role of vocational supervisors was identified clearly in the Smith-Hughes Act of 1917 and the federal guidelines for its implementation that followed. By 1926, the inservice teaching functions of supervisors were well established. Among their responsibilities were: making job analyses and assisting teachers in curriculum design; providing inservice instruction for teachers; and cooperating with teachers in the preparation of lesson outlines and text materials (Wright and Allen, 1926).

A more detailed study of the vocational supervisor's role was conducted by George Brandon (1952). Identifying over 100 specific activities, Brandon found that supervisors typically had responsibilities in the areas of planning and budgeting, staff development, curriculum management and teacher evaluation.

Teaching Functions of the Supervisor

Among the teaching functions identified by Brandon were the following:

1. Training teachers on the local level in accordance with individual needs and approved plans.
2. Providing supervised observation, participation and student teaching experience.
3. Encouraging teachers to participate in teacher improvement plans.
4. Holding group meetings, conferences, workshops and other activities for teacher improvement.
5. Holding classroom clinics, model classwork and demonstration teaching.
6. Instructing new teachers on the job.
7. Assisting teachers to locate, use and evaluate instructional materials.

In recent years, there appears to be a growing volume of literature that treats the school system like a factory. Such industrial organization terms as management by objectives, systems approaches to instruction and competency-based teaching have become common.

This trend is evident in a recent yearbook of the National Business Education Association (Conover, 1978) devoted to the administration and supervision of business education. A total of 27 articles treat a variety of topics that include history, modern concepts, human skills and group dynamics, staff selection, and responsibilities of supervisors in national, state and local settings. Despite the humanistic titles of some articles, this compendium of the business education community gives little attention to the teaching role of supervisors.

WHAT HAPPENED TO SUPERVISION?

What happened to supervision? There was a time when the supervision of vocational instruction was considered fundamental to the improvement of teaching competence and professional development. In the early days of vocational education in America, schools and state offices were liberally stocked with master teachers who were employed to improve the quality of instruction. Clearly identified in federal legislation, policy bulletins and funding formulas, these super teachers were carefully selected for their qualities of leadership, skills and knowledge gained through experience and advanced study.

Now we observe a diminished use of such people. The supervisor's role has been split up among administrative assistants, list makers, quasi-scientists and other instant experts, many of whom would not know good teaching from a pail of steam.

Has supervision truly become a lost art—a victim of change, an anomaly, a blank space in organizational charts? If so, how did the tragedy occur? Where was our leadership while it happened? And what can be done to reverse the trend?

CAUSES OF THE PROBLEM

One reason for the dimunition of vocational supervision is its loss of identity in federal legislation. Beginning with the Vocational Educaton Act of 1963 and continuing through subsequent amendments and new laws, the focus of legislation has been directed more toward the reduction of social inequities. Categorical funding prescriptions for specific target populations have led to significant new programs for handicapped and disadvantaged persons and other groups with specal needs, but the change in emphasis from instructional categories to population categories has reduced the visibility of instructional support services.

Another cause for the virtual extinction of vocational education supervision has been the dramatic growth of militant unionism among teachers. As relationships between teachers and boards of education have become increasingly formalized and polarized through the legalistic language of negotiated contracts, the role of the supervisor—traditionally one of middle management with one foot on the labor side and one on the management side—has been further compromised.

A third reason supervision has lost its place in the educational mainstream appears to be the simple fact that a good supervisor is hard to find. During the past 15 years of extremely rapid growth in vocational education, there have just not been enough good experienced people to serve as supervisors. State and federal offices, college departments and local school organizations have filled their job openings with people who, since they often have had limited vocational teaching experience, are poorly prepared to help others in the front ranks of teaching. Unfortunately, some of these new people seemed to have a single talent—the ability to fit any job classification and to move abruptly from one area of responsibility to another in tune with the exigencies of changing bureaucratic organization, management policy or legislative fiat.

REVERSING THE TREND

If we accept the idea that supervision is a needed adjunct to vocational teaching, specific actions will have to be taken to insure that it regains its legitimate role. To reverse the trend toward its oblivion, concerned individuals must initiate a renewed awareness of supervision and its critical importance to the teaching process. Among the actions that can be taken are those to:

1. Provide testimony in legislative hearings that supports the inclusion of vocational education supervision in federal and state regulations.
2. Strengthen and support professional organizations devoted to the improvement of supervision in various program areas.
3. Identify the roles and functions of supervision in national, state and local settings.
4. Provide graduate school programs designed specifically to prepare experienced teachers for supervisory positions.
5. Insure that the teacher support role of supervisors is identified clearly in regulations and in collective bargaining materials.
6. Budget adequate funds for supervisory activities that include provisions for travel and visits to local school and college settings.
7. Conduct research studies that examine various aspects of the supervisory process.

SUMMARY

We have presented the position that supervision, especially the part designed to help teachers improve their instruction, is in jeopardy, even though it is indispensable. Also discussed have been some unique aspects of vocational education, the special qualities of the vocational teacher, and reasons vocational education supervision may have lost its place in the mainstream.

Finally, some suggestions were made for reversing the trend. Because it is always more difficult to halt and reverse a change than to initiate a new one, it is suggested that concentrated energy, intelligence and persistence will be needed.

There should be considerable hope that this reversal can be accomplished. First, it is so logical and simple—if teaching is indeed the lifeblood of the educational process, then it seems clear that a significant portion of the resources designed as support services should be allocated to the improvement of teaching. Another reason for optimism comes from the fact that the rapid proliferation of new vocational schools and programs has apparently run its course. Now, in a period of more stability and less frantic expansion, vocational educators should again have time for internal improvements. Let us take action, then, to help insure that supervision of vocational teaching is saved from extinction.

Vocational Instruction

REFERENCES

Barlow, M. L. (Ed.) *Vocational education: The sixty-fourth yearbook of the National Society for the Study of Education.* Chicago, Ill.: University of Chicago, 1975.

Brandon, George Louis. An appraisal of the preparation of industrial education supervisors in Ohio colleges for teacher education. Unpublished doctoral thesis, Ohio State University, 1952.

Conover, Herbert (Ed.) *Administration and supervision in business education.* Reston, Va.: National Business Education Association, 1978.

Cremen, L. A. *The transformation of the school: Progressivism in American education, 1876-1957.* Reston, Va.: National Business Education Association, 1978.

Law, G. F. Strategies for change through career education. *Inequality in education.* Cambridge, Mass.: Cambridge Center for Law and Education, Harvard University.

Lucio, W. H. *Supervision: A synthesis of thought and action.* New York, N.Y.: McGraw-Hill, 1962.

Marks, J. R. *Handbook of educational supervision: A guide for the practitioner.* New York, N.Y.: Allyn and Bacon, 1971.

Sergiovanni, T. J. *Emerging patterns of supervision: Human perspectives.* New York, N.Y.: McGraw-Hill, 1971.

U.S. Department of Health, Education and Welfare, Office of Education. *Vocational education: The bridge between man and his work.* Washington, D.C.: U.S. Government Printing Office, 1968.

Wright, J. C. and Allen, C. R. *The supervision of vocational education of less than college grade.* New York, N.Y.: John Wiley, 1926.

II

PLANNING AND DEVELOPING
THE CURRICULUM

1.

CURRICULUM PLANNING IN VOCATIONAL EDUCATION

Ralph W. Tyler

All curriculum planners must answer four basic questions in developing their programs:

1. What subject matter should be taught?
2. What should the students do to learn this subject matter?
3. How should learning experiences be organized?
4. How should the effectiveness of the curriculum be appraised?

There is no particular sequence in which the four guiding questions should be examined, although most persons start with the question of objectives (What should be taught?). In developing answers to each question, one may gain information and recognize implications that lead one to modify the answers to questions considered earlier. For example, the difficulty or impossibility of devising practical learning experiences for a certain objective may lead one to eliminate that objective. Or an appraisal showing that the students are not attaining an important educational objective may lead to a revision of the learning experiences.

Each of the four questions should be answered in terms that are consistent with the other three. This means that the planning, implementation and evaluation of a curriculum involves continuing review of all basic questions.

WHAT SHOULD BE TAUGHT?

Curriculum planners usually state this question as: What educational objectives should the curriculum seek to attain? Educational objectives provide guidelines for developing, conducting and evaluating an instructional program. They represent the kinds of behavior patterns that teachers should consciously try to help students learn. Since objectives have such an important part to play in planning a curriculum, they should not be selected without careful consideration.

The chances that decisions about objectives will be wise and that goals will be significant and appropriate are increased greatly if relevant facts are available to those making the decisions. For example, information about what students have learned before enrolling in a program may suggest to program planners the need to focus objectives on patterns of behavior not acquired previously. As another illustration, information about the tasks performed by a medical technician is useful in selecting, as learning objectives, knowledge and skills to be taught in a curriculum designed for such technicians.

Related subject matter is another source for ideas on objectives. For example, educational objectives for a curriculum to educate electronics technicians are based partly on principles formulated by electronic engineers and physicists that can help technicians understand the operations of electronic instruments and other equipment.

Objectives obtained from these three sources—studies of students, task analyses and other studies of occupations, and the content of related subjects—need to be reviewed critically to make sure they are in harmony with the philosophy of the educational institution and are consistent with what is known about the psychology of learning.

Using Occupational Information

All curriculum planning must consider the present and future environment of the students in determining educational objectives. Of concern in curriculum planning are the present and future demands of the environment on the student and the opportunities it provides for him or her to satisfy needs, to stimulate and encourage personal interests, and to achieve personal goals. For example, current and future employment opportunities must be considered by curriculum planners.

More specifically, studies of a given occupation furnish information useful in vocational curriculum planning. Task analyses are particularly useful.

Each occupation involves the performance of certain tasks essential to accomplishing its mission. For example, practical nursing involves such tasks as taking and recording the temperatures of patients, helping patients handle their fears constructively, bathing patients and giving prescribed medications.

Task analysis is a simple matter when the task is a straightforward one that can be performed successfully by developing a skill, but many technical tasks require a knowledge of certain principles and skill in applying these principles in various situations. A practical nurse, for example, must understand certain psychological principles relating to the control of fear, recognize the cues that indicate the patient's emotional condition and apply these psychological principles in devising the appropriate approach to help patients handle their fears constructively. In this illustration, the educational objective suggested by the task analysis is not simply "to learn to calm patients' fears" but "to understand the psychological principles that are relevant to the control of fear, to recognize cues that indicate the emotional state of a patient, and to devise and employ an approach that will help the patient handle fears constructively."

If an occupation is largely characterized by standardized and routine tasks, the skills to be learned are fairly simple. In this case, the task analyses become educational objectives. The curriculum simply provides the opportunity to learn what tasks are to be performed and the chance to practice performing these routine tasks. But as an occupation becomes more complex, tasks are involved that are not performed effectively by routine practice.

The professional needs to understand principles to recognize various conditions that require adaptation of procedures, to recognize problems not solved by standardized practices and to utilize a problem-solving approach to these situations. These educational objectives are inferred from an examination of task analyses and judgments about how these tasks are performed effectively.

Using Needs Assessments

Since students often differ in their interests, needs and knowledge, it is commonly recognized that studies of students can yield helpful information about what they need to learn in a particular program. This is often called a needs assessment.

What is a need? One use of the term refers to the gap between a desirable norm and the situation as it actually exists. In this sense, *need* is the gap between what is and what should be. A second use of the term *need* comes from psychologists who say that fulfilling a need means to bring tensions in the organism into equilibrium so that a normal, healthy condition can be maintained.

The argument for using the student needs as an important source for educational objectives runs somewhat as follows: The day-by-day environment, in the home and in the community generally, provides a considerable part of the educational development of the student. It is unnecessary and unwise for an educational program to spend time duplicating educational experiences already provided adequately. Its efforts should be focused instead upon serious gaps in the development of students.

Hence, studies that identify these gaps or needs to which education can make a contribution are necessary to furnish a basis for the selection of objectives that should be given an important emphasis in the curriculum.

Studies of students or prospective students in a program can furnish information not only about their needs but also about their aspirations, interests, habits and practices, all of which provide a basis for inferring what the students can and should be helped to learn. A curriculum that is not designed to serve its particular students is likely both to duplicate what has already been learned by the students and to omit knowledge and skills they need to learn.

Using Related Subject Matter

In curriculum planning, subject matter is considered for three different purposes: (1) to prepare students to specialize in the subject field, (2) to prepare students for an occupation that requires the use of some of the content from one or more subject fields, and (3) to provide general education for people who may not become specialists in the field or use the content in their occupations. Subject matter, therefore, needs to be examined with one of these purposes clearly in mind.

Subject matter specialists can help curriculum developers decide what content to use from a given field. But it is important to make sure that the specialist understands the use of the subject that is contemplated. Otherwise, one is likely to receive suggestions that apply only to the student specializing in that subject.

FORMULATING THE OBJECTIVES

Analyses of the occupation, studies of the students and examination of relevant subject matter usually yield far more objectives than can be included in the educational program. Furthermore, some of the objectives will be inconsistent with others. For an effective curriculum, there should be a relatively small number of highly important objectives that are consistent.

To select a group of a few highly important, consistent objectives, it is necessary to screen the heterogeneous collection of objectives obtained from the three sources in order to eliminate the unimportant and contradictory ones. The educational and social philosophy of the vocational educator can serve as the first screen.

Fundamental Questions

This philosophy should provide the basis for answering several important questions such as the following:

1. Should vocational education seek to prepare a student for a specific job or should it help to open up a variety of occupational options?
2. Should vocational education focus on teaching rules for dealing with occupational problems or should it help the student to develop problem-solving skills that can enable him or her to work out the procedures for new occupational situations encountered? Or both?
3. Should vocational education emphasize specific occupational skills or help the student understand and use generalized principles and skills in occupational situations?
4. To what extent should vocational education emphasize the acquisition of information and to what extent should the development of familiarity with dependable sources of information be relevant to the occupation?

5. Should vocational education include the development of a comprehensive understanding of the role of various occupations in meeting human needs and the relation of productivity to wise consumption?
6. Should vocational education stick to its role in preparing people for occupations or seek to help the student integrate general and occupational education?
7. Should the vocational education curriculum be designed only for initial employment or should it be conceived as a major part of lifelong learning?

Answers to fundamental questions like these serve as standards for judging the consistency and the importance of proposed educational objectives. To serve in this way, a philosophy must be stated clearly and the implications for educational objectives may need to be spelled out. Such a clear and analytical statement can then be used to examine every proposed objective, noting whether each is in harmony with one or more main points in the philosophy, whether it is in opposition or whether it is unrelated to any of the points. Those objectives in harmony with the philosophy will then be identified as important.

Using Psychology of Learning

The suggested objectives should be examined to determine whether they are in harmony with the psychology of learning. Unless these educational ends are in conformity with conditions intrinsic to learning, they are worthless.

At the lowest level, a knowledge of the psychology of learning enables us to distinguish those changes in human beings that can be expected to result from a learning process from those changes that cannot. For example, young people can develop good health habits through a learning process. On the other hand, they cannot increase their height directly by a learning process.

At a higher level, a knowledge of the psychology of learning enables us to distinguish goals that are feasible from those that are likely to take a very long time or are almost impossible to attain at the age level contemplated. It has been shown, for example, that to change the basic attitudes of children requires continuous work extending over several years. In general, basic attitudes are not affected markedly by one, two, three or four months of instruction. In similar fashion, data have been obtained regarding the time involved in bringing about fundamental changes in ways of thinking and study, basic habits and practices, interests and the like. Psychological knowledge of this sort is useful in suggesting the length of time over which particular objectives will need to be emphasized.

Multiple Outcomes

One of the most important psychological findings for curriculum planning is the discovery that most learning experiences produce multiple outcomes. For example, a student who is working with an arithmetic problem may also be acquiring certain knowledge about the materials dealt with in the problems. In addition, the student is also developing certain favorable or unfavorable attitudes toward arithmetic. He or she is developing or failing to develop certain interests in this area.

In practically every educational experience, two or more kinds of educational outcomes may be expected. This is important in curriculum planning because it suggests that greater efficiency of instruction is possible by capitalizing on the multiple results possible from each experience.

To use psychology of learning in selecting objectives, it is helpful to write down the important elements of a defensible psychology of learning and then to indicate what possible implications each main point might have for educational objectives. When checked against this statement, possible objectives may be selected as appropriate or rejected as unattainable, inappropriate to the age level, too general or too specific, or otherwise in conflict with the psychology of learning.

Stating Objectives Clearly

The preceding steps described above should have produced a small list of important objectives that are feasible to attain. Because they have been obtained from several sources, they are likely to be stated in various ways. In organizing a single list of important objectives for a program, it is desirable to state them in a form that makes them most helpful in selecting learning experiences and guiding teaching.

Objectives are sometimes stated as tasks for the instructor, such as to present the theory of electric circuits or to demonstrate how to take blood pressure. These are not statements of educational ends, since the real purpose of education is not to have the instructor perform certain activities, but to bring about certain changes in the student's behavior. The statement of objectives should include the changes to take place in the students. With such a statement, it is possible to infer the kinds of activities the instructor might carry out in an effort to attain the objectives.

A second form in which objectives are often stated is in listing topics, concepts, generalizations or other elements of content that are to be dealt with in the program. Such a list indicates the content areas to be dealt with by the students, but it does not specify what the students are to do with this content. Is it to be memorized? Does it indicate a topic that the student is to study? Does it suggest situations in which skills are to be acquired? The list itself does not define what the students are expected to learn.

A third way in which objectives are sometimes stated is in the form of generalized patterns of behavior. For example, one may find objectives stated as "to develop critical thinking" or "to develop social attitudes." Objectives stated in this form indicate, in general, the kinds of changes the educational program is expected to bring about in students. However, from what we know about transfer of learning, it is very unlikely that efforts to attain such highly generalized objectives will be fruitful. It is necessary to specify more definitely the content to which this behavior applies or the area of life in which this behavior is to be used.

The most useful way to state objectives is in terms that identify both the kind of behavior the student is to be helped to develop and the content or area of life in which this behavior is to operate. For example, the objective, "familiar with dependable sources of information on questions relating to nutrition" includes both an indication of the sort of behavior, namely, familiarity with dependable sources, and the content, namely, those sources that deal with problems of nutrition.

A satisfactory formulation of objectives indicates both the behavioral aspects and the content. Hence, it provides clear specifications of the educational job. By defining these desired educational results as clearly as possible, the curriculum planners have the most useful set of criteria for selecting content, suggesting learning activities and deciding on the kind of teaching procedures to follow—in fact, for carrying on all the further steps of curriculum planning.

PLANNING LEARNING EXPERIENCES

When the curriculum objectives have been defined, curriculum planning is then concerned with the means for attaining these ends. Essentially, learning takes place through the experiences the student has—that is, through the reactions he or she makes to the environment.

In planning an educational program to attain given objectives, experiences must be selected or devised that are likely to help the student attain these goals.

Several general principles are helpful in selecting and devising learning experiences. The essential one is that for a given objective to be attained, a student must have experiences that give him or her an opportunity to practice the kind of behavior implied by the objective. For example, if one of the objectives is to develop skill in problem solving, this cannot be attained unless the learning experiences give the student ample opportunity to solve problems.

A second general principle is that the results of the learning experiences should give the student satisfaction. For example, in the case of learning experiences to develop skill in solving health problems, it is important not only that the experiences give the student an opportunity to solve these problems, but also that effective solutions shall be satisfying to him or her. If the experiences are unsatisfactory or distasteful, the desired learning is not likely to take place.

Helping the Student Go Beyond

A third general principle is that the reactions the student is expected to make in the experience should be within the range of possibility for him or her. To quote an old adage, "The teacher must begin where the student is, but help him go beyond." If the learning experience calls for a kind of behavior of which the student is not yet capable, then it fails in its purpose. If the experience involves nothing new for the student, he or she can learn nothing from it.

Clearly, the process of planning learning experiences is not a mechanical method of setting down definitely prescribed experiences for each objective. Rather, the process is a more creative one. As planners consider the desired objectives, they begin to outline a series of possible learning experiences and materials that might be used. As the list is developed, specific items might be outlined in more detail.

The tentative draft of learning experiences should then be checked carefully against the desired objectives to see first whether the proposed experiences would give an opportunity for the students to carry on the kind of behavior implied by the objectives, whether they would be satisfying to the students and whether they are appropriate for the students.

Revisions can then be made so the experiences will be more effective. If the experiences are largely inadequate in terms of these criteria, then the tentative formulation should be dropped and others developed. Such a procedure furnishes opportunity both for creativity and for careful evaluation before setting up definite plans for the instructional program.

ORGANIZING LEARNING EXPERIENCES

After devising a number of learning experiences for a program, the teacher must decide how to organize them. Important changes in human behavior are not produced overnight. No single learning experience is likely to have a profound effect upon the student, but if experiences are well organized, their cumulative effect can be great.

In organizing learning experiences, the teacher should consider their relationship over time and from one area to another. Experiences can be organized to furnish a continuing sequence, each experience building on but going beyond the earlier ones. This is commonly called vertical organization. The relationship between the learning experiences a student has in this course and those he or she has in other courses and outside the school during the same period is called horizontal organization.

Virtues of Horizontal Organization

The importance of a sequential vertical organization is generally recognized in curriculum planning, but the value of a greater integration in the horizontal organization is not so well understood. When it is considered, it is commonly seen as an opportunity for the student to use a skill that he or she is learning in one course in another or to practice outside of school the skills being taught in the classroom.

These tactics are, of course, helpful in making the curriculum more effective, but the goals should be more ambitious—that is, they should help the student perceive all experiences as part of a whole so he or she recognizes in what ways the things taught in different courses are similar, supplementary or focused on different purposes.

So far as possible, everything a student is learning should help him or her to understand and deal with the world more adequately. He or she needs to avoid putting knowledge in little compartments, each isolated from the rest. Integration of knowledge requires more cooperation among instructors in planning, but it is worth the effort in terms of the marked increase in cumulative learning that results.

EVALUATING CURRICULUM EFFECTIVENESS

Even when a curriculum is planned with great care and on the basis of ample information, it is not always as effective as hoped. The only way to insure a continually effective educational program is by maintaining a continuing evaluation of objectives, learning experiences and the organization. The principles and procedures of evaluation are so important that they occupy a section of this yearbook.

PARTICIPANTS IN CURRICULUM PLANNING

Traditionally, curriculum planning was carried on by special persons not directly responsible for instruction, but we have learned over the years that a curriculum handed down from a district or state office or formulated by a project group is rarely implemented in the way intended. Two researchers in the field of science found, for example, that less than one-third of the teachers they observed who were using new curricula developed nationally employed these materials as they were intended. Typically, materials intended to stimulate or to guide inquiry learning were being treated as material for students to memorize. It has become clear that fully effective implementation of a curriculum requires that all the essential actors (1) understand the objectives and believe them to be important, (2) believe that the curriculum offers a constructive way for them to use their efforts, (3) know what is expected of them, and (4) can and do perform their roles.

Most curricula require actions by teachers, students, parents and administrators, so the four conditions listed above refer to all of these people. It would be difficult, if not impossible, for all these persons to participate constructively in the educational program if they had no part in planning it. For this reason, the involvement in one or more phases of curriculum planning by all those who are expected to participate in the operation of the program is recommended.

Include Employers

In the case of vocational education, employers should be included among the participants in planning because of their knowledge about occupational needs and opportunities and because they will often be responsible for providing employment for students and graduates of vocational programs. It is also important to involve other community leaders in the planning, since they will have a significant voice in shaping policies relating to the transition of youth from school to work. They may also be able to contribute information and advice regarding what should be taught and how it can be learned. Furthermore, their involvement should help them gain an understanding of the educational program as it relates to employability and the related role of on-the-job training and other learning experiences outside of school.

Two Criteria for Participants

In general, the selection of persons in curriculum planning should be guided by two criteria: Whether they can furnish helpful information for curriculum planning and whether they will have a part to play in the implementation of the program. Teachers have contributions to make in all phases of planning because they have relevant information about students, content and learning, and they also will be the persons who conduct the program.

Students have a part to play in deciding what is to be taught because they have information about student needs and interests. They have a part to play in devising and selecting learning experiences because they have views on the kind of learning experiences that have been helpful to them in the past.

Parents have a part to play in deciding what is to be taught because they are aware of their children's interests and activities. They should participate in planning learning experiences because they need to reinforce curriculum objectives through their attitudes and activities in the home.

Administrators, particularly principals, have a part to play in all phases of curriculum planning because they have helpful information and because they are involved in the implementation of plans. Supervisors and consultants can also contribute much through their expertise.

Finally, but of great importance, are local advisory councils that include employers, unions, educators and other local leaders. The councils can furnish information about jobs in the local area where students are and where most of the transition from school to work will take place. They can also help to devise and select learning experiences both for the school and for on-the-job training. They can assist in developing a sequence of learning experiences involving both school sites and work sites, shaping evaluation procedures and interpreting evaluation data. They can also be a rich resource for curriculum planning.

CONCLUSION

In conclusion, curriculum planning is a comprehensive and continuing process that distinguishes an educational program developed systematically by professionals from ad hoc programs. Not all of the necessary steps can usually be taken at one time, but a schedule can be developed to insure that the program will be periodically reviewed and improvements made where problems are identified.

PLANNING AND DEVELOPING
THE CURRICULUM

2.
PUTTING COMPETENCY-BASED
INSTRUCTION IN PERSPECTIVE

Carl J. Schaefer

Writings about competency-based instruction seem to be in vogue. The popular media make passionate pleas for achievement at minimum competency levels. Professional educational journals abound with articles about organizing instruction to achieve predetermined minimum competencies.

Make no mistake about it, parents and students alike are looking upon educators with a critical eye as the dispensers of certain competencies. Even more critical, vocational educators are being judged by business and industrial employers for their ability to produce minimum student competencies. And those in high government positions who have been instrumental in providing federal dollars to assist our programs appear somewhat disillusioned with our efforts.

These events raise the question, "Is competency-based instruction in vocational education fact or fantasy, bogus or real?" I, for one, think we should pursue competency-based instruction to the utmost, and it is my intent to argue that we vocational educators have survived far too long without having to prove to our various publics that graduates from our programs are indeed more competent occupationally than those graduating from nonvocational programs.

TEACHING AS AN ART

Few would dispute the statement that the teacher is central to the educational process. Given a good teacher, learning takes place. Given a poor or mediocre teacher, less learning can be expected. Test this statment by asking students in which classes they feel they are learning. There is a direct correlation between teacher and student and make no mistake about it.

But all teachers are not alike—even those who teach the same subject. We have known for a long time that students vary in ability and learning style, but for some reason we have not recognized that teachers likewise vary as individuals and as dispensers of knowledge. They have their own preferences, interests, subject matter expertise, teaching styles and ability to establish rapport with students. Anyone who has ever attended or taught school knows that most teachers relate better to some students than others, that they are most functional within a particular setting involving a certain type of student population and learning environment.

Moreover, students themselves have long been sensitive to teacher preferences. They quickly "size up" the instructor's likes and dislikes, temperament and expectations. Thus, in many respects, teaching is more of an art than a science. The ability to capture student interest, to hold it, and to mold and develop innate talent requires creativity and skill. There is no formula, teacher training program, inservice training or discipline that can assure the successful transmission of subject matter to all students equally by all teachers. The performance of teachers will always be varied.

Yet minimum competency achievement on the part of each student is expected, both by our society and by the profession itself. To fail repeatedly in such an achievement is to have failed as a professional.

A LOGICAL ARGUMENT FOR CBVE

If we accept the proposition that vocational educators are responsible for helping students attain minimum occupational competencies, the question arises as to how this can be best accomplished. As Mager and Beach (1967) put it:

> The plumber fails if he cannot stop a leak. The machinist is useless if he shapes metal but doesn't shape it according to the blueprint . . . and the surgeon fails if he operates but removes the wrong part.
>
> So too, the instructor fails if he goes through all the motions but can't (or will not) demonstrate that his students can perform according to course objectives.

Competency-based vocational education (CBVE) starts with certain achievable and required competencies and then measures them to see if they have been acquired. Many maintain we have been doing this all along in vocational education. Yet our critics appear less than convinced that we are producing program graduates who can demonstrate mastery of a body of competencies (even the most basic) that places them at an advantage in their quest for jobs.

If nothing else, the advantage of CBVE is its emphasis on program measurement of achievement.

A LOGICAL ARGUMENT AGAINST CBVE

In the development of a product, certain specifications are set forth. Usually the best minds possible are brought to bear on the product specifications before the product is placed into production. Even then, there have been product failures, and manufacturers have gone broke because the cost was too high, the product didn't last or the design wasn't attractive. CBVE encompasses many of the hazards of any product development.

A major problem is reaching agreement on what competencies ought to be taught. Some would argue that even basic occupational competencies in a given field or trade vary significantly, especially from geographic area to geographic area. Carpentry is not the same in the New England states as it is in California. Building codes, merchandising procedures, food production and business practices vary to a major extent from locale to locale. How then can the competencies themselves be determined?

Second, the specifications of CBVE are difficult to construct. Questions exist not only on what to measure (the content involved), but on what forms the measurement should take. Should the specifications include performance measures or merely measures of knowledge? How much of each should be required if both are to be specified?

Third, the target population needs to be identified. What kind of student input is needed to meet the specification measurements? Do we have any control over this raw material input and, if not, can the product be developed even by the best of teaching?

Overcoming the Problems

These and other problems could give teachers a legitimate way to avoid the CBVE concept. It could be argued that there are too many uncontrolled variables and one must just do the best job possible within a situation without being concerned about the end product of the process.

My view is that some form of CBVE is essential. Because vocational education has its roots in the content of various occupations, the competencies taught stem from the technological makeup of occupations. Thus, agreement must be reached on what current, up-to-date competencies are required, what can be taught to beginners and how these competencies can be measured as having been learned. All of this is an integral part of competency-based instruction.

SOME THOUGHTS ABOUT ACHIEVEMENT

Achievement takes place as a result of persistence or endeavor. Emphasis on accomplishing something is evident throughout our daily lives. This is why we are a nation of sports enthusiasts, lovers of champions and admirers of those who achieve. Achievement is a way of challenging the individual to want to learn. Yet we tolerate and label individuals as nonachievers. What an admission for educators to make!

Goal Setting

Achievement starts with setting realistic goals. Goal setting may be viewed as the blueprint or sketch of the final product. After all, the architect doesn't write the specifications until the overall plan is drawn.

Vocational Instruction

Vocational educators depend on the process of occupational analysis to set educational goals. The logic here is to use the trade or occupation as a blueprint or sketch to direct the achievement deemed necessary. There are, of course, a number of techniques for making an occupational analysis, several of which are discussed elsewhere in this yearbook.

Product Specification

What the teacher can do to help students meet occupational goals depends on a variety of factors over which the teacher has some control. Unfortunately, one hears vocational educators say only too often that they cannot possibly make a mechanic out of a student because he or she does not meet the required specifications, i.e., can't read, write or do mathematics. Frequently, one also hears complaints about lack of motivation or interest, a problem that may be caused in part by deficiencies in the teacher.

Setting specifications or standards almost always means some failures. No standards are met by 100 percent of those who try to attain them. Unfortunately, those who judge education often believe that it must be 100 percent effective and the profession has complied by using what has been called social promotion. Thus, those who persist eventually graduate, only to fail at the next educational level or during the employment selection process.

Rarely is the graduate of a vocational program provided with verification of what specifications he or she has met in the occupational curriculum pursued. Evidence of what the student can do to meet or surpass a standard might assist him or her in finding employment.

Contrast this situation with the effort that has gone into achievement measures for those who want to get into college. Here, specifications are set so any postsecondary administrative officer can determine whether or not a student meets the standard set by the institution. How unfortunate for the vocational graduate that he or she does not have evidence of having met certain specifications—mainly because vocational education has never set any.

Program Assessment

Doesn't it seem strange that vocational education has, at times of high employment and at times of high unemployment, based its achievement mainly on how many graduates were placed in jobs for which they were trained? Everyone knows job placement is a function of job availability. When there are a lot of job openings, most people, including vocational graduates, are placed readily. On the other hand, when jobs are not readily available and unemployment is high, vocational graduates suffer along with others and are not placed in high numbers. For example, in 1976 the placement of secondary school vocational graduates employed in the field trained for was 58.1 percent (U.S. Office of Education, 1978), whereas in 1973 it was 62.1 percent (U.S. Office of Education, 1974). The difference of four percentage points could well be attributed to economic conditions at the time and not to a drop in effectiveness of the vocational program.

This leads us back to competency-based vocational instruction as a measure of program quality. CBVE specifies the competencies achieved at the end of the program even if job opportunities are not readily present upon graduation. As a criterion of achievement, placement is just too variable during any one year for vocational education to be held accountable on that basis alone.

Additional measures that are too often overlooked are improvement in basic skills through pre- and post-testing procedures, related technical knowledge, achievement through paper and pencil instruments, manipulative (psychomotor) skills through performance measures and affective behaviors (attitude) through additudinal scales.

Admittedly, if goals are not reached, the teacher may not have delivered. Judgment as to the fault—whether it be the student input, curriculum or the way the instruction was presented—is possible with the use of CBVE.

KEY QUESTIONS

The state of the art in CBVE appears acceptable to the profession, but key questions remain to be answered. The notion of measuring achievement has always been a paramount goal of vocational education, but what and how to measure have been the problems. Probably there never will be a nationally adopted curriculum for vocational education. Each state has its own system of delivery and each holds to its respective brand of accomplishment.

But even after granting administrative and organizational differences, there remains a great deal of commonality in goal setting, specifications and the instructional process itself.

Probably the closest vocational education has come to a common understanding of what is desired in its graduates can be seen through the student organizations. For example, the Skill Olympics (now a worldwide competition) show the impressive achievement of members of the Vocational Industrial Clubs of America.

But what about the average vocational graduate—one who does not share the limelight of local, state or national competition? What competencies will be required of such a vocational graduate? How will his or her achievement be recognized? Who will set the minimum standards for the occupation being studied? How and when will they be measured? What will be done with those who are judged deficient? All of these are key questions that need to be answered before CBVE can become a full reality.

THE POTENTIAL OF CBVE

The exciting thing about CBVE is its potential for raising the image of vocational education from a "catch all" for the student who is not college bound to one of "know how" in the occupational world. For the first time, vocational education through CBVE could give an edge to its graduates in finding and retaining employment because they could attest to occupational competency. The high school diploma would remain the mere piece of paper it is today and the record of competency would become the benchmark of vocational achievement.

Some Pieces in Place

The use of CBVE on a broad scale may not be far in the future. Several pieces of the puzzle are already in place.

Vocational-Technical Education Consortium of States. The principal objective of the Vocational-Technical Education Consortium of States (V-TECS) is the production of catalogs of performance objectives and performance guides for use in the development of vocational-technical curricula. Eighteen states, the U.S. Air Force and the U.S. Navy form the Consortium through which more than 40 catalogs have been developed.

Catalogs are developed in relation to the three-digit occupational groups in the *Dictionary of Occupational Titles* (4th edition) and the process includes validation by incumbent workers. Here are several uses of V-TECS materials:

1. Performance objectives may be compared to existing programs for inclusiveness.
2. Performance objectives may be used for curriculum development.
3. Performance objectives may be shared with the student before instruction, revealing the anticipated competencies that will result from instruction.
4. Performance objectives attained by students may be revealed to potential employers, thereby describing the tasks the student can perform and how well he or she can perform them.
5. Performance objectives may be used as a basis for developing criterion/reference test items.
6. Performance guides may be used to identify prerequisites such as minimum reading abilities, the ability to discriminate between colors and physical requirements.
7. Performance guides may be used to assist in sequencing instructional units.
8. Performance guides may be used as intermediate learning checkpoints that must be addressed in preparing the student for task accomplishment (Vocational-Technical Consortium of States, 1978).

Thus, it is not difficult to see how V-TECS can contribute to the CBVE process of instruction and accountability.

National Occupational Competency Testing Institute (NOCTI). Another piece of the emerging CBVE concept rests in some of the work being done by the National Occupational Competency Testing Institute, which is also a consortium of states. NOCTI works with about 45 states in the development and administration of occupational competency instruments to measure minimum competency for preservice and inservice teachers in the areas of trade, industrial and technical education. The approach here is to provide achievement testing of related technical knowledge and performance skill ability to assure expertise in the subject one is going to teach.

About 25 NOCTI tests have been developed and are administered annually and semiannually throughout the country in 42 test centers. Teacher certification and the granting of college credit by examination are the main purposes being accomplished by NOCTI (National Occupational Competency Testing Institute, 1978). Again, the tie-in with CBVE for secondary and postsecondary vocational education remains an intriguing thought.

Ohio Achievement Program. Ohio has distinguished itself in the achievement area by developing achievement tests in trade, industrial and technical education. Last year these instruments were administered to more than 50,000 secondary vocational students in 16 different occupational areas. As paper and pencil measures, the Ohio Achievement tests help verify the acquisition of basic occupational knowledge and assist in improving the curriculum and updating instruction (Ohio Trade and Industrial Education Service, 1972).

What Needs to Be Done

Agreement will never be reached on the "how" of teaching. Pedagogy is an art more than a science and the teacher must be left to dispense knowledge and skill in his or her own way, making the learning a creative and exhilarating experience.

But the "what" of teaching is another matter. This is where CBVE comes into the picture. With the aid of V-TECS, NOCTI and the Ohio Achievement Program, a comprehensive system could be formed. Once and for all, the vocational graduate might be able to say, "I can do these things and do them well." This is a far cry from our past and present difficulties in demonstrating our accomplishments.

What is needed is leadership by teachers and administrators and a will to move ahead in making CBVE work for the benefit of all.

REFERENCES

Mager, Robert F., and Beach, Kenneth M., Jr. *Developing vocational instruction.* Palo Alto, Calif.: Fearon Publishers, 1967.

National Occupational Competency Testing Institute. *Fifth annual report.* Albany, N.Y.: NOCTI, 1978.

Ohio Trade and Industrial Education Service. *Achievement test program.* Columbus, Ohio: State Department of Educaton, 1972.

U.S. Office of Education. *Summary data: Vocational education, fiscal year 1973.* Washington, D.C.: Bureau of Occupational and Adult Education, Division of Vocational and Technical Education, 1974.

Vocational Instruction

U.S. Office of Education. *Summary data: Vocational education, fiscal year 1976*. Washington, D.C.: Bureau of Occupational and Adult Education, Division of Vocational and Technical Education, 1978.

Vocational-Technical Education Consortium of States. *Fifth annual report of V-TECS*. Atlanta, Ga.: Commission on Occupational Education Institutions, Southern Association of Colleges and Schools, 1978.

II.

PLANNING AND DEVELOPING
THE CURRICULUM

3.
THE VOCATIONAL-TECHNICAL EDUCATION CONSORTIUM OF STATES

Herbert Bruce, Jr. and Robert Spillman

Too many students are leaving school without the basic skills necessary to function as contributing members of society. Parents and society in general are questioning the accountability of our educational system, and considering the mood of society, there is little chance of getting an increase in taxes to support education.

Vocational education is also receiving its share of criticism for ineffectiveness. This alarming situation raises some very basic issues. What should be included in the school curriculum? How should teachers determine when students have reached learning objectives? How can one determine which competencies students have attained at the end of a program or at a given point in the program?

Competency-based education (CBE) has emerged as one workable approach to improving education and making it accountable to society. A number of educators, who are interested not only in accountability but in developing and promoting sound vocational education, have taken significant steps toward implementing competency-based programs. This chapter defines competency-based education, gives a brief rationale for the concept and describes a program that provides a basis for the development of CBE.

Determining curriculum content through occupational task analyses, establishing student performance standards, developing and providing open-ended curricula, and designing appropriate learning activities for students are not new activities in vocational education. In fact, many vocational educators have been following these sound educational practices for years. The principles of competency-based education are new to a majority of teachers, however, and the approach therefore constitutes a revolution in the delivery of vocational education.

A DEFINITION OF COMPETENCY-BASED EDUCATION

A number of definitions for CBE have been written during the past few years. (For our purposes, CBE and PBE [performance-based education] are used interchangeably.) A widely used definition is that of Elam (1964) who used three levels of descriptors: (1) essential elements, (2) implied characteristics, and (3) related or desirable characteristics. He states that:

> Competencies (knowledge, skill, behaviors) to be demonstrated by the students are derived from explicit conceptions of teacher roles; stated so as to make possible assessment of a student's behavior in relation to specific competencies; and made public in advance.

Elam's (1964) assessment of the student's competency uses his or her performance as the primary source of evidence; takes into account evidence of the student's knowledge relevant to planning for, analyzing, interpreting, or evaluating situations or behavior; and strives for objectivity.

The student's rate of progress through the program, according to Elam, is determined ". . . by demonstrated competency rather than by time or course completion. The instructional program is intended to facilitate the development and evaluation of the student's achievement of competencies specified."

Several other characteristics included in Elam's list of essential elements are found often in competency-based programs:

1. Instruction is individualized and personalized.
2. The learning experience of the individual is guided by feedback.
3. The program as a whole is systemic.
4. The emphasis is on exit requirements rather than on entrance requirements.
5. Instruction is organized into modules.
6. The student is held accountable for performance, completing the preparation program when and only when he or she demonstrates the competencies that have been identified as requisite for a particular professional role.

Less central than the essential elements and implied characteristics, according to Elam, are several other related and desirable characteristics:

1. The program is field centered.
2. There is a broad base for decision making.
3. The materials and experiences focus on concepts, skills and knowledge that can be learned in a specific instructional setting.
4. Both the teachers and the students are designers of the instructional system.
5. The program includes a research component and is open to change.
6. Preparation is continued throughout one's career.

Though Elam speaks of competency-based teacher education, most of the concepts are applicable to competency-based vocational education.

In another attempt to define CBE, Fardig (1975) states that: "Competency-based education, then, is a total system for planning, developing and implementing a curriculum designed to insure that students acquire the knowledge, skills, and attitudes essential for successful job performance."

V-TECS—A SYSTEMATIC APPROACH

The Vocational-Technical Education Consortium of States (V-TECS) provides a systematic approach to determining the competencies students need to be competent workers in specified jobs. The system has been accepted by a group of 17 states that comprise the consortium: Alabama, Florida, Georgia, Illinois, Indiana, Kentucky, Louisiana, Maryland, Michigan, Mississippi, New York, Pennsylvania, South Carolina, Tennessee, Virginia, West Virginia, Wisconsin.

In addition, there are three associate members: The U.S. Air Force Training Command, represented by the Community College of the Air Force; the U.S. Naval Educational and Training Command; and the U.S. Army Training and Doctrine Command. The work of the consortium is administered by the Commission on Occupational Education Institutions/Southern Association of Colleges and Schools.

The primary purpose of V-TECS is to:

. . . develop valid catalogs of performance objectives, criterion-referenced measures, and performance guides for learners in vocational-technical education. Methods and procedures carefully planned and tested are used to insure that the products developed will be of high quality. Since uniform procedures are established throughout the consortium, the result has been a high degree of confidence in the materials on the part of the member states and agencies sharing them. This advantage, plus assurances that the materials will require a minimum amount of adaptation by users, has enhanced the transportability of the product (Vocational-Technical Education Consortium of States, 1977).

The V-TECS model for developing catalogs of performance objectives and criterion-referenced measures has well-defined steps and quality control processes for monitoring each step from identification of priorities through diffusion and the revision cycle. (For a specific description, consult the *V-TECS Technical Coordinator's Handbook,* V-TECS/Commission on Occupational Education Institutions, 795 Peachtree Street, N.E., Atlanta, Georgia.)

V-TECS DEVELOPMENTAL MODEL

State priorities for the production of catalogs are identified by studying manpower needs, program needs, employment opportunities, student enrollment and the need for curriculum development in a particular area. In addition to data found in a particular state, regional and national data are also used. The V-TECS board of directors discusses the priorities established by each member state before setting consortium priorities.

Each member state finally selects and with approval develops a minimum of two catalogs per contract period. This step is taken to make sure duplication does not occur and that each state has the opportunity to bargain for specific catalogs in which it may have a particular interest.

After priority areas have been identified and catalog assignments made to member states, the first step in the development process is to conduct a thorough state-of-the-art review. This is an effort to identify all available materials in the area for which a catalog is being developed. Using the results of this review and interviews with workers on the job, a comprehensive list of task statements is developed. The resulting task inventory is used to conduct an occupational survey and an occupational task analysis.

The Occupational Survey

The occupational survey is conducted by asking a representative sample of workers in the selected occupational area to verify the task statements. Thus, data is gathered to determine the tasks performed by the worker, the relative amount of time spent on each task, and the tools and equipment used.

On the basis of this information, decisions are made on the selection of tasks to be assigned performance objectives and criterion-referenced measures. The objectives and measures are written by a team of carefully selected people. Quality control standards are established for the composition of both the writing team and the performance objectives produced by the team. Before the final printing of the catalog, the performance objectives are field tested and revised.

It has long been recognized that utilization of materials is much more difficult to achieve than production of materials. Each member state and agency is required therefore to develop and submit a diffusion plan. These plans are designed to help teachers, supervisors and administrators in managing performance-based instruction. In line with this broadened interpretation, the plans include inservice education, program supervision, organizational structuring and resource allocation to support performance-based vocational education.

The Revision Cycle

Even though the V-TECS program is relatively young, curriculum revision to keep up with technological developments has been written into the V-TECS model and is now being planned. While specific procedures have not been established, a three-to-five-year revision and updating cycle is part of the program.

The revision cycle completes the model, which can be summed up as (1) the identification of priorities, (2) the writing of a domain study, (3) the completion of a task analysis, (4) the validation and writing of objectives, (5) the diffusion of the product, and (6) the planning for revision of the materials. Built into this model is a sound system of curriculum development that combines the efforts of the participating states and the military services to develop valid catalogs of performance objectives, criterion-referenced measures and performance guides.

ORGANIZATIONAL STRUCTURE OF V-TECS

V-TECS is operated by the Commission on Occupational Education Institutions (COEI) and Southern Association of Colleges and Schools. It is organized with a board of directors consisting of one person from each participating state. The board serves as the policy-making body of the consortium, providing advice, technical assistance and policy direction to the executive director.

Each state also has a technical coordinator, who (1) acts as liaison between the state projects and the central staff and (2) serves as a technical resource person for project personnel in the state and assists the technical coordinators and the central staff. The working relationship of these people must be rather close so that acceptable levels of quality for products, personnel training and procedures used to develop catalogs can be maintained.

The other key people involved in the consortium are the project directors, who are responsible for the actual production of the V-TECS products in their states.

IMPLICATIONS FOR CURRICULUM DEVELOPMENT

The V-TECS materials have many implications for curriculum planning and program development in vocational education.

First, there is the assurance that objectives have been developed that are congruent with tasks performed by workers in the occupations for which students are preparing to enter.

Second, the instructor has a validated instrument or technique for determining when the student can perform the specified objectives.

Third, data are available to indicate the tools and equipment used by workers in the occupation. Consequently, educators will know what tools and equipment must be available for training purposes.

Fourth, the V-TECS program will provide a structure for both vertical and horizontal articulation. Vertical articulation is possible because a record of individual student achievement can be maintained and transferred from one level of education to another. Horizontal articulation will be possible because the objectives the student completes will be on record, eliminating the requirement to repeat instruction when transferring to another program.

It will also be possible for students to get credit for competencies developed outside the school setting. The V-TECS system of curriculum planning will in fact permit students to develop competencies in whatever setting is most efficient.

Fifth, V-TECS provides a tool for program evaluation that makes it possible to conduct accountability studies in depth. This same tool may also offer better opportunities to evaluate teaching techniques.

SUMMARY

Though it may be true that the V-TECS program does not encompass all the elements of a competency-based educational program, it does provide a research-based, validated set of performance objectives that can be used as the basis of competency-based vocational education programs. The V-TECS materials emphasize competencies a student should possess upon exit from a program. The program provides a basis for organizing the curriculum into modules.

The V-TECS program is systemic in its structure and process. Students can be held accountable for competencies identified as requisite for selected worker roles. Although the V-TECS products provide a basis for the development of competency-based curricula, they can also be used in many educational programs that do not include all the elements of competency-based education.

REFERENCES

Elam, S. *Performance based teacher education: What is the state of the art?* Washington, D.C.: American Association of Colleges for Teacher Education, 1964.

Fardig, G. E. *Handbook for the development of vocational education modules.* Lexington, Ky.: Curriculum Development Center, 1975.

Vocational-Technical Education Consortium of States. *Fourth progress and information report.* Atlanta, Ga.: Southern Association of Colleges and Schools, 1977.

PLANNING AND DEVELOPING
THE CURRICULUM

4.
EXPECTATIONS AND STANDARDS FOR QUALITY INSTRUCTION

Grant Venn and Daniel E. Skutack

Though vocational educators have long endorsed and sometimes practiced many of the principles and methods needed to change instructional results, quality instruction has too often been characterized by selectivity or the rationalization of pointing with pride to those who have succeeded. As John Goodlad points out:

> Education has for too long pointed with pride to those who have "made it" while disregarding the many who have "fallen by the wayside." Although we have chosen not to notice the general ineffectiveness of education, the overall failure is glaringly apparent in dropout rates, in barely minimal learning on the part of the many who do remain in school and in growing alienation among the young of all colors and classes (1973).

This extremely harsh statement has more validity than most of us would admit. Its truth must be recognized, however, if we are to make any effort to change such conditions.

This chapter will not discuss the various principles and practices of vocational instruction known to improve learning, such as indivdualzed instruction, experiential learning outside the school, individual projects, and the application of knowledge and theory in real situations. Vocational education has led the way in this nation in applying these principles. Instead, this chapter will discuss the expectations and standards with which vocational education must deal. These factors are crucial to the creation of a learning environment necessary for quality instruction.

MEASURES OF QUALITY INSTRUCTION

Benjamin Bloom has defined aptitude as "the amount of time required by the learner to attain mastery of a learning task." This definition means simply that given adequate time and instruction appropriate to expectations and standards, students can learn. This principle should guide classroom instruction. *The degree to which all students attain minimal required standards should be the first measure of quality instruction.* The recognition of individual differences would invalidate traditional group teaching and inflexible schedules under which much vocational instruction must take place.

The emergence of education as necessary for a work life as well as a private life and a public life has caused vocational instruction to be seen by many persons as a cure-all and by some as a solution for those whose expectations have not been met through traditional educational offerings. The emergence of preparation for work as a social necessity has made vocational education an effective way to learn for an increasing number of people.

The Meaning of Quality Instruction

In America it has become necessary to prepare everyone for a productive work life or take care of them at public expense. Opportunities for work depend both on basic skills and on competencies in an occupational area. Few opportunities for work are open to the uneducated. Quality instruction must therefore be defined as the degree to which people acquire the skills necessary to function and advance in their private, public and work lives.

Quality Instruction: Past and Present

In the past, when most work was manual, repetitive and unchanging, education was little needed by most workers. Today the relationship between education and work is stronger because most jobs depend on the mastery of basic and occupational skills.

Selectivity in the past was the *sine qua non* of quality. The measures of quality instruction accepted were a selective admissions policy, a harsh grading system and a large number of prerequisites for courses.

Because the uneducated can no longer function effectively in our society, the concept of selectivity as a measure of instructional quality is destructive of society and of individuals. Everyone must learn to read, write and compute at a minimal level if they are to learn effectively. In addition to these basic skills, everyone must develop occupational skills, along with basic work competencies such as responsibility, cooperativeness and communication skills.

Equal Educational Opportunities

Recent federal legislation supports increased educational opportunities for the disadvantaged and handicapped, expanded vocational and career education, and more emphasis on sex and racial equity in education. These mandates all point up the necessity of redefining quality instruction as providing everyone with the minimal competencies needed to function in their private, public and work lives.

The original response to demands for equity in educational opportunity was to simply allow more individuals to enroll in the same programs taught in the same manner. This "solution" often created new problems, however, through the pressure of additional students who were unable to meet instructional standards when time, methods and content were the same for every student.

EXPECTATIONS AND STANDARDS

As societal expectations change, work and its supportive system, vocational education, must adapt by making adjustments that include alterations in the instructional process. In the past, expectations were based on the work ethic, which emphasized the economic necessity of productive work and direct personal rewards from work. Labor, management, the community, the family and political power structures all functioned according to the unprinted tenets of this ethic.

For many years, this work ethic was accepted by nearly everyone. Recently, however, it has been under siege. The rapidly occurring changes in work during the past few decades have not led to equally drastic changes in the educational system. Changes in expectations have been attributed to the generation gap, wars, and the failure of the home and church to teach proper moral values.

Past motivation to work and to prepare for work illustrate Maslow's needs theory, in which psychological and safety needs are the primary basis for work rewards. According to this theory, work rewards include the basic necessities of life and a few luxuries. Today these rewards are taken for granted and are easily attained through the benefits of technology and affluence.

The development of new technology also changed the nature of work and, consequently, the standards for education and for job skills. Occupational skills became something that had to be taught rather than something "picked up" on the job. The knowledge and skills required to secure, hold and advance in the work force continue to change as new technology constantly replaces some jobs with new machines.

The Effects of Structural Unemployment

These rapid changes have led to structural unemployment, i.e., the lack of persons with the skills to fill existing and emerging jobs. When this occurs, the nation's unemployment rate increases. The increase is especially noticeable among the young and uneducated because they are the least able to meet high standards for occupational skills.

The instructor must understand that in a technological society of affluence and change (as contrasted to our earlier agrarian society of scarcity and stability), expectations will change as society changes. The expectations brought to the classroom by the student constitute an important aspect of the learning environment.

Job Standards

In addition to teaching basic employability skills that will enable students to enter and advance in the work world, every vocational instructor must teach specific job skills. The specific occupational standards each student must meet are set by those outside education, i.e., employers. Too often the individual institution or instructors may believe they have the right to define what specific knowledge, theories and skills should be taught. When this happens, the result is often a conflict between what the student has learned and what the employer or supervisor needs on the job.

An earlier goal of vocational education was to develop the complete craftsperson. Increases in technological complexity now make the attainment of this goal impossible. Instead, the student develops a more specialized set of competencies, with the understanding that learning will continue as he or she continues in the occupation.

Learning in the Work Place

Opportunities to learn in the work place should be available in quality vocational instruction. Workers must constantly learn new skills and concepts as the machines, products and services demanded by society change.

A frequent criticism of vocational education is that it teaches specific skills that soon go out of date. Today quality instruction requires that specific, usable entry-level skills be taught. But nearly all employers and workers would agree that what one learns after getting into the occupation may be more significant than what one learned during the preparation period. New manuals, consumer demands for services, inventions and technology all mandate new standards for quality vocational instruction that lead to a continuation of learning as part of the job.

Changing Careers

A new competency is becoming more important to many workers—the ability to adapt to different work situations. It is now expected that most people will change jobs or even occupations several times during their work life. This kind of change often involves moving to new geographical locations, retraining for a new occupation or developing an entirely new career. Quality instruction in vocational education should prepare students to make these adjustments in their lives.

THE NEED FOR NEW APPROACHES

We cannot expect to simply improve the content, process and evaluation of instruction—we need to try some new approaches with different settings and people to improve the quality of instruction. As Goodlad points out:

> Until recently, we believed that we had only to provide some new subject matter here, inject a heavier dose of phonics there, or tighten the discipline a little, to improve both the system and society. Better schools (defined largely in quantitative terms) would mean more jobs, a brisker

economy, safer cities, and more aware, dedicated citizens. Or so we thought. Dwindling confidence in these relationships reflects both declining public confidence in the schools and the tenacity with which we cling to the "learning equals school" equation. Painfully we are coming to realize that grades predict grades, that success in school begets success in more school but is no guarantee of good workers, committed citizens, happy mothers and fathers or compassionate human beings (1973).

Student Aptitude and Motivation

All students vary in their aptitudes for learning. No vocational instructor can teach effectively unless the individual student aptitudes for learning are known. Every student can learn, given enough time and alternative ways to learn, but program planning and instruction must be based to a large degree on an assessment of student learning aptitudes.

An aptitude for learning is undeniably important. It makes little difference, however, if the student is not motivated to learn and sees the instruction as unrelated to personal career goals or rewards for effort.

The motivation to learn may have many sources other than the simple hope of securing a job. If the motivating concept is presented solely in terms of economic return, many persons will reject such reasons as inadequate. For too long this has been the only motivational technique used.

A student's personal goals can be the biggest motivator for learning. The more instruction enhances personal goals and expectations, the more student learning will be increased.

Time and Learning

Probably the greatest handicap to quality instruction is the inflexibility of instructional time. Despite great changes in educational institutions, most educators continue to believe that schedules, hours, credits or the length of time on task must be the same for all students.

If time for learning is constant, then learning must vary if there is more than one student in the class. The serious instructor must therefore find ways to vary the instructional time according to aptitudes for learning, achievements, experiences, motivation, purposes and self-concepts of the individual students.

ALTERNATIVES FOR QUALITY INSTRUCTION

Teachers are combining several new approaches with time-tried methods to improve instruction. For example, they may find that the work place is the best learning laboratory. Because responsibility is a basic competency required in all work, it may be desirable to give students full responsibility for accomplishing instructional tasks at appropriate times.

The students who learn most quickly can aid their classmates. Teachers can also join forces with parents to create better student motivation to improve learning. And because many teachers have little time to learn the newest methods, techniques and skills used in the working world, craft advisory committees can be used to keep programs up to date.

Individualized learning may be better in some instances than group instruction. Some students may learn faster without a written text or manual, and hands-on experience may be a better motivator for some than additional information. Independent study, small group study or team projects are several approaches available to the instructor.

Administrative Policies

Many states and local institutions have created new policies on graduation requirements, attendance, experiential learning, credit by examination, student participation and responsibility, alternative schools, individualized learning and classroom procedures. An instructor who wishes to create new ways to improve quality should first find out what current policies and regulations are on the books in the district or school.

CONCLUSION

It needs to be restated that high expectations and standards are both essential to quality instruction. These are continually changing. The teacher's task is to find an instructional pattern that will meet both individual needs and the standards of the work place.

Let us each remember that we can't do it alone. Teachers must use the student, the parent, the community and the educational system in every way possible to insure quality instruction. It is important to remember that even when all these resources are used, not every student can be saved.

REFERENCES

Davis, Allison. The educability of the children of the poor. In Harold Howe, II (Ed.), *The unfinished journey—issues in American education.* New York: John Day, 1972.

Goodlad, John I. The future of learning: Into the twenty-first century. *Toward accountability: A practical guide to educational change.* Palo Alto, Calif.: Westinghouse Learning Press, 1973.

Lessinger, Leon. *Every kid a winner.* Chicago, Ill.: Science Research Associates, 1971.

Maslow, Abraham H. *Motivation and personality.* New York: Harper and Row, 1954.

PLANNING AND DEVELOPING
THE CURRICULUM

5.
USING RESEARCH FINDINGS
TO IMPROVE INSTRUCTION

William B. Richardson and Gary E. Moore

A vocational teacher anticipates teaching a class into which special needs students have been mainstreamed and ponders which teaching strategies might work best. A second teacher is attempting to recruit females into a male-dominated vocational program. A state legislator is writing new education legislation and needs to determine the effects of vocational education on minority unemployment. A college professor has been assigned the task of developing an inservice program for vocational teachers. The director of a vocational school has been asked to start a new vocational program, but isn't sure if enough students would be interested in the program.

Each of these persons faces a different challenge and each wants to arrive at a workable solution. A question that arises in each case is whether research findings are available that could help solve the problem. Clearly, a common thread for finding a solution to each problem lies in the profitable use of vocational education research.

This chapter focuses on an important question: What are the effects of research on vocational education? In other words, to what extent are vocational educators using research findings to guide their work? A related question is: What needs to be done to increase the influence of research on vocational education?

WHAT IS RESEARCH?

A logical beginning point in evaluating the effects of vocational education research is to define the term *research*. Some educators view research as primarily an effort to gather facts and information. Others take a more pragmatic view, seeing research as a procedure for gathering information that is then converted into useful processes or products.

In this chapter, the term *research* encompasses a wide spectrum of activity, from scholarly inquiry to developmental and training activities. Hull (1969) provides an excellent summary of this broad definition:

... Research is conceived in its most generic sense, as a function—a function of program planning and development . . . This view conceives research not as a narrow, discipline project-oriented activity, but rather as a broad function of the educational system itself. The objective or goal of this function is to facilitate change and improvement in vocational-technical education.

It is clear that research is in a state of evolution. The research function is broader than ever before, encompassing both research (R) and development (D) activities. Vocational education has been proactive in this evolution. In fact, in vocational education, the "D" appears to be as important as the "R". Therefore, *research* is used interchangeably with *research and development* (R&D) in this chapter.

USING RESEARCH FINDINGS

Professionals involved in vocational education include teachers, administrators and teacher educators. Each group has specific needs that can be met in part by using the findings of vocational education research. Some specific uses of research by professionals are outlined below.

The Vocational Teacher

The findings of R&D are often not visible to the classroom instructor. The direct use of the findings of a research project is not a common occurrence in many areas of education. This often leads to criticism of research by persons who are not involved in the research process. Local educators may wonder why a project that terminates on Friday cannot have direct implications for instruction on Monday.

The influence of instruction by R&D activities usually occurs in an indirect manner. Teachers see, hear or otherwise find out about a new concept verified by R&D and begin to slowly adopt the findings. This process takes time and often a teacher adopts a concept after seeing a colleague use it successfully, without necessarily being aware of the source. By the time an individual teacher implements the concept, then, the direct link to an R&D effort is often lost.

If one were to ask a group of randomly selected vocational teachers whether they use the findings of vocational education research in their classroom or laboratory, the replies might be surprising. Many teachers would probably reply, No they didn't, while a few teachers would say, Yes. Yet all of these teachers are probably using research results every day in their curricula, teaching techniques and approaches to teaching special needs students.

Curriculum Development. Vocational instructors make considerable use of curriculum guides and instructional materials that are outcomes of R&D projects. Often teachers do not see the extent of R&D that goes into curriculum materials. In most cases, by the time a finished product reaches a teacher's desk, thousands of dollars have been spent on resources, professional effort and testing to validate the materials.

Many vocational education leaders have developed curriculum materials for use in their states. This effort has been so widespread that many states duplicate the developmental efforts of one another. To prevent duplication of efforts, a number of states have banded together to work cooperatively on curriculum development. This group, called the Vocational-Technical Education Consortium of States (V-TECS), is discussed elsewhere in this book.

Using the V-TECS process as a starting point, individual states are devising their own systems for developing curricula. In Indiana, for example, West (1978) developed a complicated, yet feasible model for producing and implementing performance-based curricula in secondary and postsecondary vocational programs.

The curricula developed by the various vocational disciplines and states are being used by many local vocational teachers. Yet teachers still report a need for better curricula (Stewart, Shinn & Richardson, 1977).

Teaching Techniques. Many of the teaching techniques used by vocational teachers have been validated and refined through research. More than 60 research studies on the characteristics of effective teachers have been conducted. The findings of these studies have been incorporated, in a number of cases, into vocational teacher education programs. Vocational teachers are instructed in the most effective procedures for questioning, motivating and involving students in instruction. In many cases, these teaching techniques may be used every day by teachers who do not realize they have been refined and verified through research.

Working with Special Populations. Recently teachers have expressed a need for assistance in meeting the needs of special students such as those with learning problems, physically handicapped students, bilingual students and students in correctional institutions. Lee (1978) describes national R&D projects designed to help vocational teachers work with special populations.

One of the projects will develop a guide for teachers to use in preparing individualized education programs. Another will produce a handbook on modifying existing vocational education curricula for handicapped students. A third will give states information on attracting more handicapped persons to vocational programs. A fourth will offer information on the skills vocational teachers need to teach the handicapped. Finally, films and other materials will show handicapped students the opportunities available to them through vocational education.

Research results every day in their curricula, teaching techniques and approaches to teaching special needs students.

The Vocational Administrator

Vocational administrators at both the state and local levels use the research findings in a variety of ways, such as for program planning and evaluation. Often local vocational teachers become involved with these research efforts.

Vocational Instruction

Program Planning. Researchers at the state, regional and national levels conduct research studies that administrators can cite to establish the need for vocational programs. For example, state manpower studies provide data that can be used in program planning.

Administrators use local community surveys to determine specific employment needs in a school district. Many states require such data before a new program can be approved or an existing program expanded. Administrators and instructors also employ the findings of student interest studies in planning programs.

Program Evaluation. Program evaluation research is receiving greater attention in vocational education due to mandates in the 1976 Vocational Education Amendments. Because all programs must be evaluated, administrators and instructors will be involved directly in R&D activities. That is, vocational teachers and administrators will evaluate their own programs, using the materials developed by state level program planners.

Prior to the direct involvement by local teachers and administrators, professional researchers will develop, test, refine and implement models, methodologies and related materials for use in evaluating vocational programs. This research will employ model development, surveys and validated assessment instruments. Some vocational instructors and administrators will participate in developing these evaluative materials, but most will use the materials to actually evaluate their own programs.

Research and development is developing alternative approaches to evaluating the effectiveness of vocational programs. Cost/benefit-cost/effectiveness research is one such evaluative research strategy. The movement toward cost/benefit accountability has led researchers to conduct research that will assist in determining the effectiveness of investing dollars in vocational programs.

Placement and Follow-up. The placement of students in jobs for which they are trained is an important purpose of vocational education. Research and development has established models for designing placement programs in local schools. In many states, R&D monies are being used as "seed" funds to encourage local education agencies to establish placement programs.

Through a national survey, Gibson (1975) identified effective placement activities. The findings of this federally funded project are being used by schools in many states to develop and implement placement programs.

The follow-up of former vocational students has grown greatly in the past decade. Research and development funds have been invested in projects to create effective follow-up strategies, instruments, data analysis and reporting procedures. Almost every state can point to its own individually designed follow-up system. And individual schools have developed specialized follow-up programs to fit their local needs.

These follow-up studies are important to local administrators and instructors from two perspectives. First, local personnel have input into the development, refinement and utilization of the follow-up process. Second, the teacher and administrator can and should use the results of the follow-up study to make program refinements.

An area of research related directly to student follow-up is the follow-up of employers of former vocational students. O'Reilly et al. (1978) reported on a national survey to identify the status of employer follow-up and found that procedures used for employers were less developed than those for students. Local teachers and administrators, however, will most likely see more employer follow-up in the future and will be using research findings to make program refinements. State and local vocational administrators can also use research results to improve vocational programs.

The Vocational Teacher Educator

A large quantity of research is available for use by teacher educators in preparing vocational teachers. During the past decade, teacher education in general has been under attack. The major criticism has been that teacher preparation programs are not based on what teachers need to know and that teachers are therefore not able to perform with a high degree of competence. As a result, much research has been conducted by various disciplines in vocational education on the competencies needed by teachers.

Teacher preparation programs have been developed, based on the identified competencies. This approach to teacher preparation has been identified as Competency-Based Vocational Teacher Education (CBVTE). A nationwide research and development project has been completed by the National Center for Research in Vocational Education in Columbus, Ohio, which has resulted in the development of 100 modules for the preparation of vocational teachers.

The modules are based on a set of competencies that are related to the vocational teacher. Each module provides a self-instructional learning sequence designed to provide the student with the knowledge necessary to master the competencies. Local teachers might use the modules as a part of their preservice program, in a graduate course or in an inservice program in their school. Regardless of the delivery mode, vocational instruction should be improved as a result of this in-depth R&D effort.

Research and development in teacher education is contributing to improvement in vocational instruction in many other ways. For example, the professional teacher education curriculum has in many cases been tested and verified by R&D efforts. Effective teaching strategies, questioning techniques, motivational/interest approaches and classroom management are other areas where research and development is providing help in improving vocational instruction.

THE EFFECTS OF RESEARCH ON VOCATIONAL EDUCATION

After reviewing how some research findings are being used by vocational teachers, administrators and teacher educators, one could conclude that research in vocational education is having some influence on the profession. The question now is, "Should the research be making a greater impact on vocational education?"

The under-utilization of research findings in vocational instruction has been lamented by many. Kievit (1975) reported, "In sum there is very limited . . . direct evidence of the extent to which vocational R&D has influenced teachers to change practices."

Although vocational education research has affected the profession favorably, it does appear that an even greater impact could be made by improving the dissemination of research to vocational teachers.

Swanson (1976) worded this succinctly: "If research and development in vocational education is to occur, then the results of research and development must be utilized. . . . Too much of the effort of research accumulates and gathers dust on shelves and that R&D is not, therefore, a worthwhile activity."

The point is that researchers need to disseminate the results of their efforts to consumers. Swanson suggests that vocational education needs a brokerage function "to interpret, repackage, transport and/or interpret the value of R&D to its potential customers."

Dissemination activities should use a straightforward approach suitable for the practitioner. Few teachers read the *Journal of Vocational Education Research* and other research-oriented publications. Articles written for those types of scholarly publications are not readily usable by teachers.

All too often vocational education researchers communicate only with themselves and the results of the research go unused. One way to increase the utilization of R&D by classroom teachers is to write reports directly for those teachers. The American Vocational Association has taken a step in this direction by publishing an informative but readable column called "Research in Action" in *VocEd,* its monthly journal.

SUMMARY

Research and development in vocational education should be directed toward improving instruction. Research findings can influence the teacher's instructional program either directly or indirectly. Concern about research and development in vocational education is predicted in two areas: (1) the perception of local personnel that research and development are far removed from their day-to-day activity and (2) the lack of dissemination of research findings to local personnel in a usable form.

Many problems still exist. Vocational education research is on the cutting edge of effective growth and progress (Lee, 1978). Research as specified by the Congress in the 1976 legislation must result in improved teaching. The future of R&D will be judged against the basic criterion of how much research and development is contributing to improved instruction.

REFERENCES

Gibson, R. L., and Mitchell, M. H. *School based placement program: Equal opportunity provider* (Indiana State Board for Vocational and Technical Education Grant #8-75-C-3). Bloomington, Ind.: Indiana University, School of Education, 1975.

Hull, W. L., Frazier, W. D., and Stevenson, W. W. *Research handbook for vocational-technical education.* Stillwater, Okla.: Research Coordinating Unit, Oklahoma State University, July 1969.

Kievit, M. B. *Vocational education research and development as a factor influencing teachers to change practices.* Washington, D.C.: National Academy of Sciences, National Research Council, Assembly of Behavioral and Social Sciences, 1975.

Lee, A. M. *What secretary Califano did not tell Congress.* Unpublished manuscript, Northern Arizona University, 1978.

O'Reilly, P. A., Asche, F. M., Holub, S. M., and Johnson, R. P. *The national status of vocational student and employer follow-up.* Paper presented at the American Vocational Association Convention, Dallas, Tex., December 1978.

Stewart, B. R., Shinn, G. C., and Richardson, W. B. Concerns of professionals in agricultural education. *Agricultural Education,* June 1977.

Swanson, G. I. Utilization of research and development: A question of perception. *American Vocational Journal,* February 1976.

West, B. R. *Research for performance based vocational education in Indiana: A position paper.* Bloomington, Ind.: Research Dissemination Service, Vocational Education Information Services, Indiana University, April 1978.

II

**PLANNING AND DEVELOPING
THE CURRICULUM**

6.
ALIGNING VOCATIONAL PROGRAMS WITH EMPLOYER NEEDS

Krishan K. Paul and Paul V. Braden

A recent interagency agreement signed by the Departments of Health, Education and Welfare, Labor, Transportation and Commerce has emphasized the urgent need to improve coordination between employers and training institutions (The President's Interagency Coordinating Council, 1979). Relating Training to Occupational Needs (RETONS) is a process model designed to bring about better congruence between employer needs and vocational education programs. It provides a mechanism for transmitting employer needs in a systematic way to vocational teachers, counselors and students in order to improve curricula and vocational guidance programs.

CONCEPTUAL BACKGROUND

Although vocational education has been preparing students for gainful employment for decades, only recently have serious efforts been made to assess employer needs in developing vocational programs. Since the 1968 vocational education legislation, numerous information systems have been developed, tested and implemented to assist in planning vocational programs. One feature common to almost all such systems is the assessment of current and future labor demand, defined as the number of workers likely to be hired at prevailing wage levels. Though the method of arriving at labor demand figures may vary from system to system or from state to state, all information systems are concerned with the needs of employers. Therefore, these systems offer a valuable tool to training institutions in planning programs that meet employer needs.

At the same time, industries and businesses are becoming more concerned with human resource development. There is renewed interest in job environments, job satisfaction, job restructuring, training and retraining, and more efficient use of leisure time—in other words, improvements in the quality of work life. Employers are finding that investment in human resources pays dividends in the form of a more productive work force (Mills, 1975).

Vocational education has the potential and the resources to work with employers towards human resource development and improvement of the quality of work life. To achieve this coordination, vocational education must go beyond traditional training to become more involved in the retraining of workers. This practice would not only help workers to become more productive, but would assist them in making better use of their leisure time.

Currently, however, vocational programs concentrate mostly on training youths and adults for entry-level jobs. In the United States, where jobs become obsolete on an average in eight years, and where the average worker changes occupations at last twice in a working life, retraining to acquire new skills becomes essential. At present, almost all retraining is done by industry. A shift in vocational education policy could lead to a team effort, in which vocational education would provide classroom training and industry would provide on-the-job experience. Before that can be achieved, however, vocational educators will need to win the confidence of employers by demonstrating that they can accurately assess employer needs and plan vocational programs accordingly.

Focus on Qualitative Needs

Projection of employment needs, as done by the Bureau of Labor Statistics, State Employment Security Offices and some research organizations, provides a partial assessment of employer needs, usually of a quantitative nature. For vocational education planning, it is no doubt important to know how many secretaries, for example, would be needed to meet employer demand in a given geographic area. This chapter, however, deals with qualitative needs, i.e., the types of workers, secretaries, and the skills demanded by employers for specific occupations.

Job descriptions or task analyses provide only an approximation of employer needs because they describe only the skill training aspects of occupations. They do not take into account factors such as employer expectations of communications skills, changes in technology and interpersonal skills needed to perform well on the job. If all jobs were assembly-line jobs, observation of tasks and their frequency would probably be sufficient to plan a training program. However, most jobs (particularly service-related jobs) require more than technical skills. Employers are the best judges of such requirements and it is important that they be consulted.

There are many examples of private-sector involvement in school-related career development and employment programs. The evidence of effectiveness of such efforts is mixed at best, but the faith of employers in the elixir of schooling remains substantial (DeLone, 1978). Yet many employers and employer organizations complain that vocational programs remain insensitive to private-sector concerns, a fact that is manifest in the lack of attention to employer needs in the planning and development of vocational programs.

Local and program advisory committees, though they started with great promise, have not lived up to initial expectations. Their role is defined narrowly, and their contribution depends to a great extent on the personal capabilities of the local program administrator or the instructor of an individual vocational program. A closer linkage between vocational educators and the employers of their graduates is necessary to improve the quality of vocational programs. What is needed is an information system that seeks input regularly from employers of vocational graduates, thereby forging linkages between vocational educators and the private sector. This will not only help improve vocational programs, but also will provide industries and businesses with trained personnel that are efficient, productive and capable of coping with technological changes.

OBJECTIVES OF THE RETONE SYSTEM

The overall purpose of the RETONE system is to improve the congruence of vocational programs with current job practices as perceived by the employers of vocational graduates. By enhancing the ability of training programs to meet employer expectations, RETONE seeks to improve the employability of youths and adults enrolled in vocational programs. The following are specific objectives set for the RETONE system:

1. To identify and monitor employers' specific needs in terms of technical skills, interpersonal skills, habits and attitudes of their work force.
2. To forge and strengthen communication linkages between employers and vocational educators.
3. To identify and monitor skills, career aspirations and attitudes towards work of vocational students.
4. To identify areas where improvement can be made through changes in training and counseling programs.

The conceptual framework of RETONE is simple and generally follows the basic outlines of information systems, an early prototype of which was developed in Oklahoma (Braden, Harris and Paul, 1970). The Occupational Training Information System (OTIS) in Oklahoma matched the supply of trained manpower with the demand as indicated by employers in a survey. The RETONE system, while following the same general procedure, goes beyond simple measurement of supply and demand. Qualitative assessment of both demand and supply is an important part of RETONE, which is useful as a planning and an instructional tool. Qualitative data are also useful for career guidance and counseling. In this important respect, RETONE is different and more effective than information systems currently in use in most of the states.

Important Features

As indicated earlier, the most important feature of RETONE is its orientation to employer needs rather than to those of vocational programs or students. Data are collected not only on how many workers (e.g., welders) will be needed by employers within a period of time, but also on what type of welders will be needed. Assessment is made of the characteristics, work habits and skill levels of the work force that the employer would expect to hire. At the same time, information is gathered on the wages, fringe benefits, work environment and career advancement the employers offer to their work force. This puts the labor demand into a perspective that is economic and understandable, as contrasted to the projection of numbers that has been for years the mainstay of vocational program planning at the local and state level.

In making projections for labor demand at the local and sub-state regional level, the RETONE system makes economic and community development plans a part of the data collection procedures. This is a distinct departure from the normal practice of considering national economic trends only when projecting labor demand. At the local level, at least two factors need to be considered: (1) the occupational profile of industries may be different from the national profile and (2) employment opportunities may increase or decrease significantly with location (or relocation) of industries and businesses.

At the current stage of RETONE development, there are no plans to develop local occupational profiles. However, employment opportunties created by industrial development activities are pooled, along with unemployment projections compiled by the State Department of Employment Security, to derive composite labor demand projections. These estimates are made in cooperation with local, regional and state economic development practitioners. In order to match employer needs with the right size and quality of potential work force, data are collected from all vocational students by training program. These data include the area of skill training, expectations from the first job, career aspirations and attitude towards work in general and the occupation for which each student is training.

Student Expectations Versus Employer Needs

Closer ties between employer needs and student counseling and guidance programs are needed. If it is determined that student expectations are higher than what employers have to offer, an improvement in the counseling program would be indicated. Through improved counseling and instructional programs, the needs of employers can be communicated to vocational students.

Data are also collected on the technical, communications, and interpersonal skill requirements of jobs. A comparison of employer needs with existing training programs will determine if any changes or improvements need to be made. New programs may also be identified, based on the relation between employer needs and the availability of programs in the local area.

Although the RETONE system is heavily oriented towards the employer, it is not designed to serve as a one-way communication linkage. By providing regular feedback to employers, it helps them understand local vocational programs and student expectations. In addition to the general orientation of the employers at the time of interview (or data collection), they are supplied with summary reports of student expectations and their career aspirations. This helps them understand trends among the successive generations of their potential work force.

A referral service, with the vocational schools serving as placement agents for their graduates, is also designed into the system. This communication linkage will help boost the placement rate of vocational graduates and will be a good feedback mechanism for the employer follow-up that is also a part of the system.

PILOT-TEST RESULTS

Because of funding limitations, only five occupations were chosen for the pilot-test survey in the Standard Metropolitan Statistical Area (SMSA) in Nashville, Tennessee: secretarial work, practical nursing, carpentry, welding and retail sales. The criteria for selection of occupations were (1) the projected growth in employment opportunities, and (2) the availability of vocational education programs within the SMSA. The rate of response for the sample (see Table 1) ranged from a low of 36 percent for carpenters to a high of 70 percent for practical nurses, with the overall

Table 1

EMPLOYER RESPONSE RATE BY OCCUPATIONAL TITLE

Occupational Title	Sample	Employers Interviewed	
		Number	Percent
Secretaries	157	102	65
Practical Nurses	100	70	70
Carpenters	50	18	36
Welders	52	35	67
Sales Persons	151	92	61
Total	500	317	63

Source: Paul, et al., 1979.

response rate being 63 percent. Data were collected by trained interviewers, using schedules designed by the project team.

Important Characteristics

Table 2 shows the five most important characteristics desired by the employers in their new employees. It should be noted that the employers

Table 2
MOST IMPORTANT CHARACTERISTICS OF NEW EMPLOYEES

Characteristic	Percent of Employer Responses
Personality, ability to work with people	39
Appearance, neatness	39
Skills ability, competence	36
Attitude, interest	27
Experience, work record	22

Source: Paul, et al., 1979.

rated the "ability to work with people" and the "neatness of appearance" as more desirable than technical skill. The results reported are for composite data from all occupations, though differences in ratings for different occupations do exist and are significant.

Similar results were reported in response to another question in the survey. In order to assess the importance of nontechnical skills and personal attributes, the employers were asked to check three factors they considered important in each of the five areas of skills and personal attributes. The data are reported in Table 3. In the area of academic skills, employers considered the "ability to follow instructions" the most important. Other most desired characteristics were reported as "dependability, interest in work and ability to work with others." It should be noted that only the three most important factors for each area have been shown in Table 3, though choices were made from six to ten factors in each area. Once again, the reported data are based on composite scores, with significant interoccupational differences. The trend, however, is unmistakable in all occupations. Employers consider interpersonal and communication skills very important for job performance in the five surveyed occupations.

Table 4 presents the other side of the coin—undesirable characteristics of potential employees. When asked to check important grouped factors that would result in the rejection of an applicant for a job, the employers rated "lack of interest" at the top, followed by "job hopping" and "poor attendance record." Although a good or strong recommendation was not rated very high as a factor in hiring decisions, a weak recommendation was considered a negative factor by employers. Once again, interoccupational ratings differ from the composite ratings reported in Table 4.

Data on technical skills employers expected from applicants for entry-level jobs were also collected and compiled, as were data on the job environment and career advancement potential. These data have been made available to the eight participating county and city schools and to state vocational education authorities.

Table 3

IMPORTANT SKILLS AND ATTRIBUTES AS RANKED BY EMPLOYERS

Skill Area	Factors	Percent of Employer Responses
Academic Skills	Ability to follow instructions	90
	Accuracy in using basic arithmetic	55
	Knowledge about the employer and firm's products	53
Interpersonal Skills	Ability to work with others	88
	Willingness to take instructions	77
	Ability to communicate effectively	62
Work Habits	Maintenance of a good attendance record	83
	Promptness in carrying out tasks	69
	Promptness in getting to work	53
Work Attitude	Interest in work	68
	Pride in craftsmanship and quality work	66
	Positive attitude towards employer	47
Personal Attributes	Dependability	70
	Neatness of appearance	61
	Responsibility and willingness to follow through	47

Source: Paul, et al., 1979.

Table 4

UNDESIRABLE CHARACTERISTICS OF POTENTIAL EMPLOYEES AS RANKED BY EMPLOYERS

Factors	Percent of Employer Responses
Lacks interest in job during interview	86
Has record of "job hopping"	82
Has a poor attendance record	82
Has a weak recommendation	78
Appears to be immature	68

Source: Paul, et al., 1979.

Vocational Student Survey

In order to assess the supply and quality of new applicants to the target occupations, more than 1600 vocational students in the appropriate programs were surveyed about the same time the employer survey was done. The students, mostly high-school seniors, were asked questions about the availability of guidance, counseling and placement services in their schools, their expectations from their first jobs after completion of vocational programs, their career aspirations and their attitude toward work. A total of 1,600 students were surveyed from the five relevant vocational programs in the SMSA.

Typically, students indicated that they were more likely to receive some vocational counseling in the tenth grade than in later grades and that a teacher was the most likely person to give vocational guidance but that they were more likely to find a job on their own or with the help of relatives and friends. Most students said they expected to find jobs in the occupational area of their training, and that it was important for them to get the jobs for which they were being trained. Most of the students said they enjoy working in their chosen occupations and want jobs with good advancement opportunities. Other job attributes most desired were good wages and an employer with a good reputation.

When asked what they thought would help them to be hired by the employers of their choice, students rated personality or personal appearance, education and training, work-related experience, school record, and personal recommendations as the top five factors in that order. They were also asked about their perception of the potential barriers to their hiring. The top seven barriers were the following:

1. I have too little experience.
2. I might be too young.
3. I am not qualified, since I have too little training.
4. I don't have the necessary connections to get the job.
5. There are not enough jobs like I want in this city or county.
6. I don't have enough education.
7. I am too shy and uncomfortable in a job interview.

Other potential barriers included discrimination, physical handicap, lack of transportation and poor health. There were only slight differences in interoccupational responses.

Dissemination of Results

Through a series of workshops with vocational teachers, guidance counselors and school administrators, detailed data (by occupations, skill training program and county) are being made available to the schools. Emphasis has been placed on the gaps between employer needs (and what they offer in exchange) and student expectations and career aspirations so that improvements in guidance counseling and job placement programs can be initiated during the 1979-80 school year.

Technical skill requirements data, though very useful, do not exist in sufficient detail for immediate use for curriculum revision or improvement. Improvements in nontechnical skill areas, such as communication and interpersonal skills, can and may be undertaken during the 1979-80 school year in some of the school systems.

In order to communicate the findings from the project to the students, employer expectations are being compiled into hand-out folders, which will be distributed among the students in participating schools during the 1979-80 school year. A summary of student expectations for the five skill training program areas has been prepared and made available to all participating employers. Other employers will be reached through the chambers of commerce in the SMSA.

More occupational areas are being identified to be surveyed during 1979-80. A data base for all occupational areas for which vocational programs are offered within the SMSA will be completed incrementally within a few years. An employer follow-up component to assess the rate and quality of placement of vocational graduates will be added to the system at a later date.

SUMMARY

The RETONE system currently being pilot tested in Tennessee was designed to fill an urgent need articulated both by vocational educators and the President's Interagency Coordinating Council in its April 1979 report. The purpose of the system is to bring about a congruence between vocational programs and employer needs, thereby making vocational graduates more employable in the private sector. Data collected from employers and vocational students indicate that there are significant gaps between their respective needs and expectations. The results will be used to improve vocational guidance and training program in Middle Tennessee. The system is scheduled to be completed towards the end of 1979.

REFERENCES

Braden, Paul V., Harris, James L., and Paul, Krishan K. *Occupational training information system (OTIS)* Stillwater, Okla.: Research Foundation, Oklahoma State University, June 1970.

DeLone, Richard H. Youth employment and the private sector. Paper presented at the National Commission on Manpower Policy Conference, October 19-20, 1978.

Mills, Ted. Human resources—Why the new concern. *Harvard business review,* March-April, 1975.

Paul, Krishan K., Holden, Linda B., and Hatcher, L. C. Survey of five growth occupations in Nashville SMSA. RETONE Phase I Report. Nashville, Tenn.: The Urban Observatory, June 1979.

President's Interagency Coordinating Council. Summary of employment initiatives. Washington, D.C.: U.S. Department of Labor, April 1979.

INSTRUCTIONAL STRATEGIES

1.
INDIVIDUALIZING VOCATIONAL EDUCATION

Paul Scott

From its earliest days vocational education has been viewed as an integral part of the economic system. Current trends toward humanism in education have led in recent years to a simultaneous focus on the needs of the individual. These two divergent points of view have merged in the Vocational Education Amendments of 1976 to form what Lessinger (1973) has called "disciplined caring." In short, vocational education must provide programs based on the realities of the labor market and customized to reflect the learning requirements of students ranging from mentally retarded to those with special talents.

Traditionally, vocational instruction has been group-oriented, teacher-centered and administratively convenient. A lock-step curriculum has often required each student to enter and exit the vocational program at the same time.

According to traditional methods, the instructor paces the group, all students are involved in the same unit of instruction and they move to the next unit only when the instructor feels the entire class is ready to advance. Little or no provision is made for the remediation of students who fall behind in the program or for those students who can move ahead at a faster rate.

One must conclude that a traditional approach to instruction is woefully inadequate to meet current demands on vocational education. The very nature of the traditional approach precludes the one ingredient most needed in today's vocational programs—flexibility. Flexibility is required to improve cost effectiveness, to serve special needs populations, to reach out-of-school youth and adults, and to assist youngsters who have a commitment to highly specialized occupational goals.

Alternatives to traditional instruction must be designed to provide flexibility. The purpose of this chapter is to review the concepts of individualized instruction as one means towards this end.

When the subject of individualized instruction is introduced to vocational educators, four questions are always asked: What do you mean by individualized instruction? How do you develop it? Can teachers and students use it? Is there any evidence that it works? The remainder of this chapter will address these questions.

DEFINING INDIVIDUALIZED INSTRUCTION

Many vocational educators do not understand what individualized instruction really is and how to develop it. Gilli (1975) presents a classic example of this misunderstanding. He writes ". . . individualized instruction can be a lonesome and impersonal affair for students."

Similarly, Henderson (1972) takes a very narrow view of individualized instruction, calling it a "teacherless management system" that is based on a self-study approach to learning. According to him, the self-study approach promotes fears that each student will be isolated in a cubicle with his or her resource materials, attempting to master basic skills at the expense of the broader and equally important skills of social interaction.

Individualized instruction is not the same as programmed instruction, independent study or a tutorial approach. None of these activities constitutes individualized instruction. Such innovations as independent study, team teaching, audio-tutorial instruction and programmed instruction, however, can be and often are components of an individualized program. When used alone, however, these techniques are too narrow in scope to represent anything other than a short-term learning experience.

A Monitoring Procedure

The nomenclature of individualized instruction must be coordinated with the student, teacher, subject matter content and the school environment. This is an orchestrated relationship in which each element must be designed to operate in concert with every other element. In addition, a sensitive monitoring procedure must be built into the entire system to provide the feedback necessary to maintain the natural progress of each participating student. Such a system would be based on the following concepts:

1. The system would be student-centered. This would include establishing levels of expectations for individual students that would motivate them to work at their maximum potential and allow them to select and pursue their own job goals within the occupational field.

2. The content would be empirically based in the occupation for which the student was preparing. There would be precision in the statement of each objective and in the relationship of each objective to the student's occupational goals.

3. The system would provide for formative evaluation through frequent teacher-student contact (self-checks and other appropriate

assessment techniques). Such a design would insure that each student masters the objectives selected. The whole process would be viewed as a learning cycle of diagnosing, prescribing and evaluating until the student obtained his or her goals.

4. A variety of instructional strategies and media would be fitted to the needs and learning styles of the individual students.
5. Above all, such a system would provide flexibility both in terms of time and student goals.

Individualized instruction, then, must be related to the individual student's needs, ability to learn, interests, motivation, previous educational experiences and history. The process also must allow the student to skip instructional segments already mastered and to determine, to a great extent, how many objectives he or she will attempt and in what length of time they will be learned. Such freedom does not, however, exempt the students from acquiring basic skills.

The general consensus among authorities is that individualized instruction is a process that stresses variety in teaching material, the use of multimedia and auxiliary personnel, concern for time and pace, mastery learning, socialization, diagnosing and prescribing with precision for each student, and establishing goals and objectives for each student. The process can be fully or partially individualized through varying the pace, the content or the way in which the content is presented. Such a process also gives the teacher an opportunity to establish one-to-one relationships with students, but that is not the exclusive purpose of the system. In an individualized vocational program, students will work alone, in groups and, from time to time, with a piece of machinery, each in its turn and on an as-needed basis. Finally, individualized instruction is a means, not an end in itself (Weisgerber, 1971; Finch, 1974; Bishop, 1971).

TEACHER AND STUDENT ROLE CHANGE

With the individualized instructional approach, the teacher's behavior will change. In this new role, the teacher will no longer be the sole disseminator of knowledge or the dispenser of information. Instead, the teacher now becomes manager of a learning process in which the purpose is to help students make their own discoveries. The teacher guides or interacts with the students.

With such an approach, the teacher should be relatively free of noninstructional tasks and concentrate on managing a learning environment in which the students are involved in a variety of learning activities—perhaps some of them working alone, some in pairs and others in small groups. The teacher will move about responding to questions and suggesting activities.

In the new role, the teacher must know not only the subject matter, but how students learn (King, 1973; Bishop, 1971; Duane, 1973; Bjorkquist, 1971; Tuckman, 1974; Bartel, 1971).

The student's role will also change. Students will have to become more self directing, thereby becoming responsible for much of their own learning (Talmage, 1975; Keuscher, 1973).

HOW EFFECTIVE IS INDIVIDUALIZED INSTRUCTION?

Although the notion of individualized instruction has existed since the beginning of the century, little real work has been done to make it a reality. Only in the last 20 years have the educational skills and technology been available to produce truly individualized instruction. The availability of a great deal of risk capital during this period provided the real impetus to develop individualized instruction. Most of what is now known about the overall effectiveness of individualized instruction is based on the materials developed during this era.

The current research concerning both vocational and nonvocational programs indicates that individualized instruction is not significantly better than traditional group techniques in terms of student achievement as measured by standardized tests. On the other hand, there are no reported case studies in which individualized instruction did worse than group instruction.

Many researchers believe, however, that standardized tests are simply not sensitive enough to measure total student achievement in a fully individualized program. Based on that assumption, most studies have looked beyond student achievement and found a variety of positive results, not the least of which are improved student attitudes and task orientation, reduced learning time and, above all, the flexibility necessary to accommodate a variety of student needs and goals. The teachers in individualized programs often admit that they have never worked harder, but that the whole experience is a rewarding one. Oddly enough, the criticism concerning individualized instruction usually comes from teachers who have never used it—not from those who are directly involved (Scott, 1976).

DEVELOPING INDIVIDUALIZED INSTRUCTION

In developing an individualized instructional system and materials, one should give prime consideration to the content to be learned and the target population(s).The importance of knowing the student's abilities, interests, prior experiences and possible handicaps cannot be overemphasized.

The selection of the content to be learned in a vocational program should be accomplished in a scientific fashion that includes a task analysis and the time spent on each task. This information should come initially from business and industry—more specifically, from the worker who actually performs the job functions. After the job functions have been collected and organized, an analysis should be made of the tasks to identify basis components that can be learned by the students. Objectives can then be prepared for each of these functions.

Individualizing Vocational Education

An individualized instructional system should have a basic delivery vehicle that will serve the student as a learning tool and be simple enough in design to give teachers the opportunity to develop and try out their own materials. The learning package concept meets these criteria. Such a vocational learning package (VLP) should be composed of components (the package design parts) and elements (the content to be learned).

Structural Components

To increase the utility of the VLP, the structural components should relate as much as possible to those used in the preparation of existing vocational curricular materials. The essential VLP components are described below.

Guide Sheet. This is basically a direction setting device for the students. It provides information on what is to be learned in the VLP and why, and leads the student from learning activity to learning activity and to teacher consultations.

Evaluation. The VLP should contain provisions for four types of student evaluation activities. There must be a pretest to determine whether the student needs a particular unit in the first place. Within the VLP, there should be self-tests to help keep the student on target and motivated and instructor checks to maintain student-instructor contact and to prevent the student from going in the wrong direction. Finally, the VLP must contain a post-test to confirm student mastery of the objective.

Instructional Sheets. Instructional sheets are used to support and clarify the various learning activities within the VLP. These sheets should be the same as those used in other vocational curriculum materials: assignment, information and job sheets. The assignment sheet sets forth a task or set of tasks to be performed by the student. The information sheet is used to synthesize information for the students that is not available in an appropriate form from any other source. (Do not rewrite a text or reference book description that is adequate in its own right—simply refer the student to it.)

Job sheets (sometimes called operations sheets). These guide the student through a particular activity. The job sheet should contain a step-by-step procedure for the activity, along with safety factors and tools and materials requirements. Graphic illustrations are often a useful part of the job sheet.

Resource List. A resource list should be affixed to the VLP so that it can be replaced easily when old reference books are revised and new ones added.

Media. If audiovisual media are to be used, these items should be added to the package on an as-needed basis only. Each audiovisual must serve a specific purpose and be both motivational and cost effective. Some packages may contain several audiovisual presentations, while others will have none.

Package Elements

Dispersed among these components will be the package elements that include the advanced organizers (task statement, performance objective and rationale statement), the learning activities (both theoretical and hands-on), the criterion test items (performance and cognitive items) and the specific resources for that VLP. In this blending, the developer must maintain flexibility in the package to provide for future additions and deletions and to enable it to be used by students working in small groups as well as individually.

Although the package must be linked into the total individualized system, it should also be developed as a freestanding entity. This will allow it to be replaced or dropped altogether when necessary and improve the potential to provide for open student entry and exit.

Two additional factors should be considered carefully in the preparation of learning packages. The first is a concern for time and pacing. Time can be a two-pronged villain. Some students do not attain the objectives because they require more than the usual time allowed. Other students will tend to relax, taking much longer than necessary to complete a particular learning package. Mayo (1974) suggested that an "achievement unit" be developed for each package. The achievement unit would state the average amount of time required to complete a particular package. This gauge could be used to maintain the proper task orientation in a classroom.

The second factor to consider in package presentation is the potential of the package to teach the objective. Current trends in the evaluation of learning packages for vocational programs come from the concept of materials validation developed for programmed instruction. This work in evaluation technology has been promoted by Butler (1972) and further refined for use in vocational education by Wall (1973) and Frantz and West (1974).

A TEN-STEP DEVELOPMENT PROCEDURE

Using the information presented here and the theories promoted by Gagne and Briggs (1974) and Butler (1972), a model procedure has been prepared that will expedite the development of individualized vocational materials on a large scale by development teams and on a small scale by the vocational teacher working independently. The ten-step model is described below.

1. *State the mission and priorities for each program.* This initial step requires the developers to answer the questions: What end products are expected from this curriculum? And what will be the breadth and depth of the curriculum?
2. *Perform an analysis of the occupation.* That is, the developers must list the actual tasks performed by the incumbent worker.

From the initial list, the developer must determine which tasks are performed most frequently by the entry-level worker and which tasks fulfill the curriculum mission and priorities identified in Step 1.

3. *Specify the student objectives.* A performance objective should be prepared for each task included in the curriculum. These objectives provide the terminal performance required for mastery of each task.

4. *Develop appropriate tests and checks.* Criterion-referenced test items must be prepared for each objective. The purpose of these items is to assess student mastery of a given objective. Therefore, a direct linkage must be established between the test items and the objective. There should be both cognitive and performance test items for each objective. These items can be used to prepare the pre- and post-tests, student self-checks and instructor checks.

5. *Analyze the learning for each objective and determine the learning tasks.* In this step, it is necessary to identify the specific skills, knowledge and attitudes essential to accomplish the objective and master the tasks. This activity will include the formation and sequencing of learning steps, as well as the identification of the type of learning required for each step. Learning levels or types suggested by B. S. Bloom (1956), Gagne (1974) and others can be used for this purpose.

6. *Select and/or develop materials.* The rule of thumb here is to identify as many appropriate materials as possible. These can be coded into the individualized system in their current form or adapted to fit the objectives. Additional appropriate materials are then developed to fill the remaining gaps and to provide the necessary supporting information.

7. *Package the materials.* Packaging the materials is an important step in developing individualized instruction. The package must serve two purposes. First, the package design must guide the student through the learning activities. Secondly, the package must prevent student "bottlenecking" by enabling the student to move smoothly to the next package. In effect, the package serves as the "trigger" for the individualized system. Currently, Georgia vocational programs are using a flowchart type of package that serves these purposes.

8. *Validate the materials.* A face validation of all the materials should be performed as a prerequisite to field testing. This should include a content review and a linkage check to be certain that there are direct relationships among tasks, objectives, criterion-referenced tests and learning activities.

Once the face validation has been completed, the materials are ready for field testing. In the field testing, sites are selected carefully, process logs are documented and students are assessed.

Because of its complicated nature and dependence on student involvement, an individualized program will have more than its share of bottlenecks and flaws. The time to find them is during field testing, not after the materials have been distributed widely.

9. *Revise the system and materials.* Make all revisions dictated by the field testing.

10. *Install the program.* Installing the program requires the same care that was used to develop the system. The following steps should be adhered to when installing the materials in a given program:

   a. Prepare the instructor mechanically and conceptually to use the materials.

   b. Prepare the physical facilities to support individualized instruction.

   c. Obtain the materials, special equipment and supplies.

   d. Initiate the system.

   e. Monitor and continue to evaluate the program.

BENEFITS OF INDIVIDUALIZED INSTRUCTION

The concept of individualized instruction presented here is not intended as a panacea. Individualized instruction is a means for achieving the full flexibility required of today's vocational programs, while maintaining a high level of instructional quality. Currently, it is best to define individualized instruction for vocational education as a comprehensive process that applies the theories of management and the logic of the systems approach to the design and development of instructional materials for vocational programs.

Vocational programs are now being operated on an individualized basis without sacrificing the quality of instruction or the development of social skills. Vocational programs are, in fact, gaining in some significant ways. Administrators are now more certain of program content coverage. The curriculum has become more competency based, which enhances program accountability and improves articulation between secondary and postsecondary programs. The individualized approach has also been a significant aid in providing services for handicapped students in regular vocational programs.

Perhaps of equal importance is the potential to improve the teaching capacity of the craftsman teacher. Finally, overall cost effectiveness has been enhanced by the flexibility of an open entry-open exit enrollment process made possible through an individualized curriculum.

Models and materials for individualizing vocational programs exist in several states. Any new effort to individualize should begin by reviewing the work already completed in those states (Georgia and Kentucky are two of many). It is no longer a question of whether individualized instruction will work, but how best to deploy it for the benefit of the student population.

REFERENCES

Bartel, E. V. Initiating a self-directed learning program in the classroom. *Education,* February-March 1971.

Bishop, L. K. *Individualizing educational systems.* New York: Harper and Row, 1971.

Bjorkquist, D. *What vocational education teachers should know about individualizing instruction.* Columbus, Ohio: Ohio State University, 1971.

Bloom, B. S. (Ed.) *Taxonomy of educational objectives handbook I; cognitive domain,* New York, N.Y.; David McKay, 1956.

Burns, R. Methods for individualizing instruction. *The educational technology review series* (No. 5). Englewood Cliffs, N.J.: Educational Technology Publications, 1973.

Butler, C. F. *Instructional system development for vocational and technical training.* Englewood Cliffs, N.J.: Educational Technology Publications, 1972.

Duane, J. E. (Ed.). *Individualized instruction—programs and materials.* Englewood Cliffs, N.J.: Educational Technology Publications, 1973.

Finch, C. R. Individualizing instruction: What can you learn from research. *American vocational journal,* September 1974.

Frantz, N. R., Jr., and West, B. A procedure for evaluating learning package performance. In Frantz, N. R., Jr. (Ed.), *Individualized instructional systems for vocational and technical education: A collection of readings.* Athens, Ga.: Vocational Instructional Systems, 1974.

Gagne, R. M., and Briggs, L. J. *Principles of instructional design.* New York: Holt, Rinehart and Winston, 1974.

Gilli, A. C., Sr. A personalized system for vocational education. *American vocational journal,* November 1975.

Henderson, G. L. Individualized instruction: Sweet in theory, sour in practice. *The education digest 37,* 1972.

Keuscher, R. E. Individualization of instruction: What it is and what it isn't. In Duane, J. E. (Ed.), *Individualized instruction—programs and materials.* Englewood Cliffs, N.J.: Educational Technology Publications, 1973.

King, L. Individualized instruction: Not if or when, but how. *American vocational journal,* September 1973.

Lessinger, L. M. Disciplined caring for career education. *Essays on career education.* Portland, Ore.: Northwest Regional Educational Laboratory, 1973.

Mayo, G. D. Individualized instruction: Concepts and measurements. In Frantz, N. R., Jr. (Ed.). *Individualized instructional systems for vocational and technical education: A collection of readings.* Athens, Ga.: Vocational Instructional Systems, 1974.

Packard, R. G. Models for individualized instruction: The search for a measure. *The educational technology review series* (No. 5). Englewood Cliffs, N.J.: Educational Technology Publications, 1973.

Scott, C. P. *A comparison of the effectiveness of individualized instruction to traditional instruction in heating/air-conditioning and cosmetology pro-*

grams in Georgia post-secondary area vocational-technical schools. Unpublished doctoral dissertation, Georgia State University, 1976.

Talmage, H. Instructional design for individualization. In Talmage, H. (Ed.), *Systems of individualized education.* Berkeley, Ca.: McCutchan, 1975.

Tuckman, B. W. The student-centered curriculum: A concept in curriculum innovation. In Frantz, N. R., Jr. (Ed.), *Individualized instructional systems for vocational and technical education: A collection of readings.* Athens, Ga.: Vocational Instructional Systems, 1974.

Walberg, H. J. Psychological theories of educational individualization. In Talmage, H. (Ed.), *Systems of individualized education.* Berkeley, Ca.: McCutchan, 1975.

Wall, J. E. The pervasive process of curriculum validation. *American vocational journal,* October 1973.

Weisgerber, R. A. *Perspectives in individualized learning.* Palo Alto, Ca.: American Institute for Research, 1971.

III.

INSTRUCTIONAL STRATEGIES

2.

INDIVIDUALIZED INSTRUCTION FOR MARKETING CAREERS

Gail Trapnell

It has been said that "no goal of classroom practice is more frequently hailed and less frequently achieved than individualized instruction" (Gartner and Riessman). Although individualized instruction has been incorporated to varying degrees in vocational programs throughout this century, the degree of sophistication in its utilization has left much to be desired. This chapter will examine some of the distinguishing characteristics of individualized instruction and the promise the Interstate Distributive Education Curriculum Consortium (IDECC) holds for a systematic instructional program for students seeking selected careers in marketing.

INDIVIDUALIZED INSTRUCTION

Individualized instruction can be described as a process of diagnosis and prescription. It involves the careful identification and delineation of the individual's needs, abilities, interests and learning styles in order to prescribe a program of studies tailored specifically to fit those unique characteristics.

The Diagnostic Process

In the process of diagnosis, attention is devoted to the analysis of the individual student's background, aptitudes, demonstrated abilities and interests. The stimuli that motivate the student and the style of learning most appropriate to the individual are also studied.

Diagnosis of the student's individual learning style is probably one of the most neglected areas in individualized instruction. It can be subdivided into an analysis of the learner's cognitive and affective styles. A report issued by the Teacher Improvement Project, East Lansing Schools, Michigan, defines *cognitive style* as "the way [the learner] takes meaning from the world around him, how he comes to know what he knows."

The *affective style* refers to the emotional climate and sociological needs of the student, the self-concept developed and expressed as a result of having achieved, and the self-empowering outcome of having learned. It is only through the careful diagnosis of all such factors that an appropriate program of studies can be prescribed to meet the unique characteristics of the individual.

Prescribing a Program

Once a thorough diagnosis has been made of the student's needs, a program of instruction is designed. In mapping out such a program, attention must be devoted not only to the identification of objectives, alternative learning activities and evaluation measures, but to the creation of favorable learning conditions as well.

In this context, it is important to note Bloom's assertion that 95 percent of all students are capable of learning all that a school has to teach at or near the same mastery level. The attainment of such an achievement level is, however, predicated on the establishment of favorable learning conditions that facilitate and accommodate the individual's unique characteristics. According to Bloom, this requires flexibility of time, flexibility in space utilization, flexibility in grouping, flexibility of materials and flexibility of staffing patterns (Harvey and Horton, 1977).

Just as diagnosis of the individual student's learning style is often sorely neglected, so is the prescription of a program of study designed to accommodate that learning style. Too often attention is devoted to the development of learning activities appropriate for the achievement of specific performance objectives—regardless of the student's learning style. Although learning activities may be appropriate for given objectives, they are not necessarily appropriate to the learning style of the individual student.

Edling describes four general types of individualized instruction ranging from "Individually Diagnosed and Prescribed" to "Independent Study." The two major variables that distinguish the types include who determines the instructional objectives (the school or the student) and who selects the means for achieving those objectives (again, the school or the student).

Contrary to the notion held by some people, individually prescribed learning activities may take place in a group or in an individual setting. The important criterion is that the learning activity is appropriate for each student within that setting. Indeed, it should be noted that many objectives cannot be achieved by a student studying in isolation, but only through the interaction of students within a group. This is particularly true in such areas of study as human relations and communications.

THE IDECC WAY

Many vocational educators believe the learning system developed by the Interstate Distributive Education Curriculum Consortium (IDECC) offers the best of both worlds—individualized instruction and competency-based instruction—since it provides a means for the student and the learning manager to outline a program of individual study based on the competencies required for gainful employment in a selected marketing career.

IDECC—What Is It?

The IDECC was originally organized in 1971 as a nonprofit corporation composed of 11 states under the direction of Wayne Harrison, the state supervisor of distributive education in Wisconsin. The major purpose of the organization was to develop and disseminate competency-based instructional materials for use in distributive education programs.

The U.S. Office of Education study conducted by Lucy C. Crawford, "A Competency Pattern Approach to Curriculum Construction in Distributive Teacher Education," provided the basis for the development of the original materials. The 983 competencies identified for 67 occupations were in seven employment areas: food stores, food service, variety stores, department stores, wholesaling, hotels/motels and service stations. The competencies were grouped into 10 instructional areas: advertising, communications, display, human relations, mathematics, merchandising, management, operations, product and service technology, and selling.

Learning Activity Packages

These instructional areas were retained by IDECC for the subsequent development of 500 learning activity packages (LAPs). Each package included one or more performance objectives designed specifically to enable the student to develop an identified competency, criterion-referenced evaluation measures to pretest and post-test the student's achievement of each objective, and four learning activities for each objective. Two of the learning activities were designed for group instruction and two were designed for individualized instruction. At least one of the activities for each objective was self-contained. Each package also contained handouts to accompany and supplement the learning activity packages, as well as a learning manager's guide to provide instructional tips, suggestions for using the materials, a list of resources needed, and a list of prerequisite competencies where appropriate.

After field testing and revision, the materials were printed and disseminated to the member states in 1974. In 1975, the Board of Trustees moved the IDECC headquarters from the Wisconsin State Department of Public Instruction to Ohio State University, where it is currently housed.

Recent activities have centered around the further refinement of the materials, revalidation of the competencies and subsequent revision of the instructional materials, and the expansion of the system to include more occupational clusters within marketing. Currently, IDECC consists of 23 member states that contribute either direct payment or in-kind services for the operation and further expansion of this comprehensive learning system.

THE BASIS OF A TOTAL INSTRUCTIONAL SYSTEM

Numerous uses have been identified for the utilization of the IDECC materials. They can, of course, provide the basis for a total instructional system for students whose career goals can be cross-referenced to one of the occupations included within the system. To implement the system, the student must first identify an occupational objective. To accomplish this initial step, careful guidance and counseling must be given to each student.

Of the 67 occupations within the system, only 19 are identified as "first level" jobs, 27 as "second level" jobs, and 21 as "third level" jobs. Although a student may identify a long-range career objective as becoming a "credit manager," it is important that the student first obtain the competencies required for a "first level" job such as a "credit interviewer." After achieving the competencies required for employment at the entry level, the student's instructional program can then be directed to a "second level" job such as "assistant credit manager" and finally to the "third level" job as "credit manager.'

High Degree of Articulation

By following such an orderly progression, the basis is provided for implementing a competency-based individualized instructional system for beginning and advanced students. A high degree of articulation is thereby provided for each student as he or she moves from a secondary to a postsecondary program. If competency records are maintained for each student, as recommended, an instructor in a postsecondary program can quickly determine that student's current status and outline a competency-based individualized instructional program of study that will enable the student to continue his or her advancement toward an ultimate career goal.

Upon identifying his or her occupational objective and determining the competencies required, the student then begins a program of study in any of the instructional areas required for that occupation. A pretest is taken for a specific required competency. If the student passes, that competency is recorded on the student's record and he or she moves to the next assigned competency. Should the student fail the pretest, he or she selects and completes an appropriate activity included within the LAP. Upon completion of the activity, a post-test is administered. If the student passes, that competency is recorded and the student moves to the next assigned competency.

Should the student fail to pass the post-test, he or she selects another appropriate learning activity. The cycle continues until the student has developed all of the competencies required for the chosen career ladder.

Easing the Teacher's Burden

Because of the many tasks confronting the learning manager in administering a system with 15 to 25 students in one class, the IDECC staff will furnish, upon request, a computer printout of competencies required for each student upon the identification of his or her career objective. Common competencies for all students in the class are identified and may be presented in large group instruction. Competencies unique to sub-clusters of students are also identified, which allows for small group instruction. Competencies unique for a specific occupation are identified for each student. Such identifications provide the basis for the development of a total instructional program that incorporates large group, small group, and individual instruction, all of which is competency based and appropriate to the needs of each individual student.

ALTERNATIVE USES OF THE IDECC MATERIALS

Should a teacher decide not to use the materials as a total instructional system, numerous alternative uses have been identified. One such alternative is the selection of LAPS for a specific unit or module of instruction. If, for example, the teacher wanted to incorporate a unit of instruction on advertising layout, the appropriate LAPS could be pulled out of the system for that purpose.

Since the materials are usually filed by LAP according to instructional area, a teacher may develop an entire course of instruction for a given subject such as advertising. When appropriate to the career objectives of all students in a class, the LAPS for advertising could be pulled, sequenced and used for the course.

Often a teacher will have several advanced students within a given class who have the requisite skills and are interested in or ready to develop more advanced or supplementary skills. Appropriate LAPs could be identified and used with these students.

On the other hand, there may be several students within a class who work at a slower pace, have low reading ability or score low in regular large group instructional activities. In this instance, the teacher could carefully select LAPs that are appropriate to those students' achievement levels and career interests.

Performance Objectives and Evaluation Measures

If the teacher is proficient in the development of learning activities for specific performance objectives, but is somewhat weak in stating the objectives themselves, the materials can be helpful since more than 2,000 performance objectives are included within the IDECC system. The same is true for criterion-referenced evaluation measures. If the teacher lacks proficiency in this area, the approximately 4,000 evaluation measures included within the system offer an excellent resource. These two uses may prove to be of increased value in the future, with the public demanding more accountability in education and more states and school districts moving toward the establishment of a competency-based testing program for grade promotions and graduation.

The materials can also be used in other ways: For reinforcement purposes or to insure the transfer of training profiles and training plans for cooperative plan students; to develop evaluation instruments to measure the student's progress in a cooperative training station; to give selected post-tests to verify achievement of specific competencies in the school laboratory or classroom; and to give pretests to determine the possible exemption of a given student from a specific course or instructional module.

Transparency masters included in the LAPs can be used to enhance and supplement large group instruction. Handouts included in the materials can augment learning activities developed by the teacher. The materials can be used to prepare students for the competency-based events in Distributive Education Clubs of America (DECA) and as a resource for selecting learning activities (approximately 8,000 activities are included in the materials).

In addition to the multiple uses distributive education teachers have made of the materials, teachers in other vocational service areas have found the materials helpful to them in such units of instruction as mathematics, communications, human relations, and product and service technology.

CONCERNS IN UTILIZATION

Much more extensive utilization of the LAPS has been made in several of the alternatives described than as a total competency-based individualized instructional system. The reasons for this are numerous. Perhaps one of the most restricting factors is the wide range of exclusions in the system.

In the program classification taxonomy developed by the U.S. Office of Education for enrollment reporting purposes, 22 separate programs are identified within the Marketing and Distribution taxonomy (04.00), with a twenty-third identified as "Other, Sales, and Marketing." The occupations included within the IDECC materials represent only a fraction of those in the total employment field of marketing.

As students identify career objectives in home furnishings marketing, banking, insurance, real estate, tourism and other occupations, they may find that few materials appropriate in their particular career objectives are included within the system. At this point, the system excludes more than it includes. From a more positive standpoint, it should be noted that the widest array of instructional materials available from any one source are provided for 67 of the most common occupations in marketing!

In addition to the exclusions, other factors restrict the use of the materials as a competency-based individualized instructional learning system. A recent study conducted by Dr. Roger Ditzenberger at the University of Northern Iowa (1977) found that planning time, student motivation and problems in identifying career objectives were the most commonly perceived barriers to the implementation of the system. Clerical duties, the development of adequate record keeping procedures and the lack of adequate resource materials were also identified as barriers.

Suttle and Lane (1977) refer to problems such as getting the student to assume more responsibility for learning, changing the role of the traditional teacher, depersonalization of the learning environment and classroom control. Concerns mentioned by others include cost; availability of necessary supplies, equipment and instructional resources; and the format and general construction of the LAPs themselves.

Efforts of the IDECC Staff

In an effort to offset the last concern, the IDECC staff has revised the format of the LAPs. The new version should be available during the 1978-79 school year. In addition, the IDECC staff members provide inservice training for teachers and supervisors throughout the country and offer a wide array of resources to augment the tasks of the learning manager. These include such aids as curriculum organizer cards for organizing and sequencing the curriculum, an operations handbook, a student orientation handbook, student orientation transparencies, student completion certificates, student competency records, a curriculum index file, a bibliography of instructional materials, a separate set of test keys and numerous bulletin boards.

IDECC is also developing a series of teacher education modules; offering monthly newsletters containing "IDECC Ideas" for utilizing the materials; expanding the competency lists to include identified job tasks and required competencies in such areas as transportation, apparel and accessories, real estate, insurance, and banking; expanding its subscription service to include a greater variety of materials; completing the development of a series of LAPs designed to develop a student's economic competence; assuming a more effective role in the DECA competency-based competitive event program; and developing new materials for career exploration purposes (Gleason, 1978).

THE FUTURE OF IDECC

In my opinion, the future of IDECC will depend directly upon the vocational teacher's commitment to competency-based instruction that can be individualized according to each student's needs, career interests and learning style. It is not enough, however, that a teacher be *committed* to such a process. The teacher must have the expertise to use the materials effectively and to develop a high degree of proficiency as a learning manager.

Preservice, Inservice Programs Needed

An equal commitment must be made by personnel in state departments, local education agencies and teacher education institutions to develop, provide and maintain a comprehensive, continuous program of preservice and inservice education. The development of a total competency-based, individualized instructional system can be realized only when preservice and inservice educational programs are themselves organized in this way. This requires identifying the job tasks required of a learning manager; translating these tasks into competencies; and developing performance objectives, criterion-referenced evaluation items and competency-based learning activities whereby the teacher can develop the competencies required to become proficient.

IDECC offers the best in individualized competency-based instruction as a systematic instructional program for students seeking selected careers in marketing. But the realization of the system's full potential rests squarely on the shoulders of state supervisors, local supervisors, teacher educators and the individual teacher.

REFERENCES

Ditzenberger, Roger. Perceived barriers to implementing a distributive education competency-based learning system. Unpublished doctoral dissertation, Cedar Falls, Ia.: University of Northern Iowa, 1977.

Edling, Jack V. *Individualized instruction: A manual for administrators.* Corvallis, Ore.: Oregon State University.*

Gartner, Alan, and Riessman, Frank. *How to individualize learning.* Bloomington, Ind.: Phi Delta Kappa Foundation.*

Gleason, Jim. Yesterday . . . tomorrow: IDECC's efforts. *Distributive educators digest,* Spring 1978.

Harvey, Karen, and Horton, Lowell. Bloom's human characteristics and school learning. *Phi delta kappan,* November 1977.

Suttle, Robert, and Lane, James. Alternative approaches to the LAP's. *Distributive educators digest,* Fall 1977.

Suttle, Robert, and Lane, James. *Operations handbook.* Columbus, Ohio: Interstate Distributive Education Curriculum Consortium.*

* No publication date given.

INSTRUCTIONAL STRATEGIES

3.
INSTRUCTIONAL MATERIALS AND TECHNIQUES

Hazel Taylor Spitze

One way to look at the educational process is to analyze its elements and the principles that guide us in combining them. We might identify six important elements in education: (1) the students, (2) the teacher or leader, (3) the learning environment, both psychological and physical, (4) the subject matter, i.e., the knowledge or principles to be taught, (5) the teaching techniques used, and (6) the materials, resources, references, visual aids and equipment.

What principles could be used to combine these elements successfully? I define a principle as a general, factual statement of relationship, that is, a whole sentence showing the relationship between two or more concepts. Sometimes single words are used as abbreviations for principles, and for brevity here, I shall do that, but unless the *relationships* are understood, we probably won't communicate very well.

Four possible principles I believe will be useful to teachers in combining the six elements mentioned are:

1. *Relevance.* Is the subject matter relevant for the students? Will they see the relation between the technique and their objectives? Can the teacher function effectively in the environment?

2. *Timing.* Is this the best time to teach the content? Is the teacher going too fast or too slowly? Is he or she doing things in the right sequence? Should the teacher or the student be setting the pace? Is the clock interfering with learning? Would it be better to have larger blocks of time less frequently? What should be done when some are able to complete the learning task more quickly than others? Is the time available to the teacher and students being used to the best advantage?

3. *Appropriateness.* Is the material appropriate to the environment? Is the technique appropriate to the content? Is the teacher appro-

priate to the learning situation? Is the environment appropriate to the students?

4. *Economy.* Is there another technique that would be as effective as the one being used and be more economical in time, effort, skill or money? Are the materials worth their cost? Can a demonstration area serve as well as a more costly laboratory with stations for every student? Is the proposed learning environment worth the extra cost over the old one? Is it more economical, judged by final learning results, to teach in larger groups? What changes can be made to adjust to budget cuts? Is there a simpler way that is equally effective? Will a given procedure be too costly in terms of human relationships?

TECHNIQUES FOR TEACHING

A taxonomy of teaching techniques based upon the principle of decreasing reality consists of: (1) real life situations, (2) simulations of reality, and (3) abstractions from reality (Spitze, 1979).

In vocational education we have many opportunities to teach in real life situations, in which our students are involved in paid work experience, volunteer projects, consumer activities, family membership, personal care and resource management, citizen participation and student organizations.

If we cannot teach in real life situations, the next best choice is simulations of reality, which can be provided through role playing, skits and pantomime, games, inquiry activities, demonstrations, laboratory practice and experimentation, contrived incidents, in-basket procedures and discussions.

The techniques that are most abstract, that is, most unlike our students' real life situations, are recitation, lectures, programmed instruction, supervised study, examinations, drills, certain kinds of learning packages, audio-tutorial instruction, and computer-assisted instruction.

Teaching techniques can become more effective through using the following principles in making choices (Spitze, 1979):

1. When a variety of teaching techniques are used within a class period or from day to day, it is more likely that all students will respond.

2. Student interest will be greater and achievement usually more rapid when the student is actively participating, mentally and physically.

3. Learning is more likely to continue when the student finds pleasure in the situation.

4. Success is motivating and it enhances self-esteem.

5. If a student is involved in choosing the techniques, he or she will accept the subsequent learning situation more readily.

6. Motivaton is increased when students see usefulness in the learning situation.

7. Independent learning is fostered by the development of positive attitudes toward learning.
8. If the learning situation seems real to the student, he or she will be more eager to learn.
9. If a student has a personal interest in the success of a given technique, motivation and learning are increased.
10. If the student develops skills for independent learning, she or he can continue to learn after formal schooling is finished.
11. Positive and sometimes *mildly* negative emotional involvement heightens motivation.

Techniques Make a Difference

Does it matter which techniques are used in teaching? In general, as Berliner and Gage (1976) point out, "The evidence is sufficient to support the conclusion that different teaching methods yield similar average results when achievement of knowledge is used as the criterion, but this conclusion in no way means that different teaching methods are equivalent in other ways."

They further state that "although one teaching method may not be superior to another when class averages are looked at, students with different aptitudes may very well perform differently, depending upon which method is used." These differences can include verbal ability, anxiety level and a host of other factors. In addition, we must recognize that different teaching methods may achieve their results in differing amounts of time and with differing expenditures for equipment and materials. Likewise, there may be varying effects on student attitudes and motivation.

In making judgments in matters of teaching techniques, one's educational *objectives* are crucial. If the objective is to have the student memorize information and repeat it back on a test, the teaching technique may not matter very much. But if one is trying to help a student develop critical thinking ability, one technique could be much less effective than another. Techniques may be especially crucial for some of the affective objectives and for developing skills for continuing independent learning. Bloom reported that thoughts "which have little or no direct relation to the subject under consideration are reported almost twice as frequently in lectures as in discussions" (1953). He found problem-solving thoughts recorded eight times as often in discussion as in lecture. He suggested, "If the objective is the development of abilities and skills which are problem solving in nature, the least efficient discussion is superior to most lectures."

The importance of the way we teach is suggested by Parker and Rubin (1966): "Process is the highest form of content and the most appropriate base for curriculum change. . . . The deepest objectives of education cannot be achieved by looking directly to content." One of these deeper objectives is a "well-informed mind with the capacity to think and to continuously renew itself." Some educational objectives require careful selection of content, but others can be reached only through the experiences the students have as they learn the content, i.e., the teaching techniques employed.

Many studies have shown that student-centered techniques have greater emotional and social value to the student. For example, Ruja (1953) found that "the students in the discussion sections seemed more aware of the principle that learning is an active process and were more likely to blame themselves for failure than the instructor, the examination, or the textbook."

When teachers use the discussion technique, some knowledge of effective grouping is helpful. Gall and Gall (1976) made five recommendations:

1. Though two to twenty students represents a reasonable lower and upper limit, the best group size for discussion appears to be approximately five members. They consider group size the "most critical factor in the optimal implementation of the discussion method."

2. The group should be heterogeneous with respect to abilities, attitudes and other characteristics.

3. Moderate rather than high cohesiveness helps prevent students from rejecting minority views, restricting performance of some members or ignoring the task.

4. Seating arrangements that permit eye contact and easy hearing, and removal of barriers to participation, increase effectiveness.

5. A democratic rather than an authoritarian leadership style aids discussion by encouraging free expression of views and student participation in decision making, as well as the emergence of student leadership.

STUDENT-CENTERED VS. INSTRUCTOR-CENTERED GROUPS

Rasmussen (1956) found that his test for knowledge gains showed no significant difference between the student-centered and instructor-centered groups, even though the latter had four advantages: more background courses, more graduate students, slightly higher mean IQ, and familiarity with test style and test items. Compared with estimates made by the instructor-centered classes, members of the student-centered classes estimated at the close of the course that they had learned more, that what they had learned would be of more practical use, that more attitude change had taken place, that more behavioral change would take place, and that the class had been more interesting. All differences were significant at the .01 level, and the same result was shown six months later when students were asked to indicate actual behavior changes that had occurred during that period.

Gibb and Gibb (1952) reported that their participative action class made statistically significant gains in "role flexibility, self insight, leadership and likeability ratings, and group membership skills . . . with no apparent loss of normal content acquisition as measured by traditional objective and essay examinations." Jenkins (1955) pointed out that the teacher in the group-centered class had "opportunities to do individual and group counseling within the framework of the course structure" and that the number of isolates had been reduced, while the instructor-centered class produced more than it had in the beginning.

According to Gagne (1976), "Modern research suggests that the most critical feature of instruction for the learning of any item of verbal information is the provision of a larger meaningful context with which the item can be associated or into which it can be incorporated. . . . The essential task of the teacher is to arrange the conditions of the learner's environment so that the proceses of learning will be activated, supported, enhanced, and maintained."

Maehr (1976) adds another dimension to the essential task of the teacher when he suggests that we "view the school in its ideal as a place where learning is initiated and the interest in learning fostered rather than exclusively or even primarily as a place where it occurs. Continuing motivation may well be *the* critical outcome of any learning experience." He defines continuing motivation as "the tendency to return to and continue working on tasks away from the instructional context in which they were initially confronted."

INSTRUCTIONAL MATERIALS

Instructional materials are anything that enhances the effectiveness of the technique being used. Obviously, different techniques require or are enhanced by different materials. There may be little or no relationship between the elaborateness, complexity or cost of materials and their usefulness. Well-chosen ones may save teacher time and increase student interest.

Instructional materials can be commercially made, teacher made, student made, or nature made. The latter may include everything from a stone, an egg, a leaf and a piece of ore to a bacterium, the sound of rushing water or a bird song, the walls of the Grand Canyon, the land and the stars. Materials are also needed sometimes to help us make use of other materials—microscopes, telescopes, cameras and film, projectors, tape recorders.

Materials for teaching may also be classified as print, audio, video or combinations of these. Or they may be classified as books and bulletins, charts and diagrams, drawings and photographs, exhibits and displays, machines and equipment, games and realia (i.e., objects or activities used to relate classroom teaching to real life).

None of these classifications is necessarily complete and none may be very helpful. The important thing is that we choose materials that are suitable for the student, the subject matter and the technique being employed.

If a material is to enhance the technique and make learning more effective for the student, it will do at least one and preferably several of the following:

1. Make an explanation clearer
2. Enable the student to discover a relationship
3. Permit the student to proceed at his or her own pace
4. Sharpen or extend the senses
5. Reinforce or apply knowledge gained or foster longer retention
6. Supply an example of, or an exception to, a general principle
7. Provide the student an opportunity for practice
8. Pose a problem
9. Generate increased student interest and curiosity
10. Make learning more enjoyable
11. Extend the student's experience
12. Stimulate thought and discussion
13. Suggest broader horizons or add to vision or ambition
14. Inspire to higher levels of achievement
15. Reduce sex stereotyping or racism

Rosenberg includes a useful checklist for evaluating materials in the last area in "Evaluate Your Textbooks for Racism, Sexism!" (1973). Gibson (1969) gives these criteria for judging materials:

1. Authenticity, accuracy, honesty and balance when dealing with a subject that has two or more points of view.
2. Engagement of the student in the teaching-learning process, i.e., the necessity in the use of the materials for the student to be an active participant, mentally and emotionally involved in the learning.
3. Realistic portrayal of the subject.
4. Involvement of students and teachers in preparation of the materials.
5. Ability to enlighten teachers in the subject covered.
6. Embodiment of learning theory.
7. Suitability to the individual's learning level or flexibility in adapting to different learning levels.
8. Ability to enlighten parents.

The materials should also be judged on the basis of whether they are relevant to the teaching objectives, are worth their cost and storage space, increase student interest and motivation, represent economy in the use of student and teacher time, and are suitable in terms of the sequence and frequency of their use.

An extensive instrument for evaluating instructional materials has been formulated by Eash (1974). In four parts, it focuses on the objectives, organization of the materials (scope and sequence), methodology and evaluation. Rinne (1974) offers six criteria for evaluating curriculum materials in human relations:

1. The materials must require the student to perform a task.
2. Te materials must insure that the student experiences consequences from his or her behavior.
3. The consequences of behavior must be seen by the student in the context of a larger concept or model of interaction.
4. The materials should allow the student to repeat the experience when appropriate.
5. The materials must allow all students to protect themselves from undue threat and emotional pain.
6. The materials should encourage students to relate their classroom behavior to real world constraints.

Another source teachers may find helpful is Klein's *About Learning Materials,* especially Chapter 3, "About Some Problems in Developing and Evaluating Learning Materials."

EDUCATIONAL GAMES

In the case of educational games, we need to ask some additional questions (Spitze, 1979):

1. Does winning require knowledge rather than luck?
2. Do players have to make decisions? Does playing the game require high levels of cognitive behavior?
3. Does the amount of learning justify the time required? Does the game become more important than the learning?
4. Is the game complicated enough to be interesting and challenging but simple enough for the rules to be understood quickly? Are the directions clear and concise?
5. Is the game flexible in terms of time required to play, number of students who can participate, age and ability level of students who can benefit from and enjoy playing it? Can one person play it as a game of solitaire?
6. Does the competition remain friendly? Can teams play?
7. Will the game last? If a piece is lost, can it still be played? Can lost parts be replaced?
8. Can students play and learn with a minimum of teacher involvement?
9. Is the game attractive enough to generate student interest?

Differentiating between games and simulations should be useful for the teacher. I define a *game* as a contest played by a set of rules, usually with one or more winners, which has educational objectives, and a *simulation* as simply a pretense of a real life situation enacted for educational purposes. Hence, some games are simulations and some are not; some simulations are games and some are not. All can have value if chosen carefully and used appropriately.

Seidner's review of research led her to conclude that "the most consistent finding of research with games in the classroom is that students prefer games to other classroom activities. This finding holds true for students from elementary school through high school and for both simulation and nonsimulation games" (1976). She found that student behavior showed this inclination for games even when compared to other innovative teaching techniques and that even at the college level, simulations were more successful than case studies in eliciting student involvement. She also noted that "simulation games tend to provide success opportunities for more kinds of children, including those whose control beliefs may be the most tenuous." Peer tutoring has been observed, especially when the games were played in teams. If discussion is combined with games, the teacher's skill in discussion will be important, of course, and a game-discussion-game sequence may be most effective.

READING LEVELS

I think one of the biggest problems we face in vocational education in using printed materials is the reading level at which they are written. Reading specialists say we may have students in an average high school class reading at eight or ten different grade levels, perhaps fourth grade to college level. Obviously, then, no single text will be suitable for more than a few. Some references written for youth and adults who read at elementary levels are available, but there are far too few. Some examples in consumer education are included in an annotated bibliography by VanderJagt (1971). Many of our students are frustrated constantly by assignments in books they cannot read and their self-concept sinks lower and lower as they are made to feel that they should be able to comprehend them.

We need to be aware of the reading level of the texts and references we use and of the reading levels of our students. Formulas for calculating reading level are quoted in articles by Spitze (1970, 1971). We need to provide variety in reading materials and sometimes to "translate" the principles from the eleventh grade textbook into handouts at fourth or fifth grade level to provide some students success experiences in reading as well as in acquiring information.

Reading Problem Often Severe

The extent of the reading problem is often unknown to teachers. They are surprised to learn, as we did in one instance in a suburban school in an affluent neighborhood, that not a single student in an eighth-grade vocational class could read at eighth-grade level. Or as we found in another school in a rural area, that at least 15 percent of a junior-senior vocational class could read at no more than fourth-grade level. These are more common occurrences than most people realize, and I believe that vocational teachers have two responsibilities: (1) to become aware of the problem in their own school and to provide reading materials their students can handle, and (2) to help students advance to higher reading levels by giving them a *need* to read, providing success experiences, offering praise for improvement, and working, as appropriate, with reading specialists.

INDIVIDUALIZING INSTRUCTION

Materials can have an important function in individualizing instruction. One way not mentioned previously is the use of self-teaching materials. These may be learning packages, games that can be played in a solitaire version, self-guided field trips with report forms determined in consultation with the teacher and/or materials to be collected and analyzed, or exhibits or displays the student observes. The latter may be prepared by the teacher, a resource person or a student. Or they may be exhibits in a museum or other public place. One excellent example in the foods area is "Food for Life" in the Museum of Science and Industry in Chicago, where computers are used to assist visitors in learning nutrition.

CONCLUSION

A teacher cannot be expert in everything. The choosing of techniques and materials to use may be one of the most important aspects of the job. If a teacher can inspire students to want to learn and then provide materials that can teach, she or he will have gone a long way toward success in vocational education. It is worth a considerable amount of time to become aware of what is available, evaluate critically, create what is needed and plan for storage that will make materials easily accessible to students.

Help for the teacher in this important endeavor may be found as he or she attends professional meetings and visits exhibits; reads professional journals, especially reviews of new materials; gets on mailing lists of government agencies, associations, businesses and publishers; analyzes advertisements; corresponds with other teachers to exchange ideas; attends workshops or institutes; and keeps an eye and ear attuned to needs for materials as he or she goes about the affairs of daily life.

REFERENCES

Berliner, David C., and Gage, N. L. The psychology of teaching methods. In N. L. Gage (Ed.), *The psychology of teaching methods* (Seventy-Fifth Yearbook of the National Society for the Study of Education). Chicago, Ill.: University of Chicago Press, 1976.

Bloom, Benjamin S. Thought processes in lectures and discussions. *Journal of general education,* April 1953.

Vocational Instruction

Eash, Maurice J. Instructional materials. In Walberg, Herbert J. (Ed.), *Evaluating educational performance: A sourcebook of methods, instruments, and examples.* Berkeley, Calif.: McClutchan, 1974.

Gagne, Robert M. The learning basis of teaching methods. In N. L. Gage (Ed.), *The phychology of teaching methods* (Seventy-Fifth Yearbook of the National Society for the Study of Education). Chicago, Ill.: University of Chicago, 1976.

Gall, Meredith D., and Gall, Joyce P. The discussion method. In N. L. Gage (Ed.), *The psychology of teaching methods* (Seventy-Fifth Yearbook of the National Society for the Study of Education). Chicago, Ill.: University of Chicago, 1976.

Gibb, Lorraine M., and Gibb, J. R. The effects of the use of "participative action" groups in a course in general psychology. *American psychologist,* July 1952.

Gibson, John S. Selecting and developing social studies instructional materials. In Dorothy McClure Fraser (Ed.), *Social studies curriculum development: Prospects and problems* (Thirty-Ninth Yearbook of the National Council for the Social Studies. Washington, D.C.: National Council for the Social Studies, 1969.

Jenkins, Russell L. An appraisal of teacher-counselor-adviser teaching. *Journal of experimental education,* June 1955.

Klein, M. Frances. *About learning materials.* Washington, D.C.: Association for Supervision and Curriculum Development, 1978.

Maehr, Martin L. Continuing motivation: An analysis of a seldom considered educational outcome. *Review of educational research,* Summer 1976.

Parker, J. Cecil, and Rubin, Louis J. *Process as content: Curriculum design and the application of knowledge.* Chicago, Ill.: Rand McNally, 1966.

Rasmussen, Glen R. An evaluation of a student-centered and instructor-centered method of conducting a graduate course in education. *Journal of educational phychology,* December 1956.

Rinne, Carl H. Criteria for evaluating curriculum materials in human relations. *Educational leadership,* October 1974.

Ruja, Harry. Experimenting with discussion in college teaching: A survey of recent research. *Educational administration and supervision,* October 1953.

Seidner, Constance J. Teaching with simulations and games. In N. L. Gage (Ed.), *The psychology of teaching methods* (Seventy-Fifth Yearbook of the National Society for the Study of Education). Chicago, Ill.: University of Chicago, 1976.

Spitze, Hazel Taylor. *Choosing techniques for teaching and learning* (2nd ed.). Washington, D.C.: Home Economics Education Association, 1979.

Spitze, Hazel Taylor. Slow readers in home economics. *Illinois teacher of home economics,* November/December 1970; Consumer education and the literacy problem. *Illinois Teacher of Home Economics,* November/December 1971.

VanderJagt, Gail. Bibliography of low reading/level materials in consumer education. *Illinois teacher of home economics,* November/December 1971.

INSTRUCTIONAL STRATEGIES

4.
INSTRUCTIONAL STRATEGIES FOR CAREER DEVELOPMENT

Edwin L. Herr and Thomas E. Long

Career education and *career guidance* have received much of their conceptual framework from insights originating in *career development*. In addition, as research in career development has grown more comprehensive during the past three decades, it has contributed to changing perspectives on employability, job readiness and work itself.

Theories of career development are concerned both with the structure of work-related behavior and with the changes that occur in it over time. Therefore, the intent of such theories is to explain those factors—psychological, sociological, cultural, economic—that influence, positively or negatively, such outcomes as work values, employability, self-identity, career identity, decision making and career maturity.

Career development is concerned with the factors that cause continuity or discontinuity in the work patterns (careers) of individuals rather than in the differences between clusters of work activity (occupations). The assumption of career development theories is not that work patterns and the factors that influence them are inevitable. Instead, it is assumed that differences in career development can be understood, anticipated and influenced by the individual if systematic assistance is provided to him or her through a combination of educational experiences. From this perspective, careers (or work patterns) exist only as people create them by the choices they make. Therefore, career development is related intimately to the factors that motivate or impede decisions or other personal actions that forge work-related patterns.

PRINCIPLES OF CAREER DEVELOPMENT

Though there is no one theory of career development, certain principles create a context for considering instructional strategies for career development. Adapted from Herr and Cramer (1979), these principles are as follows:

1. The concept that work is chosen for economic reasons is too simplistic. Work also provides a means for meeting individual needs of social interaction, dignity, esteem and other forms of psychological gratification. Such vocational needs, in a society where at least a minimum level of remuneration is available from any form of work, are likely to affect individual choices more clearly than does economic return.

2. Personal, educational, occupational and career maturity consist of complexes of learning that begin in early childood and continue throughout life.

3. Career development is composed of identifiable tasks with which persons must cope in each life stage. Many of these tasks are culturally defined. Successful resolution of the tasks required in each life stage is affected by the quality of the educational, psychological, local and occupational environments that the individual experiences.

4. Because of the importance to adult behavior of early childhood experiences in the family, the school and the community, interventions designed to facilitate career development need to begin during elementary school. During this period, attitudes are formed that lead ultimately to work commitment or rejection.

5. Since career choices are ways of implementing self-concepts, every individual should have access to information about his or her own aptitudes, values, attitudes. Unless the person is aware of all personal resources, he or she has no basis on which to decide among available alternatives.

6. To be most effective, career information should be provided in actual or simulated context—e.g. gaming, field trips, career-related curricula, work study, role playing, computer mediated information retrieval—in which the individual can project the self into possible work roles, act them out and test their meaning.

7. Career development insights provide content that can be translated into instructional strategies pertinent to children, youth and adults.

CAREER DEVELOPMENT CONTENT

In addition to counseling programs, individual career planning can also be accomplished through career education activities in the classroom. In fact, instructional strategies designed to facilitate career development can be implemented through academic, general and vocational education activities both within the school and in the community. In response to growing awareness that career development proceeds throughout one's life, higher education institutions and many community agencies serving adults have developed career development instructional strategies adapted to the experiences and needs of their constituents.

Instructional Strategies for Career Development

All instructional strategies should engage clients in activities that move them through stages of career awareness, exploration and and preparation. Instructional strategies for career development are usually organized around a set of tasks or themes identified by research as appropriate for the population to be served. These themes and tasks can be considered career development content.

There are many interesting and useful ways to classify career development tasks, only two of which will be cited here. One of these is the set of tasks developed by Super, Starishevsky, Matlin and Jordaan (1963) to span the ages of approximately 14 to 25:

1. Awareness of the need to crystallize a vocational preference
2. Use of resources
3. Awareness of factors to consider in formulating a vocational preference
4. Awareness of contingencies that may affect vocational goals
5. Differentiation of interests and values
6. Awareness of present-future relationships
7. Formulation of a generalized preference
8. Possession of information on the preferred occupation
9. Planning for the preferred occupation
10. Specification of a vocatonal preference

The second example is career management tasks developed by the Minnesota Career Development Curriculum Project to cover the individual from Grade 7 through postsecondary education (Tennyson, Hansen, Klaurens and Antholz, 1975). The tasks include:

Grades 7-9

1. Clarification of a self-concept
2. Assumption of responsibility for career planning
3. Formulation of tentative career goals
4. Acquisition of knowledge about occupations, work settings and life styles
5. Acquisition of knowledge about educational and vocational resources
6. Awareness of the decision-making process
7. Acquisition of a sense of independence

Grades 10-12

1. Reality testing of a self-concept
2. Awareness of preferred life style
3. Reformulation of tentative career goals

4. Increasing knowledge and experience in occupations and work settings
5. Acquisition of knowledge about educational and vocational paths
6. Clarification of the decision-making process as related to self
7. Tentative commitment to an occupation

Postsecondary

1. Development of interpersonal skills essential to work
2. Development of information processing skills about self and the world of work
3. Reintegration of the self
4. Acquisition of a sense of community
5. Commitment to a concept and career
6. Development of the determination to participate in change

Instructional strategies should be devised to achieve the mastery of this content. These tasks also provide the basis for statements of individual behavioral goals and for systems of evaluation. Beginning instructional planning from such a perspective reduces career development from an abstraction to a set of clearly defined behaviors, each of which can be the focus for specific instructional strategies. Rather than stating in a vague fashion that an instructional program will aid the career development of some population, a teacher or administrator can use a program built around career development tasks to plan, assess and explain goals to others.

ISSUES IN CAREER DEVELOPMENT

One of the primary issues related to career development is whether such behavior should be a by-product of other subject matter or sought as an educational goal in its own right. The latter seems preferable. As has been pointed out, all disciplines in education can and should promote career development. If this were accomplished, all educational pursuits would be career relevant.

Many career education efforts today are concerned primarily with promoting wise occupational choices, a laudable effort. There remain, however, several other worthy goals to be addressed in career education that have at least as much value as reasoned occupational selection. These include the development of self-awareness, identity and self-esteem, matters which are as enduring as occupational placement for most persons.

Staffing, Curriculum, Evaluation

Other issues related to career education instruction include staffing, curriculum and evaluation:

1. There is a need for trained and committed staff.

2. Some schools offer students limited curricular choices, although the range of human talent reflected in the occupational structure is great.
3. Special needs students have special career development needs.
4. Evaluation of career development instruction must be done.

The final item is particularly important. Roeber (1965-1966) said all experiences with ideas, things and people can influence career development. Herr and Cramer (1972) stated furter that such outcomes are particularly beneficial if the experiences are purposefully and systematically related to the career maturation process. It must be recognized that all education is not transmitted through certified teachers. The world is a classroom and experience with any of its elements has the potential for being instructive and career relevant.

Interactions with General and Vocational Education. When deliberating about the broader educational arena, teachers might go beyond the perspectives of their discipline or specialty, but still limit their deliberations to other educational settings. For example, they might discuss how general studies and vocational studies could interact more fully. Such considerations would be valuable if they led to stronger collaborative relationships. Teachers, for example, might readily recognize the skill relationships between mathematics instruction and machinist training and might sense a need for infusing appropriate awareness about the other into each. On the other hand, value laden biases might intervene and interfere with curricular collaboration that could promote desirable instructional changes. In such instances, opportunities to enhance career-related instructional efforts for students would be lost. Probably lost as well would be the possibilities for promoting other career development experiences such as decision making, exploration and motivation.

The reader interested in collaboratve relationships that cross subject matter areas for the purpose of career development should examine *Relationships between Career Education and Vocational Education* by Hoyt (1976). Suffice it to say that such explorations would help teachers of all disciplines search out, identify, develop and use instructional experiences that would demonstrate the career-related possibilities of all education.

Interactions with School and Community. Other efforts of teachers should be directed toward recognizing the potential of the community as an instructional laboratory. Teachers helping youth prepare for adulthood can begin understanding their needs by looking at the typical environments of both youth and adults. Though certain exceptions exist in the American social order, it is reasonable to state that most children and adults share a home life. However, other age-related experiential deficiencies exist between children and adults. For example, youth have a school life that includes few contacts with adults besides teachers, while adults have a work life that excludes youth, for the most part. Given the characteristics of the current occupational structure, insufficient meaningful part-time work exists to give youth an opportunity to participate in and try out adult work norms.

Consequently, in formal activities, many youths learn little about work and workers, and adult workers contribute little to educating youth who want to learn and make decisions about work-related matters. This valuable instruction could be accomplished by bringing representatives of business and industry to the classroom or by extending the classroom to community work settings. The shared home experience of adults and children, when addressed to career development activities, could also enrich both school and home experiences.

CATEGORIES OF INSTRUCTIONAL STRATEGIES

Once teachers are aware of the important contributions that both formal education and the broader community can make to the career development of individuals, they are ready to consider instructional strategies that can use each environment to its fullest advantage. A simple classification model which illustrates the relationships between two issues concerning the selection of teaching strategies follows.

Basically, instruction of any kind may be classified as being mediated either by the school or by the individual. Instruction can also be classified as occurring in or out of school. In the Mediation/Location Model four cells are established. Each represents a category of teaching strategies, and differences among cells can be considered in relation to several issues (see Table 1).

Table 1
MEDIATION/LOCATION MODEL

	In School	Out of School
School Mediated	School Mediated A In School	School Mediated B Out of School
Individually Mediated	Individually Mediated C In School	Individually Mediated D Out of School

Control and Locus Issues

Cells A and B would characterize activities which are largely organized, controlled or supervised by school staff. Activities in cells C and D would largely be under the control of individuals or small groups of students. Cells A and C would focus on in-school activity and Cells B and D would be community-based. Cell A would be restricted to totally school-controlled activities. Cell D would include highly independent community-oriented instructional thrusts.

138

Cost Issues

Curricular activities within the school, Cell A, or school-controlled visits to the community, Cell B, would require tax dollars for instruction, supervision, monitoring or transportation. Independent activities in school, Cell C, would include expensive (computer terminals) or relatively basic services (library). Independent out-of-school activities, Cell D, would be relatively cost free, at least to the school, or independently financed by individual students or by community resources.

Content and Grouping Issues

School-based Cells A and C relate primarily to formal educational processes of instruction, appraisal, diagnostics, remediation and evaluation. Community-based Cells B and D include home and commercial involvements such as exploration, observation, awareness, and modeling activities. It is important to note that all cells can accommodate both individual and group activities. While recognizing the many exceptions, Cell A is most clearly focused on group activities and Cell D is the most individualized.

Ancillary Personnel Issues

In the model each cell can be used to identify ancillary personnel needed and the roles they might play in group or individual, school or community-based education. Depending on the age of students, personnel availability, program efforts and community resources, teachers and students can determine the need for involvement of counselors, co-op teachers, special needs educators, vocational specialists, work experience coordinators, parents, and other representatives of the labor force. All who would be capable of contributing to the instruction to be offered or the logistics of delivering career development activities can be identified on such a four-cell paradigm.

Examples of Instructional Strategies

There is no one right way to do career development instruction. Certainly the form of mediation and the location to be used has much to do with the technique adopted. Even so, there are many possibilities that can be considered for any given condition. A list of common techniques for delivering career-related instructional content follows. While extensive, the list is not exhaustive. The only limit to teacher planning for instruction is personal ingenuity and resourcefulness.

Career Development Instructional Techniques

Curricula Infusion
Films
Discussions
Student role books
Development of bulletin boards
Self-characteristics listing and
  analysis
Analysis of student expectations
Collection of related articles
  from popular press
Theme writing
Games
Self ratings
Field trips
Chalk talks
Job analyses
Drama
Interviews
Posters
Career exhibits
Follow-up studies
Computer-mediated career
  guidance
Career logs
Case studies of career choice
Resource persons
Want ad studies
Work samples

Work-study
Part-time work
Panel discussions
Census studies of worker
  distribution
Camera studies of different types
  of jobs
Recordings of interviews with
  workers
Charting of occupational trends
Worker surveys
Shadowing a worker
Defining terms pertinent to
  self or career
Role playing
Debates about career
  development issues
Test interpretations
Library research
Newspaper article writing
Simulations
Career development contracts
Analysis of biographies of
  famous people
Decision-making courses
Plays about work
Job search skills

Using such common instructional tactics, Table 2 shows sample elementary school activities for each career development stage for each cell in the mediation/location model. It must be remembered that these activities are only examples. Any activity that uses local resources and addresses career development needs are applicable. Tables 3-7 show similar instructional activities for junior high schools and senior high schools respectively.

Table 2

**ELEMENTARY CAREER DEVELOPMENT STRATEGIES
(SCHOOL MEDIATED)**

	In School	Out of School
Decline	Discuss role of senior citizens in society.	Visit senior citizens center. Tape work histories.
Progression	Identify factors related to promotion on jobs.	Prepare posters on career ladders.
Maintenance	Invite resource visitor to discuss needs for training and retraining.	Study effects of absence, shoddy work and tardiness on the job.
Entry	Discuss types of work in local community.	Study entry-level requirements in want ads.
Preparation	Show movie on schooling and specific occupations.	Study scouting activities for report on career relevance
Decision Making	Discuss common decisions of elementary-age students.	Interview and tape employment supervisor on job decision-making and employment practices.
Motivation	Identify personal, above-average performances.	Have home reading, discussion of career success variables with parents.
Exploration	Tell others about the work of a relative.	Explore jobs held by relatives.
Awareness	Discuss "What is Work?"	Make field trip to local industry.

Table 3
ELEMENTARY CAREER DEVELOPMENT STRATEGIES
(INDIVIDUALLY MEDIATED)

	In school	Out of School
Decline	Do library assignment on retirement problems.	Spend a day with a retiree.
Progression	Write case studies on occupational progression of specific workers.	Relate licensing procedures to training required for licensing.
Maintenance	Study implications of part-time work to finance work-related schooling.	Study certification requirements of various workers.
Entry	View filmstrips on job interviewing.	Visit employment agency.
Preparation	Write a skit about training for work.	Talk with workers to learn how to prepare for a career.
Decision Making	Perform library work on decisions related to work preparation.	Discuss factors involved in occupational decision making with workers.
Motivation	Study math skill needs of various workers and self.	Determine parents' feelings about work.
Exploration	Participate in simulation game on life careers.	Study types of work done in home neighborhood.
Awareness	Read about interesting occupations.	Study work of parents, neighbors, relatives.

Table 4
JUNIOR HIGH SCHOOL CAREER DEVELOPMENT STRATEGIES
(SCHOOL MEDIATED)

	In School	Out of School
Decline	Have panel discussion on need to prepare for retirement.	Study job loss due to occupational disabilities.
Progression	Write themes on job histories of selected workers.	Visit state professional licensing bureau.
Maintenance	Listen to speaker on personality variables and occupational success.	Visit industrial retraining center.
Entry	Role play job interviews.	Survey characteristics of recent high school graduates' first jobs.
Preparation	View film on alternative schooling possibilities.	Study former students.
Decision Making	Have chalk talk by counselor on high school curriculum.	Make posters of educational variables related to occupations of interest.
Motivation	Profile personal abilities, aptitudes and interests.	Give report after interviewing workers about occupational values.
Exploration	Compare training levels of various occupations.	Do camera study of local workers.
Awareness	Discuss personal values and occupational interests.	Make busness-industry-education day visits to the community.

Table 5
JUNIOR HIGH SCHOOL CAREER DEVELOPMENT STRATEGIES (INDIVIDUALLY MEDIATED)

	In School	Out of School
Decline	Lead about occupational disabilities and their effects.	Talk with grandparents about career termination issues.
Progression	Prepare research report on career ladders.	Inquire about local job training opportunities.
Maintenance	Prepare skit about faculty work values for dramatics group.	Relate personal values to occupational satisfaction.
Entry	Read about occupational entry issues.	Talk with a local foreman about job requirements.
Preparation	Report on local training opportunities for members of school club.	Identify jobs with varying preparation routes.
Decision Making	Request aptitude measurement of school guidance program.	List personal priorities related to occupations.
Motivation	Write article on work for school newspaper.	Identify career aspirations.
Exploration	Visit the local area vocational-technical school.	Spend vacation day with local craftsman on job.
Awareness	Participate in computer-assisted instructional program on careers.	Visit father's or mother's work place.

Table 6

SENIOR HIGH SCHOOL CAREER DEVELOPMENT STRATEGIES (SCHOOL MEDIATED)

	In School	Out of School
Decline	Discuss adult leisure time and wage earning possibilities.	Have club demonstration of craft activities at senior citizens center.
Progression	Write theme on occupational failure and its causes.	Study ads permitting upgrading of employed workers.
Maintenance	Study civil service requirements for occupations of interest.	Visit civil service testing center.
Entry	Debate influence pedalling in job seeking activities.	Visit local apprentice training program.
Preparation	Discuss local proprietary schools and their offerings.	Visit local postsecondary educational institutions.
Decision Making	Play college decisions game—Go-NoGo.	Survey workers who have made mid-career changes.
Motivation	Discuss "work values: Who needs them?"	Have social studies class survey work in the community.
Exploration	Have in-school work experience activity.	Discuss cooperative programs in vocational education.
Awareness	Practice using *Diction of Occupational Titles.*	Have small group visits to community work sites.

Table 7
SENIOR HIGH SCHOOL CAREER DEVELOPMENT STRATEGIES (INDIVIDUALLY MEDIATED)

	In School	Out of School
Decline	Outline speech on pension plans for local politician.	Perform volunteer work at local retirement home.
Progression	Read about factors related to occupational upgrading.	Interview a recent industrial promotee.
Maintenance	Draw cartoons related to attitudes about work and job loss.	Question employers about their own occupations and job success.
Entry	Prepare educational experience résumés.	Collect and study industrial application forms.
Preparation	Prepare speech on correspondence courses.	Discuss military training possibilities with veterans.
Decision Making	Use *Dictionary of Occupational Titles* to study occupations of interest.	Talk with personnel manager about occupations of interest.
Motivation	Form special interest groups related to selected occupations.	Visit Junior Achievement center.
Exploration	View filmstrips on occupations.	Survey local labor market conditions.
Awareness	Work on youth group occupational information file.	Shadow a worker in an interest area (ask for permission first).

In summary, it seems advisable to point out that certain techniques seem appropriate for school settings. Others are more suitable for community-based activities, while still others are appropriate for both. Strategies relating to school activities include computer-assisted instruction, films, drama and role playing. Strategies relating to community-based activities are interviews, surveys, field trips and work study. Strategies relating to both locations include discussions, job analyses, camera studies and resource persons. While recognizing the special characteristics of certain strategies, it seems that teachers who consider local resources along with mediation and locus issues will be able to identify, adapt or structure instructional techniques to meet the career development need being addressed.

CONCLUSION

The rewards of career development instruction are diverse. The student, teacher, the educational setting and society at large can benefit. Students profit most by acquiring new feelings of purpose and the skills to plan accordingly. Teachers gain renewed insight into the relationships between the instructional material and its application in the world of work. The educational setting obtains greater credibility as its content becomes more skill-based and relevant to the challenges found in childhood. The society gains by an increase in young people or adults who have assessed and implemented a set of personal goals related to their future educational and occupational life styles. In this latter sense, many perennial tensions between education and society can be eased as new partnerships and shared responsibilities arise through implementing career development instruction in the schools and community.

REFERENCES

Herr, E. L., and Cramer, S. H. *Vocational guidance and career development in the school: Toward a systems approach.* Boston: Houghton Mifflin, 1972.

Herr, E. L., and Cramer, S. H. *Career guidance through the life span: Toward systematic approaches.* Boston: Little, Brown, 1979.

Hoyt, K. B. *Relationships between career education and vocational education.* Washington, D.C.: Government Printing Office, 1976.

Roeber, E. C. The school curriculum and vocational development. *The vocational guidance quarterly,* 1965-66.

Super, D. E., Starishevsky, R., Matlin, R., and Jordaan, J. P. (Eds.). *Career development: Self concept theory.* New York: College Entrance Examination Board, 1963.

Tennyson, W., Hansen, L. S., Klaurens, M. K., and Antholz, M. G. *Educating for career development.* St. Paul, Minn.: Pupil Personnel Services, Minnesota Department of Education, 1975.

INSTRUCTIONAL STRATEGIES

5.
USING MILITARY CURRICULUM MATERIALS

Merle E. Strong

There are extensive curriculum materials produced by the military services that are available for the asking and highly appropriate to the teaching needs of vocational and technical educators. This statement is believed by some. But is it fact or fiction?

Some vocational educators say the obstacles are too great to make use of military materials. They point to problems involved in obtaining these materials that make them, for the most part, unavailable for general use. These educators also claim that since the materials are military specific, they are virtually unusable for most vocational educators.

I will attempt in this chapter to present a point of view that falls between these two extremes, giving some constructive suggestions on how to make use of a promising source of materials.

CURRENT USES OF MILITARY MATERIALS

First, it seems appropriate to discuss briefly the present state of the art relative to the use of military-produced curriculum materials in vocational and technical education. These generalizations are drawn from an informal survey of state departments of education and regional curriculum laboratories, an Educational Resources Information Center (ERIC) search, and from my own observations and experiences over many years. Later in the chapter some promising activities will be outlined.

Military-produced instructional materials have had little impact on vocational and technical education up to now. Isolated examples can be found where such materials are in use or have been adopted. Though the military services and vocational education have carried out training programs that are parallel in many respects, there has not been a strong communications or sharing link between the programs.

One problem is that military-produced instructional materials, with a few exceptions that will be cited later, are difficult to acquire. There is no single place or even a short list of places one might contact to find out what materials are available. Generally speaking, the military has no vehicle for distributing materials to outside persons. This is not a criticism of the military because most schools do not have this capability either. Working with personnel in the various military services, one begins to realize that the system of sharing among services and schools within the military leaves something to be desired. Again, this is similar to the situation in the civilian sector.

Much of the military material presently found in vocational and technical programs has been acquired through informal processes. Often military material comes into technical programs when former service personnel are employed as teachers or administrators and bring with them copies of materials they have used in training programs. Another informal way of obtaining military curriculum materials is through personal contact. A vocational educator will get to know "John Smith" at "X" base and will acquire a copy of course materials. When asked if the material was available to other vocational school personnel, the educator usually answers, "Probably not."

It seems safe to conclude that answers have not been found, at least on a broad base, for using military-produced materials. Some promising activities for more extensive use of these materials, however, are beginning to surface.

Advantages of Using Military Materials

The advantages of adapting military curriculum materials for use in vocational and technical education have been discussed for many years. Leaders on both sides favor the idea, but the problems of availability and appropriateness of materials have hampered their adoption on a broad scale.

The U.S. military establishment is involved in the business of education in a big way. In fact, a sizable percentage of personnel in the various services undergo education or training programs on a more or less continuous basis. Though there are some combat type of occupations that are quite military specific, most military occupations have a civilian counterpart.

The military services have invested sizable resources in developing curriculum materials. For the most part, materials are developed under rigorous standards. In many instances, the necessary resources have been available to develop very effective multimedia materials to foster an efficient learning process.

Military courses are often repeated many times under controlled standards of instruction, facilities and trainee characteristics. This makes it possible to have a systematic evaluation of the materials used. Many recent curriculum materials are competency based, a fact that should make them attractive to vocational and technical educators.

Two other factors should also be mentioned. First, the military has a process for updating materials. Since this is always a problem for instructional programs, civilian education personnel should capitalize on this resource of up-to-date instructional materials. Second, the fact that the military is beginning to individualize instruction should be noted by vocational and technical educators who are striving to implement this type of instruction.

POSSIBLE PROBLEMS

In spite of the many arguments for using military curriculum materials, several problems must be overcome if substantial progress is to be made. As mentioned before, a major problem is availability.

Another problem is terminology. Jobs or occupations in the military are given different names than those in the private sector, which makes comparisons difficult. There is a lack of standardization in job titles and terms even among the various military services. Unfamiliar military terms in the materials may also cause problems if they are used in vocational and technical education.

More difficult than the problems of job titles and terminology is the fact that work in the military may be divided up differently than it is in the civilian sector. Many occupations in the military are broken down into a number of more specific jobs, allowing a person to be trained in a very short period of time. Since training can be managed to respond to very specific projected openings, it is efficient to train for the specific equipment to be used and specific systems to be maintained.

In the civilian sector, the forces that affect the structuring of jobs may be quite different from those found in the military. For example, trade unions greatly influence how some occupations will be structured. Professional organizations also influence the range of jobs developed in the civilian sector. These organizations, for example, have been very influential in the health occupations and must not be ignored by vocational educators. It will continue to be necessary for vocational educators to provide programs that are compatible with the requirements of certification and licensing bodies.

Justifiably, military curriculum materials have been based on an analysis of needs within the military, not the civilian sector. Before these curricula can be adopted or adapted, it is necessary to make sure they are compatible with the work force needs and job classifications in the civilian work force.

Some teachers object to the use of military-produced materials, an attitude that originated for many during the Vietnam era. This, hopefully, is an obstacle that can be overcome; however, those planning to implement the use of such materials should keep it in mind.

The problem of making curriculum materials available for training programs in which the number of trainees is not large has been a difficult one, whether we are talking about adapting or adopting military materials or materials from any other source. The unit cost becomes very high. Except for the occupations that have relatively large numbers in the work force, it has been difficult for commercial publishers to justify the investment needed to refine and market the materials. One project is making loan copies available. This method of distribution obviously has limitations for classroom use.

Prospects for use of military materials in vocational curricula are not all doom or gloom. Unsatisfactory, oversimplified solutions may emerge, however, unless there is an understanding of the problems involved in incorporating these materials into civilian vocational programs.

PROMISING PRACTICES FOR THE FUTURE

Though there has been a desire to use military-produced curriculum materials, there has not been a well-conceived or generalized approach to identify appropriate materials or to distribute them. Not all of the following activities can be considered entirely new. All have been initiated within the last few years, however, and add up together to a significant effort on the part of vocational educators to make use of available military materials.

There has been a desire for many years at the national level, particularly within the Vocational Education Division of the U.S. Office of Education (USOE), to make more effective use of military materials. As long as 20 years ago an informal committee made up of staff from USOE and the various military services met on occasion to discuss the problem. The results over the years were quite disappointing, for there was no particular incentive to make something happen. The effort depended upon the goodwill of the volunteer members. Several organized attempts were made to secure financial resources, but this was not accomplished.

It is gratifying to note that the problem was recognized in the Education Amendments of 1976 in Section 172 (3), which states:

> The Commissioner shall, from the funds made available to him under this section, make contracts to convert to use in local education agencies, in private nonprofit schools, and in other public agencies, curriculum materials involving job preparation which has been prepared for use by the armed services of the United States.

This provision appears in Subpart 2, "Programs of National Significance." Though the dollar resources are not particularly great to implement this subsection, the fact that it has become a part of the vocational education legislation emphasizes the need. Already several projects have been funded and it appears that the momentum will continue to increase.

Two Exemplary Projects

One of the promising projects funded through the vocational education amendments is entitled "Trial Implementation of a Model System to Provide Military Curriculum Materials for Use in Vocational and Technical Education." This project is being conducted by the National Center for Research in Vocational Education at Ohio State University under the leadership of Wesley E. Budke (1976). It is based on an earlier project at the National Center funded by the U.S. Office of Education during the years 1975-76 to design a model system for identifying, selecting and disseminating relevant curriculum materials to civilian vocational and technical education programs. The purpose of the effort is to provide materials in their present form rather than to rework them for use in vocational and technical education.

The field test suggested that only courses that have been reviewed by subject matter specialists to verify their appropriateness and those that are not available from other resources should be made available through the system. The problems of making the courses available suggest that microfiche may be the best source for review copies, with hard copy being made available on a cost-recovery basis.

The exact nature or magnitude of this continuing effort by the National Center is at this time indefinite. It does appear, however, that vocational educators will in fact have a more adequate source for identifying military materials. Through the National Center, educators will be able to get microfiche and photo copies.

A second project entitled "Department of Defense Products for Conversion" is also being carried out through the National Center under the leadership of Pascal D. Forgione, Jr. and Mollie N. Orth. This again is a pilot project with a primary goal of identifying military materials that should be converted or reworked for use in vocational education. A process will be developed through which particular courses can be identified for conversion. Funding for the actual conversion may then come from the U.S. Office of Education or other sources. Under this project, an extensive review and evaluation procedure was established, using an array of curriculum and subject-matter experts from vocational education.

To show how extensive the effort is, several of the review categories will be mentioned. First, reviewers looked at the materials in terms of need, i.e., the size of the work force in the particular occupational area and the expectation of growth in the future. The adequacy of existing materials in the field was also assessed.

In addition, reviewers noted course goals and objectives. Were they well-written and complete? Were the goals relevant to vocational education programs or were they military specific? Considering lesson objectives, the project personnel evaluated the courses in terms of a) whether they included performance objectives and b) the quality of those objectives in terms of the needs of vocational education.

Other criteria included the technical accuracy of the materials, whether they were up to date and whether the specific references were appropriate to the civilian sector as well as to the military. Instructional and management strategies were also examined. What was the main method of delivery? Did the material include practical as well as classroom work? Was the material individualized? Ease of adaption was another criterion used. Obviously, if it would be more difficult to adapt the material than to develop materials from scratch, it would not be efficient to use the existing military material.

These and other criteria were used by the evaluators in the initial year's effort, not only to identfy a system appropriate to the evaluation and selection of materials, but to provide some suggestions to the U.S. Office of Education for particular course or program areas in which materials that are available from the military should be adapted for civilian use.

Another national effort that vocational educators should know about is the work of the National Audio-Visual Center of the National Archives and Records Service of the federal government. This center is designed to serve as a central clearinghouse for all federally-developed audiovisual materials. The program gives access to some 10,000 audiovisual materials covering a wide range of subjects. *Education* is one of the subject matter areas. The materials may be purchased or rented. A catalog on vocational and technical education includes audiovisual materials in the areas of auto mechanics, carpentry, construction, drafting, electricity/electronics, photography, heating, air conditioning, refrigeration, metal workings, welding, machine shops, benchwork, plumbing, pipe fitting and safety.

The problem of equating civilian jobs to military jobs has been addressed by the Department of Defense in a publication entitled *Military-Civilian Occupational Source Book* (1978). The book is particularly helpful to anyone attempting to identify military curriculum materials for use in civilian occupations. It provides not only a statement of the components of the job in the military, but also provides the USOE cluster within which it would fall, along with an appropriate civilian job title and number from the *Dictionary of Occupational Titles*.

The book also gives job titles for each of the military services within which the jobs are found. For example, it might be helpful for a vocational educator to know what a retail store manager's title might be in the military service. This occupation obviously falls within the USOE cluster of marketing and distribution. In the Navy such a person would have the title of Navy exchange manager; in the Air Force, supply service supervisor; in the Marine Corps, exchange man; in the Coast Guard, subsistence specialist.

Another resource for vocational educators is the Aerospace Education Foundation, an affiliate of the Air Force Association. With USOE funding, this organization has identified and made available instructional packages to vocational educators. A catalog is available from the foundation and quite a number of schools have ordered materials from this source. Educators concerned with curriculum, particularly in postsecondary technical programs, should become familiar with materials provided through this organization.

All vocational educators should be aware of the Vocational-Technical Education Consortium of States (V-TECS), discussed in detail elsewhere in this book. Under this consortium, catalogs are developed for specific occupational areas. Each catalog includes performance objectives, criterion-referenced measures and performance guides for the particular occupations. The project began in 1973 and continues to expand in the number of states involved and the number of occupations covered.

It is interesting to note that the Air Training Command of the Air Force and the Research Program Development of the U.S. Navy Education and Training Command are associate members of the V-TECS consortium. In the development of V-TECS course materials, the consortium of states can therefore take advantage of Navy and Air Force materials. The Community College of the Air Force is a part of the Air Training Command, which was approved in 1972. Currently located at Lackland Air Force Base in Texas, it is an accredited member of the Southern Association of Colleges and Schools, Mission on Occupational Education Institutions.

The central idea in the development of the college was that Air Force courses and courses available from civilian colleges could be blended into a coherent, career-relevant study program. The college was thus envisioned as providing the means to integrate on-duty technical education with off-duty educational opportunities made available worldwide through the Air Force Education Services Program. This continuing effort by the Community College of the Air Force is commendable and provides one more vehicle for communication and cooperation between the military service and vocational education.

Curriculum coordination efforts are most likely to take place within individual states or between individual schools and military bases. It is difficult to identify these various efforts individually, however. It seems clear that vocational educators must strive to find ways to cooperate more fully with the military services and vice versa, if the resources committed to training are to have a maximum impact. Some of the efforts now under way suggest that accomplishments will be notable in the years ahead.

SUGGESTIONS FOR ACTION

As vocational educators strive to maintain curricula that are up to date, they may find a good ally in the American military training establishment. The sharing of quality curriculum materials has great promise as one dimension in this activity. The following are some suggestions for increasing effective efforts.

The Vocational Education Amendments of 1976 give the USOE authority to spend funds to convert military curriculum materials for us in private nonprofit and public schools. Leaders in the USOE should expand their efforts to identify and support these conversion efforts.

Vocational Instruction

The job is too big for the USOE alone in terms of human resources and funds. Therefore, strategies should be considered that would involve curriculum resources across the nation. An overall national committee should be established, with leadership from the USOE, to recommend policy and future direction. This committee should be made up of influential leaders from a cross-section of vocational education schools who can get the job done. The committee should be large enough to be fully representative of the field, but small enough to become a cohesive working group—perhaps a dozen people.

The functions of the committee might include:
1. To assess the present state of the art.
2. To suggest alternative approaches for solving the problem.
3. To suggest the level of resources required.
4. To establish priorities for conversion.
5. To suggest means to bring state and local resources to bear on the problem.
6. To become a strong liaison with representatives from the military services.
7. To be a liaison with involved professional groups, including the American Vocational Association, the American Association of Community and Junior Colleges and professional groups who should be involved in various curricular areas.
8. To play a coordinating role with present efforts and potential future contracts for curriculum conversion.

These are small starts toward the solution of a big problem. A major achievement would be to identify, secure and disseminate military-produced materials. For some materials, this step would be adequate. However, the ultimate objective should be the re-working of materials to make them acceptable and appropriate to vocational education. A further step is also needed, as those who have worked in curriculum implementation would attest. Teachers must be trained in the effective use of adapted military materials in their classrooms. Teacher educators and others who are involved in preservice and inservice teacher education programs must therefore be involved in efforts to adapt and dissminate military materials in civilian programs.

The regional curriculum laboratories, funded by the USOE, are a potential source that should be exploited. However, they are currently involved mainly in the dissemination of materials. Consideration should be given to expanding their areas of competence and operation.

Many states have well-established curriculum laboratories with a history of development, dissemination, implementation and evaluation. These laboratories can provide significant resources for getting the job done.

The National Center for Research in Vocational Education should be a continuing resource. Building on current projects, it could become the vehicle through which the effort could be managed.

Using Military Curriculum Materials

The Joint American Vocational Association-Armed Forces Committee has the potential for playing a key role in the curriculum effort. However, it would be necessary to expand its misson and evaluate the appropriateness of its current membership. From the military side, much of its membership is concerned primarily with recruitment. Similarly, the vocational education members may not represent vocational education's strongest team from the standpoint of curriculum development and implementation.

CONCLUSION

In spite of problems, the future looks bright for closer working relationships between vocational education and military training programs. Continued leadership will be needed, however, to bring about cooperation that will result ultimately in more effective education of students in vocational and technical education programs.

REFERENCES

Budke, Wesley E. *A system to provide military curriculum materials to civilian vocational and technical educators.* Columbus, Ohio: Ohio State University, June 1976.

Budke, Wesley E. *Index of military curriculum materials related to civilian vocational programs.* Columbus, Ohio: Ohio State University, June 1976.

Budke, Wesley E. *Military curriculum materials identification, selection, and acquisition strategies and procedures.* Columbus, Ohio: Ohio State University, March 1976.

Budke, Wesley E. Trial implementation of a model system to provide military curriculum materials for use in vocational and technical education—final report. Columbus, Ohio: the National Center for Research in Vocational Education, 1978.

Dogier, Earnestine A., Russell, Earl B., Schroeder, Paul E., Maurer, Susan A., and Budke, Wesley E. *Utilization of military-developed curriculum materials in civilian vocational programs.* Columbus, Ohio: Ohio State University, June 1976.

Kaapke, Lyle D. The Air Force systems approach to curriculum design. *American vocational journal,* September 1976.

Military-civilian occupational source book. Fort Sheridan: United States Military Enlistment Processing Command, January 1978.

National audio-visual center vocational/technical. Washington, D.C.: National Audio-Visual Center, National Archives and Records Service, General Services Administration, 1978.

Rogers, William A., Jr., and Nisos, Michael J. An inventory of U.S. Navy courses suitable for use in training civilian personnel in basic technical skills. Annapolis, Va.: Aerospace Educational Foundation, 1975.

Spillman, Robert E., and Bruce, Herbert, Jr. V-TECS: The push to competency-based curriculum. *American vocational journal,* September 1976.

Straubel, James H. The evaluation of three U.S. Air Force instructional systems within civilian education: A supplement to the final report. Washington, D.C.: Aerospace Education Foundation, 1970.

Vocational Instruction

Strong, Merle E. Storehouse of sophisticated materials at vocational educator's door. *American vocational journal,* September 1976.

U.S. Air Force. Catalog of occupational courses. Washington, D.C.: National Laboratory for the Advancement of Education (a division of the Aerospace Education Foundation), 1978.

Vocational instruction systems of the Air Force applied to civilian education. New York: Praeger, 1971.

III

INSTRUCTIONAL STRATEGIES

6.
USING INSTRUCTIONAL MEDIA IN VOCATIONAL PROGRAMS

Sally Mathews

Many educators are trapped by two common misconceptions about instructional media. First is the tendency to use the term *media* interchangeably with the term *audiovisual*. This usage is not completely wrong, just misleading. Audiovisuals are one form of instructional media. Machine-based instruction, games, demonstrations and textbooks are other forms. The big push for the term *media* to indicate both audio and visual qualities is most likely a carryover from the struggle of radio and television to separate themselves from the realm of print, giving rise to the popular references to the "electronic media" as opposed to the "print media." In this discussion, *media* is used as the plural of *medium,* which is defined as "a channel of communication." Therefore, a film can be a channel of instructional communication, and so can a transparency, a model, an exhibit and an instructor.

The second and most serious misconception is that teachers teach one way and instructional media another. This belief is demonstrated by the high percentage of teachers who select and use audiovisuals in lieu of giving a lecture. The "I don't feel like teaching" syndrome exemplifies the notion that when instructional media are introduced, the visual causes and effects of teaching and learning come to a standstill. Such thinking will continue to shortchange our vocational students, in terms of learning alternatives, until educators recognize that instructional media are actually extensions of themselves as communicators. It must be realized that an instructional medium, whether it is a chalkboard, game, specimen or symposium, is a channel of communication most efficient when selected with the same consideration and planning as any other part of the instructional process.

INSTRUCTIONAL RESOURCE CENTERS

Today many state vocational agencies are moving to provide specialized instructional resource centers to aid instructors in the location, selection, development and use of various learning media. This growing recognition of the importance of proper media selection and use is a very positive step towards improving the learning options of our vocational students.

Indiana is one state which has taken such action. In 1975, the Indiana State Board of Vocational and Technical Education funded the Curriculum Materials Center. The Indiana center is one of approximately 25 such centers around the country and one of 13 offering some type of instructional media services (Bottoms, 1978).

Indiana's center maintains two instructional media libraries. The Audiovisual Library contains films, filmstrips, slide/tapes, transparencies and video tapes in the areas of agriculture, business and office, marketing and distributive education, health occupations, home economics, special needs, trade and industrial education, vocational guidance and other related topics. The Consumer and Homemaking Library is a separate system of games, kits and learning packets. Materials in the libraries are available for one to two weeks on a free-loan basis to vocational educators throughout the state.

Three Types of Assistance

As a separate section of the Indiana Curriculum Materials Center, Media Services offers three types of instructional assistance. The aforementioned loan libraries are currently the most popular offering, with the remaining two services, Local Production and Referral and In-Service, maintaining approximately equal use.

Local production services include scripting, storyboarding, graphic design and development, audio production, photography, slide duplication and a number of other production-related activities involved in the design and development of instructional media. Production services are available to state board projects, as well as to a limited number of instructor-originated projects determined to be potentially useful to vocational educators across the state.

The third area of media assistance is Referral and In-Service, which tends to function as a catchall for service requests not fulfilled elsewhere in the center. The referral component is anything but sophisticated—rather, it is an informal attempt to keep a running tab of the offerings of educational and commercial media producers and distributors. Most referral information is exchanged via the telephone in a manner similar to the way in which libraries provide ready-reference information. The in-service component of services holds the brightest promise for extensive growth. Programs are designed and presented to school faculties, project personnel, vocational association affiliate groups, conditional clock-hour classes and a variety of other vocational education groups. Information is provided on the center and its services, as well as on available instructional resources and methods of selecting and using media in the classroom or laboratory. Meetings with vocational educators are both an important center service and an opportunity to collect information on a personal, one-to-one basis. In addition, vocational instructors are questioned periodically to formally assess the needs and directions of the various programs around the state in terms of materials and assistance needed.

The design and operation of the media services section of Indiana's Curriculum Materials Center is still in a developmental stage. Since it is neither the first or the latest state-funded vocational resource center, its operations and functions are neither original nor exclusive but rather as individual as any other service with a similar purpose. Such centers vary greatly not only in name, but in services. Media centers, instructional materials centers, resource centers can all be names given to basically similar support services. Such centers are found in individual schools and corporations, offices of school districts, joint school districts or regions, and at centralized locations serving entire state school populations. Though many of the basic philosophies and goals of these centers are similar, their operations and organizations are quite individual.

The school-supported center serving one or two buildings, or perhaps an entire corporation, is likely to be the most familiar of such media services. This type of media center tends to concentrate activities in the area of production and equipment supply. Instructors are assisted in developing or provided with transparencies, charts, graphs, still photos, audio tapes, slide/tape programs and possibly video tapes. Such materials are generally designed by instructors with the aid of a media specialist. The second area of major concern is equipment services, which usually involves the scheduling, maintenance, repair and delivery of projectors, cameras, screens and so on.

Media centers also purchase or loan commercially prepared materials, usually via some type of arrangement with the library department. In many cases, the media center is a section of the school or school system library, and determining where one activity stops and another begins can be difficult.

State-funded centers operate quite differently, in part because they serve a vastly different consumer population. A second important reason for different organization and operation is that centers serving an entire state must rely on postal dissemination of their loan materials. This in itself necessitates different scheduling, delivery and retrieval procedures. State centers must also consider broader aspects of potential use in determining what to produce. Indiana's center, like other state vocational media services, must consider the relevance of a proposed product to existing materials, the number of potential users of the product, and the potential use-life. The necessary production time and the price of cost recovery must also be considered. Such state centers also differ from local centers in that they seldom, if ever, are involved in equipment supply or service beyond the point of inservice sessions on techniques of use.

Vocational Instruction

Because of the many individual differences among school, regional and state media centers and services, vocational educators should first get to know their own school media personnel and center. Those services closest to home should never be overlooked. Second, it should be determined whether the state funds or supports a specialized vocational curriculum or resource center that offers media services. If such services are available, teachers should become familiar with their nature and extent, which may well vary from loan of materials to production.

Though state-funded media centers for vocational educators are still relatively scarce, those in operation tend to provide a wide span of beneficial support services. They often will be able to provide a service that a local media operation is neither funded nor directed to provide. Whether a vocational educator is working with a local or state media professional, he or she must become well acquainted with basic instructional media classifications and factors in their selection and successful use. The following pages will provide a brief overview of three basic media categories; some suggested selections and use; a rationale for the strategic placement of instructional media selection in the development of vocational education classes, courses and curricula; and a call for a new commitment to improved instructional communication.

MEDIA CLASSIFICATION SYSTEMS

There are countless media classification systems from which to choose—some are based on the amount of teacher control, while others are based on the number of people required to participate. Presently there is little or no standardization of such classification systems. This may well be an advantage, in that it allows media professionals to develop systems designed specifically for their own operational needs. Therefore, the following three categories are not hard and fast groupings, but represent a system culled from experience and found to be workable.

Human-Based Media

Speakers	Lectures	Demonstrations
Symposiums	Practice	Problem solving
Debates	Field Trips	Role playing
Dramatics	Games	Discussions
Kits	Interviews	Book Reviews
Exhibits	Simulations	Learning Packets

Human-based media such as those listed depend primarily on group (two or more students) presentation and participation. Health occupations instructors frequently employ role playing and simulation activities for instructional units such as handling the disruptive patient, legal implications of nursing and various aspects of staff relations. Learning packets consisting of games, discussion activities and problem-solving exercises are popular in many consumer and homemaking courses. The media in this classification are also quite popular in many work and job-survival skills programs. Games, simulations, role playing and problem solving are good methods of actively challenging and involving the student in the learning process.

The Guest Speaker. The lecture, while still popular, is steadily giving way to a growing spirit of experimentation in vocational education. The "talking head," a term borrowed from instructional television, is no longer able to compete in the never-ending contest for the student's attention. One offshoot of the lecture that is gaining popularity is the guest speaker, who can offer both variety and up-to-date technical information about selected areas of business and industry. The guest speaker can introduce the student to local community employment representatives, as well as employment opportunities and requirements. This activity has strong roots in cooperative vocational education and is finding growing interest in other areas as well. If selected and organized effectively, a program advisory committee can provide such speakers. For the most part, committee members respond favorably to an invitation to participate in the vocational classroom or lab and are well received by the students.

The Interview. Another good instructional medium is the interview. It is a creative and interesting way to give the student physical and verbal stimuli in situations designed to represent any occupational situation. If designed with imagination, the interview can effectively challenge written, verbal and nonverbal communication skills, and its use need not be limited to the traditional employer-employee exchange. Customer-proprietor and supervisor-employee interactions can also be represented. The interview is used in occupational-objective identification and goal clarification exercises, as well as in programs intended to build communications skills. Many instructors record such activities on either audio or video tape to allow the students an opportunity to witness and evaluate their own performance.

Demonstration and Practice. The staples of many vocational programs are demonstration and practice. Though both of these are essentials, care should be taken not only to avoid overuse, but also to insure correct use. A demonstration that "feels good" to the demonstrator can, in fact, leave the student more confused than curious. A demonstration without adequate attention to technique can cost both instructor and student hours of relearning incorrectly practiced tasks. Video tape technology has contributed much to the improvement of instructional demonstrations, but simple instructor practice before a mirror can also yield improvements. Another way to improve the quality of demonstrations and subsequent practice is to appoint student demonstrators. This technique allows the instructor an opportunity to view the demonstration along with the members of the class, identifying and correcting problems immediately, so that practice of a faulty technique does not take place. Care must be taken, however, not to embarrass the student who is acting as a student demonstrator.

Instructor Control. In concluding this brief review of human-based media, some words of caution are in order. For the most part, this category requires instructor design and development. Most media centers maintain a variety of commercially prepared activities such as problem solving, discussion guides and so on. Media professionals can provide suggestions and ideas for modifying such pre-prepared materials to tailor them to a particular situation such as an OSHA (Occupational Safety and Health Administration) inspection of the machine shop or a fire drill in the day-care center. The important factor to remember is that regardless of program area or subject content, the instructor must not only thoroughly plan the activity, but control the experience. If care is not taken, a discussion can become a marathon of pooled ignorance; a field trip, a Sunday outing; and a simulation, a situation comedy. This does not mean that conversation intensity or spontaneity should be limited by strict rules, but that an effective instructor will guide and direct the activity to its intended conclusion as defined by the lesson's objectives. As in all cases, it is essential to make the students aware of those objectives so they can also assume responsibility for the activity's success.

Non-Electronic Visual Media

Books	Study Guides	Bulletin Boards
Magazines	Chalkboards	Maps
Charts	Workbooks	Newspapers
Graphs	Realia	Flash Cards
Models	Manuals	Specimens
Catalogs	Photographs	Teacher Handouts

The key to effective use of non-electronic visual media is creativity. Many of the media listed can be self-sufficient, meaning that they can be placed on a counter, stood in a corner or hung on a wall while still conveying some sort of message. With a little time and effort, however, an instructor can create a complete learning environment by turning otherwise static media into active media.

Models, specimens and flash cards are excellent active media that can provide detailed, technical representations of virtually any reality. These three are often popular in occupational child care programs and medical technology programs. Flash cards made of either drawings or color photographs are excellent for instruction in plant identification in vocational horticulture classes. Most media centers offer an abundance of school- and commercially-prepared nonelectronic visual media such as photographs, maps, charts, models and magazines. Quality school-produced visual products are often more abundant and more functional than more expensive purchased materials.

The Bulletin Board. One vastly underestimated non-electronic visual medium is the bulletin board. Though nearly every vocational class or lab is equipped with one, it is usually found in some corner covered with magazine or newspaper clippings and school announcements. It is generally a collector of various sizes, shapes and colors of paper unarranged and for the most part regarded as a leftover from elementary education. When it is used as a learning station, however, a bulletin board can provide welcome relief to an over-burdened instructor.

A bulletin board placed in a prominent location is ideal for posting assignments, definitions, study guides, unit reviews, test questions and answers, photographs, etc. The bulletin board can also be a maintenance-free testing station, a record keeper of job progress, and an information displayer of potential employment opportunities. Even without fancy flowers and cut-out letters, the bulletin board can become an indispensible means of communication. One instructor in a special needs machine trades program posts safety reminders, employment applications and tax forms on a rotating basis to provide students with general information, as well as additional reading opportunities.

Since many of the non-electronic visual media are self-sufficient, they can free an instructor from hours of review and repetition. The availability of different subject matter and representation is virtually limitless both for commercially-produced and school-produced materials. Instructors should by no means hesitate to take their own photographs, develop their own charts and graphs, or design their own handouts. Local media center personnel can provide assistance by aiding in the location of already existing materials and in the production of instructor-designed products. However, throughout the process of location, design, production and use, creativity will remain the key to success.

Audiovisual Media

Audio Tapes:	Overhead Projection:	Film:
Cassette	Transparent	Super 8
Reel-to-reel	Opaque	16 mm
Records	Video Tapes	Filmstrips
Radio	Computer-based	Slide/tapes

Traditionally, there are three auditory instructional media: records, radio and audio tapes. Similarly, there are three traditional electronic visual media; slides, filmstrips and overhead projection. The combination of these six is the basis of the largest percentage of today's audiovisuals. This is not to overlook the importance of other media offering both sound and sight via one format, such as the video tape and film technologies, nor the development of equipment such as slide/sound projectors capable of recording and projecting sound as well as slides. However, for the most part, the slide/tape or record, the filmstrip/tape or record, and overhead projection are still the traditional audiovisual staples in most educational settings.

Overhead Projection. One of the greatest advantages of overhead projection is that both commercially-produced and school- or instructor-produced materials can be used. This is a major asset in light of the monetary shortcomings of many educational institutions. A beautiful collection of commercially produced transparencies can be assembled in nearly any vocational program area, if funds are available. If they are not, a little effort and imagination on the part of an instructor or media professional can beget an equally functional collection at a much lower price. Another important benefit that locally produced transparencies have over those made commercially is that they can be custom designed to meet the instructor's specifications. In areas where personal taste or style are key factors, such as subject emphasis in photography or selection of typefaces in advertising, an instructor may well prefer to use his or her own materials.

Still another factor in the popularity of the overhead is that instructors can face the class or lab area throughout its use. This is invaluable in much step-by-step instruction, as well as when working with hearing-impaired students. Overheads, both transparent and opaque, are also useful when working with visually-impaired students, since they permit great magnification of presented materials. Opaque projection is excellent for displaying real objects, especially those with minute parts such as sewing needles with varying eye sizes. Acetate rolls can also allow the slower reader an opportunity to recheck what has been presented at the conclusion of the class period, an option that is certainly difficult to offer when the teacher uses the chalkboard. Overhead projectors can also be teamed with prepared audio tapes to allow individualized instruction, still another alternative not offered by the chalkboard. In fact, it has been suggested by both regular and special class instructors that the overhead projector replace the chalkboard as the primary classroom medium (McKay, Schwartz and Willis, 1976; Laird, 1978).

Filmstrips. Though some filmstrip/record sets are still sold and used, generally the cassette tape has replaced the phonorecord. From the standpoint of media centers relying on postal dissemination of their loan materials, audio tapes are by far the safer option since records are easily damaged in both use and shipment. Captioned filmstrips, in combination with an audio tape, are also becoming more popular because they can enhance communication opportunities for not only the hearing impaired, but regular students as well.

Perhaps the greatest drawback to the basic filmstrip format is its lack of instructional flexibility. This drawback, however, is usually discounted in favor of its ease of use, compact size, long life and relatively low cost. Commercially distributed filmstrip sets are available in most vocational program areas at varying qualities and prices, so they remain a favorite in most media and resource centers.

Slide/Tape Programs. The slide/tape program is generally the easiest of the audiovisuals to produce. It offers most advantages of the transparency and the filmstrip, for when commercially acquired, slide/tape programs are reasonably priced and available in most vocational program areas. After purchase, they are easily repaired and revised. Perhaps the biggest drawback is the possibility of lost or misplaced slides, but duplicates are easily produced, stored and supplied as needed.

To locally produce a slide/tape program, a camera and tape recorder are the bare necessities required. The combination of slides and tape allows the producer to be as basic or as elaborate as desired. Audible tones, inaudible tones, dissolve units and multi-screen units provide the designer a great latitude in production choices. The popularity of today's 35 mm cameras and cassette tape sets makes this medium one at nearly everyone's fingers.

Many instructors use the slide/tape program to show a process—for example, the steps involved in lighting a torch, squaring a block in a vise or making a bed. Pictures taken over the years can be combined easily with a recorded tape and made available to students on an individual basis, saving the instructor hours of repeating and reviewing. Such time savings are an important consideration in light of the size and diversity of many of today's vocational classes. The potential for using the slide/tape, the filmstrip/tape and the overhead/tape for independent and individualized instruction is an obvious reason for their popularity in classrooms, laboratories and media centers.

Film and Video Tape. Both film and video tape also play major roles in our present instructional system. Their advantages and costs are often great. Both media are becoming accepted and expected items in many educational budgets. Though video tape technologies continue to make rapid advances in equipment capabilities and reduced cost, film has yet to reach instant accessibility. This presents a problem for vocational educators because the time from film conception to finished product can be quite long. This tends to reduce the usefulness of the film in portraying current practices and to increase the costs. This problem is especially serious in areas of rapidly advancing technology such as computers, medicine and electronics. The "current practice" factor must be given ample consideration as more and more education budgets are trimmed. Many schools that already have video tape facilities are encouraging vocational instructors to produce their own programs, with the aid of local business and industry, rather than purchase films. Some industries are even willing to share their own in-house video programs with local vocational programs. Such an arrangement can be a valuable product of a well selected and carefully organized advisory committee.

A Word of Warning. Too often educators get swept away by the idea of using complicated instructional media to capture the student's attention. This tendency is certainly understandable in light of our rapidly changing and growing technologies. Obviously, it can be impressive for a school or vocational media center to be able to boast of shelving 120 films, 250 video tapes and 300 slide/tapes. As we all know, however, quantity is never an indication of quality, or even more importantly, an indication of use. Complicated equipment and fancy materials can do little, if anything, to improve inadequate instructional planning.

The vocational instructor should never hesitate to design and produce his or her own instructional materials. Those who do are likely to broaden their knowledge of the subject area, more closely evaluate the content of their programs and become more systematic in their instruction. They are also likely to use their own materials more frequently than those that have been purchased from commercial distributors (Dayton, 1978). After all, it is the individual instructor who knows precisely what he or she wants to communicate to the student.

MEDIA SELECTION AND INSTRUCTION DEVELOPMENT

As indicated earlier, more times than not the "I don't feel like teaching" syndrome is the most prevalent reason for media selection in the vocational class or lab. Ideally, media selection is based on a variety of considerations such as the learning objectives, the type of information to be presented (affective, cognitive, psychomotor), the rate and time schedule of the instruction, the space and facilities available, the learning characteristics of the students and the teaching style of the instructor.

Perhaps the greatest challenge to media educators involved in vocational education is to establish general recognition that instructional media must support objective learning. If the learning objective is to demonstrate correct procedures for hypodermic injection, any medium not clearly showing the precise actions involved is a waste of both student and instructor time. Similarly, if the objective is to demonstrate the removal of exterior dents from the interior of a car via the pull-rod method, the showing of a film on sanding techniques, while perhaps interesting, is obviously not supportive of the objective. Instructional communication must enable the student to achieve the stated objective, not provide him or her with entertainment. To do this, the selection and use of instructional media must be an integral component of every instructional process from curriculum development to lesson planning.

Instructional Development Models

There are probably already as many instructional development models to choose from as there are vocational educators. There are also countless models for the integration of learning media. Most experts would agree that media educators demonstrate a strong commitment to the strategic placement of media selection and development in their models representing mediated instruction. It would also be agreed that such commitment is not demonstrated by many vocational instruction models. However, one model of vocational instruction that does incorporate such strategic placement of media selection is Indiana's Model for Performance-based Vocational Education (West, 1978).

Though not fully described here, the West model illustrates the sequential placement of media selection necessary for both effective and efficient instructional design. Specifically, the instructional designer (curriculum specialist or instructor) would:

1. Select tasks to be included in the lesson, course or program.
2. Analyze selected tasks to determine the necessary task skills and knowledge.
3. Develop criterion-referenced test.
4. Develop or write performance objectives (enabling and terminal).
5. Select instructional strategies (student- or teacher-centered).
6. Select or develop instructional media.
7. Design the learning experience.

This model is cited for two reasons. First, it is a model developed by vocational educators, not media educators. As such, it represents a commitment to effective instructional communication by vocational educators. Second, this model illustrates a solid recognition of the role of media in student achievement of instructional objectives. The placement of the selection or development of instructional media as the sixth step of this seven-step process is paramount.

As an instructional designer advances through the process, each component builds upon the preceding ones. It is essential that the instructional media be chosen after both objectives and strategies have been determined. It is also essential that the channel of communication chosen enables the student to attain those objectives. It is obvious at this point in the process that a thorough knowledge of the individual advantages and limitations of a medium becomes fundamental. Even the best plans will run amiss if the wrong medium is chosen to communicate a message. If a film is selected when a demonstration is needed, or a book when realia is needed, or a simulation when practice is needed, it only follows that the results will be unsatisfactory (Gerlach and Ely, 1971). Therefore, media selection emphasis must be placed at the curriculum development level, the program selection level and the classroom/laboratory implementation level. Media educators must actively participate in the entire development process.

CONCLUSIONS

Many state vocational agencies and nearly all schools, elementary through university, have media professionals trained in the selection and use of instructional media. Though many of these people are not vocational education experts, they are communication experts. Their purpose is to assist vocational educators in improving their instructional communications through selecting, adapting, producing and using effective media.

Instructional media in the classroom or laboratory are not an easy way out of teaching. Their effective use requires thorough planning and control. Ineffective use, while common, tends not to be the fault of the viewer, participant, or even the medium itself, but rather an inadequately prepared instructional unit. Vocational educators must realize that the mere introduction of an instructional medium other than a chalkboard, lecture or textbook is not a guarantee of either improved teaching or learning. The expectation that a medium will "teach" without careful consideration of the learning objectives and the medium's limitations will result in lost time, money and interest for all involved. Vocational educators must accept and practice a philosophy that instructional media are extensions of themselves as communicators. Such media are not panaceas. If the lesson's objectives are vague, unclear, or nonexistent or if the selected medium was chosen without regard to the objectives, the effort will be in vain.

Until media selection and use become givens within every instructional unit, vocational educators and their students will only experience the basic channels of instructional communication. The concept of instructional media must be expanded beyond audiovisuals, and the "I don't feel like teaching" syndrome must be replaced with a real commitment to providing diverse learning alternatives. Above all, the vocational educator must develop and adhere to a professional identity as an effective communicator. To do so, he or she must realize that a selected medium is an extension of the communicator and that the medium can only be as effective as the selected message.

REFERENCES

Bottoms, Gene. Your SLR is just a call away. *American vocational journal,* May 1978.

Dayton, Deane. Teacher made materials: why bother? *Indiana media journal,* Fall 1978.

Gerlach, Vernon S., and Ely, Donald. *Teaching and media: A systematic approach.* Englewood Cliffs, N.J.; Prentice Hall, 1971.

Laird, Nicola R. Which media do teachers use most? *Audiovisual instruction,* September 1978.

McKay, Richard, Schwartz, Linda, and Willis, Kathy. The instructional media center's function in programs for special needs children at the middle school level. *International journal of instructional media,* January 1976-77.

West, B. R. A plan to organize performance-based auto mechanics programs and deliver learning content. (Information Series, no. 4). Bloomington, Ind.: Indiana University, 1978.

INSTRUCTION FOR STUDENTS WITH SPECIAL NEEDS

1.
INSTRUCTIONAL STRATEGIES FOR HANDICAPPED STUDENTS

L. Allen Phelps

Recent legislation such as the Education for All Handicapped Children Act of 1975 (P. L. 94-142) and the 1976 Vocational Education Amendments (P. L. 94-482) has greatly expanded the attention given to special needs populations in vocational education. This legislation reflects a growing awareness of the need for full and effective participation of special groups in the labor market, schools and society in general.

National and state policies, plans, rules and regulations control the operation of vocational programs. Vocational education's overall effectiveness in serving students with special needs will depend to a large extent, however, upon the quality of vocational education personnel in designing and delivering instruction that leads to productive and meaningful employment.

This chapter is about the instructional process. It describes a system for developing instruction and outlines several techniques and strategies for teaching students with special needs.

WHO ARE SPECIAL NEEDS STUDENTS?

For some, the term "special needs" is unfamiliar or somewhat confusing. Over the past five years it has become recognized by vocational educators as a term that includes the handicapped, disadvantaged, persons of limited English-speaking ability, native Americans, and the gifted and talented. Essentially, it refers to any student who has difficulty succeeding in a regular vocational program and therefore requires special assistance or a modified program.

For example, students identified as academically disadvantaged often are found to have reading and math problems. First, agreement must be reached that the student is having trouble succeeding in school because of his or her reading or math skills. Once the specific nature of the problems are discovered, the appropriate remedial instruction can be provided.

Table 1

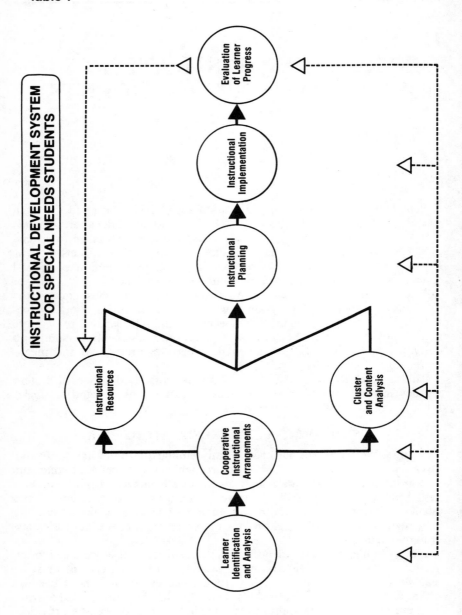

INSTRUCTIONAL DEVELOPMENT SYSTEM
FOR SPECIAL NEEDS STUDENTS

172

For purposes of federal reimbursement, special needs students cannot be identified and claimed unless special services are being rendered.

In this chapter, the following operational definition of a special needs student will be used:

> . . . an individual who is having difficulty succeeding in a regular or special, career-oriented educational program due to the effects of a disability, disadvantage, and/or dysfunctional school placement, and who therefore requires:
> 1. Individually prescribed, unique and more powerful teaching techniques,
> 2. Supplemental or supportive services that vary in type and extent depending on individual need, and
> 3. Additional resources from society for his or her education and for acceptance by society (Phelps, 1976a).

AN INSTRUCTIONAL DEVELOPMENT SYSTEM

A systematic approach to developing instruction for special needs students is extremely critical. There are a multiude of factors to consider such as the nature and severity of the special need, supportive services already being provided, etc., that have to be part of an overall instructional plan for the student. Table 1 presents a systems model for the instruction of special needs students (Phelps, 1976b).

This system should be viewed in the context of individual students. All seven components are essential in developing an effective vocational program for the individual student. However, some of the components are less critical for individualization than others. For instance, "Instructional Resources" and "Cluster and Content Analysis" do not focus directly on the individual student, but on school and community resources and the cluster of occupations being analyzed.

Special Features of System

Most teachers and coordinators are already designing and providing instruction in a manner similar to that suggeted by the system. Though the basic functions and ideas suggested by this system are not new to education, there are several special features of the system that make it appropriate for special needs students.

The system for developing instruction begins by identifying and analyzing the special educational needs of a student. Then a cooperative instructional arrangement involving vocational educators, special educators and other key professionals is organized. This cooperative instructional team assesses the identified educational needs in greater depth. Following the collection of information on available resources and the competencies required, an individual program is planned, implemented and evaluated by the team.

Evaluative information is fed back continuously to each of the components to improve services and instruction. For instance, if sufficient educational progress was made over a semester or school year so that the student is no longer considered handicapped, this information could alter the student's identification status. Similarly, if a student was assisted by funds from a new, private foundation, this information would be fed back so that the name of the foundation would appear on the list of instructional resources.

There are, of course, other ways in which to arrange the components of this system. Some educators would suggest that the system begin by identifying the available instructional resources or analyzing the knowledge and skills needed for employment. Based on field testing of the system with teachers and coordinators, however, the system presented here provides a productive plan of attack for designing and implementing programs and services for the special needs student.

INSTRUCTIONAL STRATEGIES

The actual process of instruction involves several key strategies and considerations. These include: individualization principles, analysis of student differences and needs, task analysis, consideration of occupational specializations, utilizing the student's strengths and obtaining resource assistance (Wargo, 1977; Adelman and Phelps, 1978).

Individualization

To be successful, methods used in teaching a special student must be individualized. The broad range of handicapping conditions dictates that *there is no one method or technique* that will fit a certain special need or that will fit all special need classifications. Even persons with limited ability in using their hands as a result of cerebral palsy will vary in the nature and extent of mobility from others with the same disability. Thus, every unit of instruction must be "tailor-made" for each student.

Student Analysis

If methods and techniques are chosen to help individualize a student's program, certain basic information will be needed to describe the student's disability and strengths. With the help of special education teachers, an analysis should be made of (a) vocational aptitudes (manual dexterity, work capacity, etc.), (b) basic skills (reading, writing, numerical and communication skills), and (c) occupational interests and aspirations. In some situations, other factors such as social and perceptual skills may also be important.

Task Analysis

In addition to analysis of the student's needs, an in-depth analysis should be made of the specific occupational competencies the student will be learning. First, a set of competencies and tasks should be selected that closely match the student's occupational interest. Second, job tasks can be identified and broken down to match the student's strengths. From

174

this breakdown of tasks, specific instructional goals and objectives can be developed.

Occupational Specializations

For some special needs students, instuctional objectives may be focused on one specialty within the trade or occupation. For example, the training could result in preparation of an automotive alignment specialist instead of an automotive dealership mechanic. Or an employee could be trained as a machine operator rather than an apprentice machinist. Specialization in vocational education is very appropriate for students who have limited academic skills, but who can learn to read and interpret work orders and have good manipulative skills. Training in a meaningful specialty instead of the total occupation or cluster of occupations will result in the student having marketable occupational skills that enable him or her to become a contributing member of society.

Using the Student's Strengths

The major focus must be on what the student can do rather than what he or she cannot do. In one vocational program, a group of educable mentally retarded students, who at first glance were extremely deficient in hand-eye coordination, were given hammers and nails and helped to develop the psychomotor ability to drive nails. With some individual instruction and guidance, the students were able to master the needed hand-eye coordination to drive nails safely. From there the students were led through measuring, installing screws, gluing, sawing and painting. Eventually, using mass product techniques, the students manufactured a number of child-size lawn chairs and small benches.

Obtaining Resource Assistance

In working with special needs students, many vocational instructors have found special education teachers and consultants of valuable assistance. These professionals have sophisticated skills in using individualized teaching techniques, adapting special instructional materials and assessing student progress. In a team teaching role, they can teach and reinforce vocational concepts such as measurement, tool identification, chart reading, trade terminology and other important information. As consultants, they can assist with developing or adapting instructional materials and special equipment, choosing appropriate teaching techniques and providing important information about the student's family background, disability and learning style.

Special Techniques

A number of specialized teaching techniques and strategies have been demonstrated as effective with special needs students in vocational programs. Many were developed originally by special educators in the 1950s and 1960s.

Vocational Instruction

Peer Tutors, Volunteers and Aides

Students who are enrolled in advanced vocational courses can often be used to work individually with a special needs student. Students of the same age with or without the same disability are often capable of establishing a rapport with the student. Such tutoring arrangements can often be part of student organization activities.

Various types of aides and volunteers can also be used. In most states, federal funds for the handicapped and disadvantaged can be used to hire aides, paraprofessionals or other resource persons who can assist the teacher with students who require more attention and instruction. Community volunteers, retired persons, college students and student teachers can all be helpful in this situation. In selecting tutors, care must be taken to insure that the individual is: (1) familiar with the occupational competencies being learned by the student, and (2) capable of understanding and dealing with student's disability.

Techniques for Students with Hearing Problems

Listed below are a series of special techniques for teaching deaf or hearing-impaired students. As suggested earlier, the use of specific techniques will depend upon the nature of the student's hearing loss.

1. Make extensive use of visual media instead of auditory media. Captioned films, charts and overhead transparencies should be used whenever possible.
2. Make sure amplification is available.
3. Use interpreters in the classroom or lab when appropriate.
4. With a student who lipreads, attempt to look directly at him or her as frequently as possible during lectures or conversation.
5. Remind students to turn down the volume of their hearing aids before entering noisy shop areas.
6. Install lights next to switches to indicate when machines are running.
7. Connect bells on typewriters, timers, fire alarms and other equipment to flashing lights.
8. Consider using a total communication approach that includes speech, careful listening, sign language, finger spelling, gesture and mime.
9. Consider learning manual communications (sign language and finger spelling).
10. Precede instruction with individual demonstrations whenever possible.

Techniques for Students with Visual Problems

Here are a number of techniques found to be effective with blind and visually-impaired students:

Instructional Strategies for Handicapped Students

1. Convert printed materials to braille, enlarged print or thermoformed print.
2. Use electronic scanning equipment to transform letters and words from print into raised images.
3. Transcribe essential text information onto cassette tapes.
4. Find out whether volunteer or paid reader services are available.
5. Let students examine equipment and tools while you give a verbal description so the student can develop a "mental blue-print."
6. Obtain special tools such as braille micrometers and audible multimeters.
7. In shop areas, use slightly raised lines around dangerous operating equipment to avoid accidents.

Facility and Equipment Modifications

The following are some possible facility and equipment modifications for students with cerebral palsy and other types of physical impairments:

1. Use ramps instead of stairs to provide easier access for students with wheelchairs and crutches.
2. Install handbars on walls next to machines, water fountains and benches.
3. Leave ample space between aisles and around equipment and desks for wheelchairs.
4. See that floors are nonskid so crutches and wheelchairs can be handled safely.
5. Obtain book holders, mechanical page turners and other types of special equipment as necessary.
6. Alter the height of work benches and storage cabinets if necessary. Working surfaces may have to be lowered or recessed to accommodate a wheelchair.
7. Install special guard plates on equipment as appropriate.
8. Find out if tools need to be modified or machine operating controls relocated.

REFERENCES

Adelman, F. W., and Phelps, L. A. Learning to teach the handicapped learner. *American vocational journal*, April 1978.

Phelps, L. A. *Instructional development for special needs learners:* An inservice *resource guide.* Urbana: University of Illinois, Department of Vocational and Technical Education, 1976a.

Phelps, L. A. Someone with special needs: An alternative definition. *Illinois career education journal*, Winter 1976b.

Wargo, W. D. Individualizing instruction for special needs students in industrial education. *Industrial education*, November 1977.

IV.

INSTRUCTION FOR STUDENTS WITH SPECIAL NEEDS

2.
A NEW ERA
FOR HANDICAPPED STUDENTS

Lloyd W. Tindall

Many people are asking the question: Why should handicapped people work at all? And since employment is the ultimate goal of vocational education, many also ask: Why vocational education for handicapped people? Basically, the answer to both questions is: To enable handicapped people to enjoy the personal and economic gains from employment. Work has a therapeutic value for handicapped people and their families. It creates a sense of belonging and acts as a stimulus to further effort. Society also gains from the investment in helping handicapped people become productive, contributing members of the community. The next questions are: Who are the handicapped people and what progress has vocational education made in serving them?

Handicapped persons may have physical, mental, hearing, visual, emotional, learning, speech or language disabilities. Persons with drug and alcohol abuse problems and ex-offenders may also be included on the list of disabled learners. In addition, one might find that economic, social, educational and cultural conditions have created disabled learners. Those with mental, emotional and learning disabilities comprise the largest number of handicapped students in the nation.

To measure the progress of vocational education in serving handicapped people requires more than a simple assessment of vocational programs. Progress must be measured in the attitudes and commitment of vocational educators, administrators, public school personnel, employers, state and federal agency staff, and communities in general. Of utmost importance are the linkages that vocational educators have established with other groups who are also serving handicapped people.

A FOUR-STEP PROCESS

All of us are at different stages in providing vocational education to handicapped people. At least four of these stages can be identified:

Vocational Instruction

1. Awareness of the characteristics, needs and capabilities of handicapped persons.
2. Acceptance of the philosophy that handicapped people can be educated and have a right to education, followed by a commitment to take immediate action.
3. Modification of educational programs and services to help handicapped people achieve to the best of their ability.
4. Employment of handicapped people through changes in attitude, identifying the work that handicapped persons can perform and redesigning jobs accordingly.

Progress in this four-step process must start with individuals and spread throughout the community, which includes teachers, administrators, agencies, employers, families and others who are directly or indirectly involved in the lives of handicapped persons.

Spreading the Word

We know a good deal about the needs, characteristics and capabilities of handicapped people. With the help of special educators, vocational educators have developed models for the delivery of services, as well as individualized and competency-based programs for handicapped people. They are engaged in research to identify barriers to education, successful teaching strategies, and job placement techniques. In most areas of the country, we find success stories of how handicapped persons have overcome physical, mental, emotional, social and educational barriers.

We now have a good idea of the levels of achievement that can be expected of persons according to type of handicap and how to help them achieve to the maximum. We know, for example, that bright, learning-disabled students who lack reading ability have done well in vocational classes when audio, visual and tactile modes of communication were used in place of reading.

Techniques and strategies that work with the mentally retarded and the emotionally disturbed have been identified and practiced in vocational programs. Mechanical and electronic communication services have been developed for the hearing and visually impaired, quadraplegics and the cerebral palsied. The design of physical facilities for persons in wheelchairs is well advanced. Doors, entrance ramps, water bubblers, elevator buttons, telephone locations, restrooms and classrooms are being altered gradually for better access by handicapped people.

Accepting Handicapped Students

Acceptance is on an individual basis or by groups. Progress stops at this point unless acceptance is followed by a commitment to help and by immediate action. It is surprising and disheartening how many fledgling programs fail because of lack of commitment. Programs also fail because appropriate support and follow-up services are not provided. The program may be the school's token commitment to serving the handicapped and may therefore struggle along until it eventually goes under.

Acceptance and commitment are vital for obtaining and maintaining funding for further program development. It is the comprehensive support of the community that will make the difference to handicapped students. We can start by securing the cooperation of all vocational educators, not just those engaged in special education projects. An important step in this direction was taken when the National Association of Vocational Education Special Needs Personnel was organized at the 1974 annual convention of the American Vocational Association (AVA). Committed both to disadvantaged and handicapped students, this group promotes not only the acceptance of handicapped and disadvantaged students, but also the modification and development of vocational programs for these students.

In 1976 the Division of Career Development was formed in the Council for Exceptional Children. A counterpart to the AVA group, this division is committed to the career development of handicapped students. These two national organizations are making significant progress in the promotion of better education and career development for handicapped students by alerting educators and others to their specific needs.

The Association for Children with Learning Disabilities (ACLD) is another organization extremely active in promoting vocational education for students with learning disabilities. In recent years the ACLD international conferences have dealt increasingly with the vocational education aspects of secondary and postsecondary learning for disabled students. The American Personnel Guidance Association and other organizations are also placing an increased emphasis on vocational education for handicapped students. This new emphasis and the links among educators in these various professional organizations are very important steps towards improved vocational programs for handicapped students.

Program Modification

The greatest progress in program modification so far has been made in vocational programs for students whose handicaps are most visible—for example, students with physical handicaps or visual and hearing disabilities. Students with less visible handicaps such as mental retardation, learning disabilities, emotional disturbance, and drug and alcohol abuse have not received sufficient attention. Successful vocational programs for these people are becoming more abundant, however. Educable mentally retarded persons, who are the most numerous, probably need more attention than other groups.

Vocational education for severely handicapped persons is virtually nonexistent. These persons have intense physical, mental or emotional problems. They may have a combination of problems that require educational, social, psychological and medical services beyond those offered by regular school programs. They include, for example, mentally retarded persons with severe hearing or sight defects and trainable mentally retarded persons with severe physical disabilities. The question of how vocational education would benefit these and other severely handicapped persons has not been answered fully.

Development of diagnostic services is under way, especially for persons with learning and mental handicaps. There is a need for broader diagnostic services, however, and for cutting down the time required to perform them so that appropriate modifications in the vocational program can be made quickly. Confidentiality of information restrictions frequently prohibit the flow of needed information about the handicapped student from those persons performing the evaluation to the teachers of the students. This is especially true at the postsecondary level. Teachers need to learn diagnostic strategies so they can identify needs of handicapped students in their programs. Individualized teaching programs should be a natural product of good diagnostic services, but few are in operation.

Some mainstreaming is being done. But many educators are finding out too late that to merely place a handicapped student in a regular classroom without increased services and support personnel invites failure. Mainstreaming means more, not fewer, services and personnel. Yet federal legislation requires that handicapped students receive vocational education that is as similar as possible to the vocational education received by nonhandicapped students.

Many current programs for handicapped students were started with seed money under the 1968 Vocational Amendments. Much of this money was spent on prevocational and avocational areas. Though this expenditure of funds was justifiable—actually, a vital prerequisite to vocational training—we must be sure that students move on to vocational training. The Education Amendments of 1976, Education for All Handicapped Children Act of 1975 and Rehabilitation Act of 1973 (Sections 503 and 504) will help insure that all handicapped students have access to vocational education in the future. In addition, the completed and current vocational projects for handicapped students must be evaluated in order to glean the successes and eliminate repetition of failures.

Curriculum Modification

Vocational teachers are usually not trained to adapt their programs to the needs of handicapped students. When one thinks of the many types of disabilities and literally hundreds of subject matter areas in vocational education, one realizes how much work needs to be done in current curriculum modification. Teachers need training in methods of modifying curricula for students in each disability area.

The best curriculum modifications have been made by innovative teachers to fulfill specific needs of handicapped students in their programs. As a result, the best of the modified materials are not readily accessible to the majority of vocational educators.

Publishers in the past have not seriously tackled the problem of adapting their curriculum materials to the needs of handicapped students. Now, however, they are finding it more profitable to produce handicap-oriented materials as more vocational teachers request them. Materials are beginning to specify the type of handicapped student for which they are intended. Vocational concepts are being placed in formats that will facilitate their understanding by the mentally retarded and other handicapped students.

Preparation of vocational teachers to teach handicapped students is increasingly becoming part of the regular teacher education requirements. A few universities are now offering courses to certify vocational teachers to teach handicapped students. Other universities are beginning to infuse the strategies for teaching handicapped students into existing teacher preparation courses. Both types of courses are normally taught by special needs personnel.

More and more appropriate inservice programs on how to teach handicapped students are being made available. Few states have added the certification requirements that are essential to updating the competencies of current teachers, however.

Employment of the Handicapped

"Hire the handicapped" is a slogan familiar to everyone. Though employment of the physically handicapped has been reasonably successful, finding jobs for the educable mentally retarded and those with learning and emotional disabilities continues to be a real problem. One innovative approach has been to identify skills handicapped students can learn that will be usable in a broad range of jobs. Employers are then asked to redesign jobs so that handicapped employees can use their skills. The parts of the job the handicapped employee cannot do can be assigned to another employee. The handicapped employee should and can produce the same quality of work required of the nonhandicapped employee. The aim is to expand the awareness of employers about the skills handicapped people can master and to identify skills commonly demanded by a variety of employers. The end result should be increased employment of handicapped persons. To complete the task will require greater cooperation from employment services, employers and educators in designing and creating jobs that handicapped persons can do.

Employment of handicapped persons calls for intensified communication and understanding among community members. Employers must have our help in redesigning and modifying jobs for handicapped persons. Unemployment among handicapped people is high and times of high national unemployment are especially hard on handicapped people. For these two reasons, it is vitally important that we not delay their vocational training.

The Cutting Edge

The cutting edge in vocational education for handicapped people is in the modification of programs and curricula to enable them to succeed in regular vocational classrooms. Commitment, along with awareness and acceptance, must increase if progress is to continue. As mentioned earlier, federal legislation now mandates access to vocational education for handicapped students at the secondary and postsecondary levels. This means that vocational education programs, especially postsecondary programs, will have many more handicapped students seeking services. Preparation to admit and provide services for these students must begin now.

Sufficient research, information and materials are available to start new programs and improve existing ones. Diagnosis of problems and prescription of solutions must be stepped up. Vocational education of handicapped students must become part of the regular teacher training curriculum and certification requirements. New ways to dispense information and provide inservice training to teachers are needed. Existing courses and support services may need to be modified. We have come a long way since the 1968 Amendments. To delay now will compound the problems we are trying to solve.

In reality, most of the barriers to the vocational education of handicapped people are down or are surmountable. We now ask these questions: How will vocational educators react to the present situation? Will we use this opportunity to develop and modify vocational education programs for handicapped students? Will we accept the demand for leadership? A positive response will fulfill a golden opportunity and open up a new era in the lives of the nation's handicapped people.

IV.

INSTRUCTION FOR STUDENTS WITH SPECIAL NEEDS

3.
TEACHING STUDENTS WITH MENTAL HANDICAPS

Camille G. Bell

Recent federal legislation mandates a national commitment to equal educational rights for the handicapped. As a result, vocational teachers have an increased responsibility to develop competencies needed to teach the physically and mentally handicapped.

The Handbook for Vocational Education for the Handicapped (1978) identifies 13 major competencies for vocational teachers of the handicapped.

1. Assume the professional role of vocational teacher of the handicapped.
2. Function as a professional team member in the education of handicapped youth.
3. Develop effective vocational education for handicapped students.
4. Determine the potential of handicapped students selected to participate.
5. Manage the behavior of handicapped students in vocational education.
6. Plan instruction.
7. Instruct handicapped vocational students.
8. Manage laboratories for vocational students with handicaps.
9. Determine educational needs and progress of handicapped vocational students.
10. Provide personal and career guidance to handicapped students.
11. Establish effective school-community relations that will benefit handicapped vocational students.
12. Manage vocational programs for the handicapped.
13. Advise a student organization for handicapped vocational students.

Although all of these competencies are important to teachers of any student with a handicap, this chapter focuses upon the practical realities of planning programs and instructing students with mental handicaps who are eligible for special services. It should be kept in mind, however, that many of the suggestions for this population are also applicable to teaching physically handicapped or emotionally disturbed students.

PLANNING THE CURRICULUM

Curricula for mentally handicapped vocational students should be based on the overall goal of making each student employable. According to Kirk (1972), there is no unique curriculum for mentally retarded students. Elements of the regular curriculum may need to be adjusted, however, to make them more meaningful to handicapped students.

Reynolds and Birch (1977) give three patterns that have been used to adapt curricula: (1) slowing the regular curriculum down, (2) simplifying the regular curriculum and (3) breaking the regular curriculum into smaller learning segments. A newer approach to the problem is designing curricula especially for the learning characteristics of mentally retarded students.

Individualized Education Programs

The individualized education programs (IEPs) required by recent federal legislation are important in shaping vocational curricula for handicapped students. The IEP is defined as a written statement about the objectives, content, implementation and evaluation of a child's educational program. It is not legally binding, but is a joint planning effort of teachers (regular and special), one or both of the student's parents, a professional representative of the local school district (other than one of the student's teachers), and the student. The program specifies educational objectives, how to attain them and how to evaluate the results.

The required period of time to be covered by the IEP is one year. The program should include the following: a description of the student's current educational status, a look at goals that may be a year or more away, a sequence of short-term instructional objectives leading to each goal, a list of instructional and service requirements needed, the criteria and schedule for evaluation of program effectiveness and a statement of the role of the parents. The IEP gives structure to individualized instruction, providing for flexibility and uniqueness.

A PROPER MIX OF CURRICULUM ELEMENTS

According to Reynolds and Birch, curricula for students who show slow cognitive development should consist of a proper mix of the same elements in curricula for other students. These elements are subject matter, objectives, learning experiences and evaluation. Brief descriptions of how these curriculum elements can be adjusted for handicapped vocational students follows:

Teaching Students with Mental Handicaps

Subject Matter

In addition to job skills, the vocational curriculum should give information and experiences to help handicapped students learn to cope with everyday problems (Kirk, 1972). They should have an opportunity to develop a positive self-identity, practice safety habits, develop an understanding of community responsibility and relate to other workers. In short, the curriculum should help handicapped students broaden their experiences, as well as develop good attitudes and personality traits that will make them employable.

In selecting subject matter for the curriculum, the teacher must consider the wide variety of needs, interests, backgrounds and abilities of students. The strengths of the students should be emphasized. It should be remembered that handicapped students are capable of learning if the curriculum is adjusted to fit their abilities. Subject matter must have high interest for the student, be presented in small, interlocked steps, and be accompanied by reinforcers with high appeal to the student (Jones, 1971).

Objectives

Objectives should help students achieve the overall goals in the chosen occupational area. They will differ according to state program standards and the abilities of the students. A major requirement of using behavioral objectives efficiently is the capability of breaking a somewhat general skill into tasks (Meyen, 1972). This process is referred to as a job analysis. In turn, the procedures required for the job are broken down into teachable steps through task analysis.

Task Analysis

Task analysis is vital to developing curricula for handicapped vocational students because learning must be presented in small, sequential steps. The following outline shows how to conduct a task analysis (Smith and Bentley, 1975):

1. Determine the behavioral objective you wish to achieve.
2. Review resources that pertain to the objective.
3. Distinguish between the dependent and independent behavior components of the objective.
4. Sequence the steps in logical order.
5. Analyze the steps in logical order.
6. Determine prerequisite skills or knowledge needed.
7. Evaluate student progress.
8. Alter the tasks and sequence as needed.

Learning Experiences

Mentally handicapped vocational students differ greatly in physical and mental abilities, personal needs, strengths and interests. This wide variation necessitates a wide range of learning experiences to reach one student.

Vocational Instruction

Effective learning experiences should have clear, concise directions (Neff and Pilch, 1976). Different types of instructional materials help stimulate interest and overcome the problem of students' limited attention span. Some of the audiovisual aids that have proven most effective in learning experiences are: magnetic boards, actual objects, films, filmstrips, slides, television, radio, records, tapes, videotapes, graphs, charts, diagrams and flip charts.

Using as many of the students' senses as possible (multisensory learning) is vital to effective learning experiences for many handicapped students. For example, a student who is dependent upon the auditory mode may be able to follow verbal but not written instructions.

Evaluation

Evaluation can be an effective tool for helping mentally handicapped students see their own growth in vocational education. Data and information used in evaluation should be obtained through sound measurement procedures and should lead toward self-evaluation. Since written tests are difficult for a majority of handicapped students, simple projects, reports, self-evaluation instruments, oral and performance tests are usually more effective to use as a basis for measuring student growth. If a pencil-and-paper test is simple and requires very little reading and writing, however, it can be used to evaluate some cognitive skills.

Evaluation should be a continuing process, enabling teachers to determine the student's progress and readiness for the next learning experience. Mastery of instructional objectives specified for a student should be evaluated at designated periods throughout the year. A criterion-referenced evaluation system should be used whenever feasible rather than focusing on the speed of learning compared to other students (Reynolds and Birch, 1977).

Meyen (1972) agrees with the concept of criterion-referenced evaluation and recommends that teachers develop skill inventories. This technique requires that the teacher identify the behavior to be achieved and establish a criterion level that will be acceptable as evidence of the student's successful performance of the task. The next step is to structure a situation requiring the student to perform the task under conditions that can be observed and evaluated.

The evaluation of IEPs is vital to an ongoing vocational program for the handicapped. Reynolds and Birch (1977) stress that the evaluation of IEP goals should be ongoing. The group that plans the program ought to check periodically on each short-term instructional objective to find out whether it has been accomplished within the time limit planned. If not, alterations to relevant parts of the IEP should be made. If criterion-referenced evaluation of the IEP proves it is inadequate, the program should be amended by the same process that brought it into being in the first place.

INSTRUCTING THE MENTALLY HANDICAPPED STUDENT

Teaching Methods

Basic teaching methods for handicapped vocational students do not differ greatly from good teaching methods for all students. Teachers need to discover and diagnose learning problems without labeling or categorizing the student (Neff and Pilch, 1976). On the other hand, mental retardation is characterized by a reduced ability to form stable perceptions and concepts as well as by restricted thought processes (Kirk, 1972).

Here are three methods of instruction that have been effective in modifying the behavior of mentally retarded students (Kolstoe, 1970):

Verbal Instruction. The teacher instructs the student verbally on the behavior desired. If he or she behaves in the desired manner, the teacher will generally smile, nod or compliment the student verbally. Generally, mentally handicapped students respond more readily to visual and verbal signals than to written stimuli (Altfest, 1975).

Identification. After observing the model, the student usually imitates its behavior. However, many handicapped youth have not been exposed to models of successful workers, especially handicapped workers, at home or in the community (Altfest, 1975). Thus, handicapped workers from the community should be used as models for the student. These workers can describe adaptations they were required to make in order to find and retain employment. Simulation games and role playing can also help acquaint students with the world of work.

Reinforcement. The teacher rewards the student systematically when desired behavior is exhibited. By raising the standards for receiving rewards, he or she can shape the students' behavior until it meets acceptable norms. The rewards are then scheduled regularly until the desired behavior becomes stabilized.

Teachers should capitalize on students' ideas to increase participation, interest and learning (Altfest, 1975). By making sure each step is understood and mastered before proceeding to the next step, teachers can help students achieve success.

The type of instruction used will depend on the program and the students involved. A flexible environment and a variety of media and instructional resources will help enrich learning and also prove to be invaluable to motivating students to learn (Taylor, 1976).

Teaching Techniques

Each vocational teacher should find an instructional style that is effective and comfortable. However, the following instructional practices seem to help handicapped students learn (Neff and Pilch, 1976):

1. *Use a minimum of language.* Instructions must be clear, simple, concise and direct. Too many words can confuse mentally handicapped students, for they do not have the ability to pick out the necessary information.

2. *Work from the concrete to the abstract.* An opportunity to manipulate concrete objects makes it easier for the student to deal with abstract concepts. In fact, some students cannot deal with abstractions without going through concrete, semiconcrete and semiabstract experiences.

3. *Provide many short but frequent repetitions.* Many short repetitions of a task scattered throughout the day are better than long periods of repetition given less frequently. An example is using flash cards to study key words at the beginning of each class period for several days. Such a simple activity is not time consuming, but provides frequent opportunities to practice and aids retention.

4. *Control the quality of work and length of work periods.* Mentally handicapped students can usually work for relatively short periods of time. Try to determine by observation how long a student can work at one sitting. Then plan an activity the student will enjoy after the completion of work. Gradually lengthen the students' work session until he or she can work for the desired period of time.

5. *If a strategy does not work, change it.* If students are not able to achieve objectives, go back to your analysis of the task and look at the kinds of errors that are occurring. Has a word been misunderstood? Is a procedure not mastered? Never let a student fail. Keep trying until the student finds success at his or her optimum level.

MANAGING THE BEHAVIOR OF HANDICAPPED STUDENTS

Many mentally handicapped students demonstrate undesirable behavior and attitudes in school .One possible reason is that they become frustrated easily because of limited abilities and experiences (Altfest, 1975). In addition, the insecurities of daily living, a history of failure in school and inner tensions caused by family conflicts may contribute to a hostile or apathetic attitude toward education.

Interpreting Student Behavior

It is essential for vocational teachers to gain skills in observing, recording and interpreting student behavior (Reynolds and Birch, 1977). After becoming familiar with a student's record, teachers can record behavior continuously to produce a student profile that will help in managing the behavior of the student.

Data such as anecdotal records, profile sheets, charts, graphs, checklists and rating scales are also helpful in interpreting student behavior. The vocational teacher may wish to consult others such as special education teachers, vocational adjustment coordinators, physicians or other professionals when analyzing the student behavior data. Upon completion of data analysis, teachers can formulate more effective plans for managing student behavior.

Preventive Discipline

The following general classroom management principles are suggested for teachers of mentally handicapped students (Neff and Pilch, 1976):

1. Set up, with the aid of the students, clear rules for daily routines, classwork and independent work. The reasons for rules should be discussed in detail.
2. Plan independent activities as well as group work, but be sure students have something else to do when they have finished.
3. Stress positive rather than negative statements and classroom behavior. Everyone finds it more rewarding to be told what to do rather than what not to do.
4. Praise behavior that is good.

Behavior Modification Strategies

Behavior modification strategies can be used to change behavior, maintain or increase present behavior, and establish new behavior. Berman (1971) suggests that dramatic changes have occurred, even with the most deviant students, when the external environment has been restructured so that students are motivated for appropriate behavior. Behavior modification focuses only on behaviors that are observable, measurable and need improvement. The three basic components for behavior modification are (Hall, 1970):

Reinforcement. The key to behavior modification is that desirable behavior is rewarded or reinforced, while undesirable behavior is not. Two types of reinforcement can be used: (1) tangible reinforcement, which involves giving some object such as tokens, candy, toys or food, and (2) non-tangible reinforcement, which is interpersonal and includes verbal praise, smiling and attention.

Extinction. Ignoring a problem until it goes away is referred to as extinction. It neither reinforces nor punishes behavior. This method of modifying behavior is particularly effective for dealing with discipline problems that would, if handled otherwise, cause an interruption of learning. A teacher must be careful not to overuse extinction or control will be lost.

Punishment. Punishment is adding something bad or taking away something good (such as a privilege). The only way to determine whether the stimulus is perceived as a punishment is to observe its effect on behavior. It should be used in the classroom only as a last resort, usually to halt a behavior that is potentially dangerous or one that is interfering with the appropriate behavior of other students.

Vocational Instruction

SUMMARY

Curriculum content in vocational education for mentally handicapped students is not drastically different from that for other students, but each element needs to be adjusted to be appropriate. Vocational teachers of handicapped students should develop specific methods and techniques that will help match instruction to each student's needs, abilities and behavior.

Vocational educators are beginning to reach out to mentally handicapped students. In doing so, they are learning deep respect for this special population. They have also begun to realize that an exciting opportunity exists in helping these handicapped students become useful citizens.

REFERENCES

Altfest, Myra, (Ed.). *Vocational education for students with special needs.* Washington, D.C.: Mid-East Regional Resource Center, 1975.

Berman, Mark. *Motivation and learning.* Englewood Cliffs, N.J.: Education Technology Publications, 1971.

Brown, Duane. *Changing student behavior: A new approach to discipline.* Dubuque, Iowa: William C. Brown, 1971.

Hall, Vance. Behavior modification: Basic principles. *Managing behavior,* Part II. Meriam, Kansas: H & H Enterprises, 1970.

Handbook for vocational education for the handicapped. Lubbock, Texas: Home Economics Instructional Materials Center, Texas Tech University, 1978.

Jones, Reynold L. *Education of exceptional children.* Boston: Houghton Mifflin, 1971.

Kirk, Samuel A. *Educating exceptional children.* New York: Houghton Mifflin, 1972.

Kolstoe, Oliver P. *Teaching educable mentally retarded children.* New York: Holt, Rinehart and Winston, 1970.

Meyen, Edward L. *Developing units of instruction for the mentally retarded and other children with learning problems.* Dubuque, Iowa: William C. Brown, 1972.

Neff, Herbert, and Pilch, Judith. *Teaching handicapped children easily.* Springfield, Ill.: Charles C. Thomas, 1976.

Reynolds, Maynard C. and Birch, Jack W. *Teaching exceptional children in all America's schools.* Reston, Va.: The Council for Exceptional Children, 1977.

Smith, Pamela, and Bentley, Glee. *Participant manual learning styles: Mainstreaming mildly handicapped students in the regular classroom.* Austin, Texas: Educational Service Centers, 1975.

Taylor, George, and Jackson, Stanley. *Educational strategies and services for exceptional children.* Springfield, Ill.: Charles C. Thomas, 1976.

IV.

INSTRUCTION FOR STUDENTS WITH SPECIAL NEEDS

4.
TEACHING STUDENTS WITH SPECIAL NEEDS

Ronald L. Redick and Sharon S. Redick

The Education for All Handicapped Children Act of 1975 and the Rehabilitation Act of 1973 have had a powerful impact on the American educational enterprise. Handicapped persons now have the legal right to a free public education in a setting most appropriate for their unique needs.

Public Law 94-142 has four major purposes:

1. To guarantee the availability of special education programming to handicapped youth who require it.
2. To assure fairness and appropriateness in decision making about special education for handicapped youth.
3. To establish clear management and auditing requirements and procedures regarding special education at all levels of government.
4. To financially assist the special education efforts of state and local governments through the use of federal funds (Ballard, 1977; Torres, 1977).

The primary management tool for attaining these purposes is the written individualized education program (IEP). The act requires that such a program be developed for every student who must have special education and related services. The term *individualized* means the program must be designed for an individual student rather than a group of students. *Education* means the program is limited to those aspects of the student's education that are specifically special education and related services as defined in the law. And *program* refers to what will actually be provided the student rather than general guidelines from which a program can be developed (Ballard, 1977; Torres, 1977).

The vocational teacher plays a significant role in the development of a handicapped student's IEP. He or she will be a member of the IEP team, which also includes an administrator, the student's parents or guardian, and, when appropriate, the handicapped student.

BASIC CONCEPTS

A part of the act that will have great impact upon educational programs states that each handicapped student will be educated in the "least restrictive environment." The intent of the law is to place handicapped students in the most appropriate learning environments for their unique needs. Increasingly, that will mean "mainstreaming," i.e., placing handicapped students in educational settings with nonhandicapped peers (Ballard, 1977; Torres, 1977). As mainstreaming gains momentum, handicapped students who have previously been educated in isolated, segregated settings will enter regular classrooms.

The benefits of this movement can be immense. In many cases handicapped students will be able to live with their families at home rather than attending residential schools designed for students with particular handicaps. Nonhandicapped students will have the opportunity to learn with and from their handicapped classmates. The costs of education for handicapped students may be reduced as their need for full-time special services diminishes. As more handicapped persons are provided with educational opportunities, more will join the work force and leave welfare status. The education for handicapped persons legislation and the mainstreaming movement will succeed, however, only if educators, parents, community members and students work together.

ROLE OF THE VOCATIONAL TEACHER

Vocational teachers will play a vital role in the mainstreaming movement, for current trends indicate that handicapped students are frequently placed initially in regular vocational education classrooms. If they find success there, other classes may then be added to their schedules. Thus, if vocational teachers play a leading part in the mainstreaming movement, it is essential that they be well prepared both academically and attitudinally to accept handicapped students and help them achieve success.

A first task of the vocational teacher will be to assist in the development of an IEP for each handicapped student in his or her vocational education program. Fundamental to this undertaking is a basic understanding of the needs of handicapped youth.

Identification of Needs

Teachers have indicated that an understanding of the educational needs of handicapped students is a prerequisite to providing appropriate instructional programs for them in the mainstreamed classroom (Redick, 1974). Administrators and teachers have identified five areas of educational needs for handicapped students, although the degree of need varies according to individuals (Redick, 1976a).

Socialization Skills. Because many handicapped students have had limited opportunities to socialize, they need to develop socialization skills. In vocational education classrooms, these skills can be promoted by

194

planning activities that provide an opportunity to practice social skills. Instruction can be given in social skills and students can be encouraged to participate in co-curricular activities such as vocational student organizations.

Positive Self-Concept Development. Many handicapped students experience more failure than success in their educational efforts. Therefore, there may be a need to help them gain a more positive self-concept. Sequencing learning activities and content from the simple to the complex, with success factors built in along the way, could help handicapped students to see themselves in a different light. Helping these students develop skills and increasing their ability to be independent is a direct way to build positive self-images.

Daily Living Activities. Many handicapped youth have been deprived of daily living experiences that others take for granted. For example, handicapped students are frequently not permitted in the work areas of the family home such as the kitchen, workshop, garage or utility room. Furthermore, numerous handicapped students have not been allowed to participate in everyday activities in the community at large. Vocational education teachers have an unrivaled opportunity to build experiences of daily living into the curricula through laboratory sessions, field trips, community projects and other extended learning situations.

Developing Independence. A primary goal of handicapped persons is to gain the maximum degree of independence their handicap will permit. Through vocational education (for example, home economics), handicapped students can learn skills such as resource management, food planning and preparation, clothing selection, laundry techniques, home design and care, and other skills that can grant them greater independence.

Employability and occupational skill development. Independence for the handicapped person also includes the pursuit of vocational opportunities. In vocational education, these students can learn employability skills that are prerequisites to job training. Instruction in time management practices and promptness, along with development of the ability to think critically, make decisions, organize and follow through can help handicapped students increase their readiness for job training. In addition, handicapped students in vocational education programs can be introduced to career opportunities, as well as be trained for specific occupations.

A teacher who is aware of the needs mentioned (i.e., development of socialization skills, gaining a positive self-concept, experiencing daily living activities, becoming independent, and developing employability and occupational skills) can plan and implement instructional programs designed to be responsive to handicapped students' inadequacies in these areas.

MANAGING THE LEARNING PROCESS

A positive approach to meeting the needs of handicapped students would require vocational education teachers to analyze carefully the characteristics of their particular classroom situations to ascertain how best to provide educational services to handicapped students under their guidance. Teachers should critically examine the organizational and management elements of their curricula and instructional arrangements, consider the extent and kind of control they exercise over the learning environment of their students, and decide whether they are placing priority on the appropriate organizational and management factors in their instructional programs.

Organization and Management Skills

An analysis such as the one suggested will likely reveal that vocational teachers need to concentrate on developing their classroom organization and management skills if they are to successfully integrate handicapped students into their classes. Critical to the success of organization/management schemes is an understanding of administrative and instructional variables over which vocational teachers have direct control.

Managing Time. Though vocational teachers may decry the inflexibility of the "lock-step" daily schedule of classes and set length of class periods typical of secondary schools, it is far more productive for them to concentrate on utilizing the control they have over blocks of student time during a year, semester or quarter, week and day. Organizing and managing student time on a daily basis without a view of the total time available for that student to deal with course objectives prevents the optimum use of this organization/management variable.

Managing the Learning Process. There may be little the vocational teacher can do about changing the school's grading policy, but it is worthwhile to review those aspects of student learning over which the teacher retains jurisdiction and which provide the basis for the assignment of grades. The vocational teacher determines the student learning objectives to be mastered, presents students with content and learning activities related to those objectives, develops the assessment devices used to measure and evaluate student accomplishment of the objectives, and reports student progress in realizing the objectives.

Managing the Grouping Structure. The teacher may have negligible influence on the procedures followed in assigning students to vocational education classes. But the teacher does have authority over intraclass grouping which can be employed to facilitate student achievement. That is, students can be grouped in large groups, small groups, or in other arrangements within a class.

Models of Classroom Management

An attempt has been made to establish the idea that vocational teachers can structure student time and employ intraclass student grouping arrangements to better meet the needs of various types of handicapped students in their classrooms. Construction of organization/management models of instruction based upon those concepts would use the following variables: (1) learning objectives, (2) content and learning activities, (3) time allotment, (4) evaluation methods and (5) grouping patterns. These five "flexibility variables" can be manipulated to provide variations in classroom organization/management patterns that can take into account the needs of all students in a class.

Examples of organization/management models built upon the relationships among the five flexibility variables follow:

Model 1. In this model, the flexible variables are student grouping and learning activities. Students initially spend 10 minutes in a large group session, during which the teacher focuses on establishing set for the day's work. They are then divided into small groups, where learning activities are designed specifically to meet their needs. Though learning activities vary, objectives, content, time spent in particular groups and evaluation methods remain the same for each student.

Model 2. Students are divided into three small groups for the major part of the class period, but form a large group for the last 15 minutes of work. Group 1 starts with a teacher-directed activity for 15 minutes and then has 20 minutes of individual study. Group 2 follows the Group 1 schedule in reverse order, while Group 3 spends 35 minutes in individual study. The flexible variables in this situation are student grouping, content, learning activities and time spent in particular groups. All students are expected to meet the same objectives and are evaluated on a similar basis.

Model 3. Again, students are divided into three groups. However, each group covers the same content over the same time period. Objectives, learning activities and evaluation methods differ for each small group.

Model 4. Here the class is divided into three groups, with each group participating in a teacher-directed activity, a small group activity, and individual study. But the sequence of these activities varies, with each group spending equal time in the same activity. In this model, content, learning activities, objectives, and evaluation methods are specifically designed for each group.

Model 5. This model is uniquely suited to programs where learning packages are used and basic core concepts are taught by the teacher. In a five-day instructional cycle, on Day 1 the teacher directs a large group session that concentrates on course core concepts. On Day 2 the class is divided by interests into small groups and on Days 3, 4 and 5, students study independently or in small groups in either classroom or laboratory settings. The one variable that remains the same for each student is a study of the basic core concepts. All other flexibility variables depend on the interest or determined need of the student.

These five models provide examples of how teachers can organize and manage a classroom through the control of selected variables, i.e., student grouping patterns, learning objectives, learning activities, content, time allotment and evaluation methods to meet the varying needs of all students. Though the teacher can manipulate these variables to effectively organize and manage the mainstreamed classroom, consideration should also be given to choosing the teaching techniques in a given model.

EFFECTIVE TEACHING TECHNIQUES

The learning styles of handicapped students are as diverse as those of their nonhandicapped peers. Thus, it is unwise to list or suggest only a limited set of teaching techniques. Using an interview format with a sample of teachers whose primary responsibility was to teach handicapped students in a variety of settings, an attempt was made to isolate techniques that had been proven most successful (Redick, 1974; 1976).

Individualized Approaches

A majority of teachers indicated that any technique predicated upon an individualized approach tended to be more successful with handicapped students. Specific techniques mentioned were demonstrations performed on a one-to-one basis, tutoring, peer tutoring, learning packages, learning centers and precision teaching. Through these types of teaching techniques, provisions can be made for the visual learner, the auditory learner and the kinesthetic learner. Special emphasis can be placed on reading levels and communication skills to adapt each technique for the individual student.

Student Involvement

Though the individualized approach meets the needs of student learning styles and varying levels of ability, it does not meet the need for handicapped students to develop socialization skills through direct interaction with their nonhandicapped peers. With this in mind, it is understandable that many teachers said techniques that stimulated active student involvement were effective. They cited examples of learning situations that permitted students to apply knowledge or practice skills. These examples included student exposure to laboratory experiences, role playing, problem solving and precision teaching.

Varying and Modifying Teaching Techniques

As in any group learning environment, it is recommended that a variety of teaching techniques be employed to meet the diverse needs of individual students in mainstreamed classrooms. Teachers indicated that in these classrooms it was helpful to incorporate a great deal of repetition of content, using a variety of teaching techniques. It was also found helpful to employ techniques emphasizing short sequential learning steps, thereby enabling students to experience success at several stages rather than only at the conclusion of an activity. Learning centers and packages could be designed to provide such built-in achievement factors. It should be noted that the modification of equipment and materials may be required for physically handicapped students.

A highly successful strategy for adapting content and learning activities is task analysis (Redick, 1978). Teachers have found this an excellent method of analyzing content and learning activities and modifying them to meet the needs of individual students.

Many teachers stated that specific teaching techniques were not as important as providing a stimulating, positive learning environment in which handicaped students felt comfortable and free to learn. When this atmosphere is present, many handicapped students can discover the appropriate adaptations necessary for them to become involved in learning activities. The following guides are offered to promote this type of learning environment.

Guidelines for Working with Handicapped Students

The following guidelines have been suggested by teachers of handicapped students to serve as a basis for establishing effective programs (Redick, 1976; 1978).

Meet Student. Meeting with each handicapped student before the beginning of classes can help the teacher begin to establish rapport as well as provide an opportunity to gather pertinent data. At this time the teacher can learn about the student's functional ability and prior educational experiences related to the course content.

Arrange Tour. Before classes meet, the teacher can allow the handicapped student to tour the classroom facilities in order to discover accessibility problems. It is particularly important that physically handicapped students have this opportunity.

Learn about Handicapping Condition. The teacher can become familiar with the student's condition by reading and meeting with family members and school personnel. The most pertinent information to obtain is how the handicapping condition affects a particular student, the student's acceptance of the condition and his or her degree of functional ability. It is best to stress the student's abilities rather than disabilities.

Accept the Student. Accept and respect the handicapped student as a unique individual. It is crucial to recognize individuality among similarly handicapped students.

Avoid Over-Protection. It is important not to overly protect the handicapped student, while recognizing individual needs. Of course, safety factors are of paramount concern at all times.

Adapt Tasks. Many handicapped students can participate in most classroom activities, but some tasks require adaptation. When this is necessary, ask the student for suggestions. Having lived with the handicapping condition, he or she may have made adjustments previously for similar situations.

Provide Time. Time is a primary factor. Because of the nature of their conditions many handicapped students require more time to complete some tasks. Models of classroom organization/management that provide flexibility in time allotment are most useful in these situations.

Encourage Independence. Sometimes it would be easier to perform a task for a handicapped student rather than to teach the student to perform the task or allow him or her the necessary time to accomplish it. Encourage independence by permitting each student time to develop individual skills.

Seek Help. Be aware of and seek help from qualified consultants. Teachers can benefit greatly from the input of other professionals, including medical personnel and therapists, as well as psychological, vocational and educational personnel. Each of these professionals can help the teacher be more effective in planning and implementing educational programs for handicapped students.

SUMMARY

As handicapped students enter the mainstream of education, vocational educators have a unique opportunity to help them gain independence and function at their maximum level. Educators who are aware of the pertinent legislation, student needs, barriers to effective mainstreaming, models of classroom management and techniques for effective teaching are better prepared to meet the challenge of teaching students with special needs. The very nature of vocational education's content, learning activities and learning environments make it an appropriate educational program for many students. For the student with special needs, it can make the difference between dependent and independent living.

REFERENCES

Ballard, Joseph. *Public Law 94-142 and Section 504—understanding what they are and are not.* Reston, Va.: Governmental Relations Unit, The Council for Exceptional Children, 1977.

Redick, Ronald L. *Adapting and implementing curriculum for special populations.* Presentation made at the United States Office of Education National Vocational Home Economics Conference. Minneapolis, Minnesota, October 23, 1978.

Redick, Sharon Smith. *Selected characteristics of home economics teachers and programs for physically handicapped students.* Unpublished doctoral dissertation, Iowa State University, 1974.

Redick, Sharon S. *The physically handicapped student in the regular home economics classroom: A guide for teaching nutrition and foods.* Danville, Ill.: Interstate Press, 1976a.

Redick, Sharon S. *The physically handicapped student in the regular home economics classroom: A guide for teaching grooming and clothing.* Danville, Ill.: Interstate Press, 1976b.

Redick, Sharon S. *The physically handicapped student in the regular home economics classroom: A guide for teaching housing and home care.* Danville, Ill.: Interstate Press, 1976c.

Redick, Sharon Smith, and Lazzell, Kathaleen M. *The handicapped: Our mission.* Washington, D.C.: Home Economics Education Association, 1978.

Torres, Scottie (Ed.). *A primer on individualized education programs for handicapped children.* Reston, Va.: The Council for Exceptional Children, 1977.

IV.

INSTRUCTION FOR STUDENTS WITH SPECIAL NEEDS

5.
WORKING WITH
MINORITY STUDENTS

N. Alan Sheppard and D. Lanette Vaughn

There are times when each of us feels left out or included. Other times we may feel inferior to or better than someone else. Sometimes we feel different from others, while at other times we feel we are just like everyone else. In these universal feelings lie our sameness and our common humanity. There is an Indian proverb that says we cannot judge another person until we "have walked a mile in that person's moccasins." This chapter is intended to provide assistance in the instructional process by helping the reader take a few steps in someone else's moccasins. Above all, it is our hope that through this chapter, vocational educators will see students (whether classified "disadvantaged," "special needs," or "special populations") as individuals to be treated with dignity and humanity rather than as members of certain categories to be treated as objects.

Our purpose is to assist vocational educators with little or no experience in working with minority or so-called "culturally different students" (Blacks, Hispanics, American Indians and Asian Americans). We hope the chapter will serve as a review for vocational educators who have had experience with minority students on a day-to-day basis, but have yet to scrutinize their degree of success, whether large or small.

DEFINITIONS OF MINORITY STUDENTS

In this chapter, the term *special populations,* used interchangeably with *culturally different,* refers to minority groups such as Blacks, Asian Americans, American Indians and Hispanics. Although it is difficult to make accurate generalizations about such diverse groups, it is possible to consider their common experiences and backgrounds and how these factors affect them in the cultural setting.

All culturally different minorities are not disadvantaged. However, members of the groups just identified—especially Blacks, Hispanics and American Indians—have been systematically denied advantages enjoyed by the majority culture in this affluent nation. This nation is still only vaguely aware of the geographic concentration of Mexican-Americans in the Southwest, of the Indians on the reservations and of Blacks trapped in the Mississippi Delta. Programs for change must inform the nation as a whole of the urgency of the problems of ethnic minorities. They must also prepare culturally different individuals for life in the larger society—that is, beyond their immediate environment or cultural milieu.

By definition, culturally different students behave differently from individuals of the dominant culture. An individual born into a subculture learns the appropriate behaviors of the subculture, which may not be appropriate for functioning successfully in the dominant culture. The dominant culture usually controls the political, educational and other systems of the society. Educators are most often members of the dominant culture.

PARTICIPATION OF MINORITIES

According to Project Baseline data (1976), Blacks make up a little more than 10 percent of the nation's population and 15 percent of the vocational education enrollment. Nearly 6 percent of all vocational students are Hispanic, which is probably higher than the percentage of Hispanic people in the total population. American Indians and Asian Americans are small minorities, but in both cases, they are better represented in vocational education than in the total population. As is the case with women, it would be essential to know what programs these minority groups are enrolled in to say with any assurance how well they are being served.

As it is, all the groups appear to have slipped a little in their proportions of the total vocation education enrollment over a three-year period. The last year in which ethnic data were required by the U.S. Office of Education was 1971-1972. At that time, the proportion of Blacks enrolled was 16.61 percent, compared with 15.13 percent in 1974-1975. Hispanic enrollments made up 6.06 percent of the total vocational education enrollment in 1971-1972, compared with 5.70 percent three years later. American Indians dropped from 0.84 percent to 0.79 percent. Only Asian Americans increased their percentage from 1.00 percent to 1.09 percent.

Special Problems

"Problems of subculture students," "overcoming problems of disadvantaged students," and "dealing effectively with shortcomings of students from ethnic groups" are all examples of statements one may find in reviewing literature concerned with teaching special population students. Note that these statements all emphasize student problems and none directly address teacher problems.

What are some of these problems? For example, what are the misconceptions of teachers who realize suddenly they have students from various cultural and ethnic backgrounds in their classrooms? And do teachers always understand student differences that may influence educational success or failure? These problems are not applicable to all teachers or situations. However, they are often mentioned by teachers of culturally different students.

Perhaps the most ominous problem facing the teacher of minority students is an attitudinal one. Teacher attitudes toward students determine how those students are treated. This treatment affects student attitudes toward school, which in turn, affects student performance and success. Attitudes stemming from such stereotypes as "Mexicans are lazy," "Indians are slow," or "Blacks have criminal tendencies" all fit into this attitudinal cycle. Many teachers have seen the results of this cycle, although probably indirectly. A teacher just has a feeling that John isn't the brightest student and unwittingly conveys that feeling to John. And sure enough, he doesn't do very well.

Individual teachers do not deserve all the blame for these stereotypic attitudes. It has long been socially acceptable to use degrading stereotypes for anyone a little different. In fact, some years ago, the Polish were categorized officially by U.S. immigration laws as being morally lax, inclined to insanity and incapable of learning. Some of these stereotypes have likely been perpetuated by misconceptions concerning the cultural background of students from special populations. For example, teachers are often at a disadvantage when they attempt to teach inner-city Blacks or Mexican-Americans because they lack basic understanding of the cultural backgrounds of these students.

Again, teachers are not entirely to blame for lack of knowledge pertaining to minority students. As mentioned before, much emphasis has been placed on the problems these students have. Teachers also need to be aware that these students have some strengths. Of course, all students are individuals and each is unique. But teachers of minority students report that these students have positive characteristics that can help them succeed in school. These strengths include: (1) acceptance of responsibility at an early age, (2) ability to learn through concrete experiences, (3) adherence to collective (family and group) rather than individual values and (4) good physical coordination and visual orientation (Sheppard and Vaughn, 1977).

Some of the problems traditionally attributed to minority students can be viewed from a slightly different perspective by teachers. Students may have a fear of school that has developed through unpleasant experiences and a lack of success. Teachers also experience fear when attempting to teach students from special populations. They may associate these students with a lack of success and unpleasant experiences. Teachers may realize that these students are often afraid to try and therefore feel apprehensive about teaching them.

Teachers have probably also heard of the poor health, drug and alcohol problems, poor housing and home conditions of these students. They may feel unable to deal with these problems and be unaware of support services in the school and community that can assist in alleviating the problems.

The Language Issue

Teachers should become familiar with the language of students who come from various ethnic backgrounds. Obviously, a teacher who understands Spanish is in a much better position to teach Hispanic students than a teacher who is not bilingual. Unfortunately, there is a shortage of such teachers, especially in vocational education.

Basic communication in English sometimes presents a language problem in the classroom. Teachers who do not understand the nonstandard English used by students may find themselves at a disadvantage. It is, to say the least, uncomfortable to be on the outside of a conversation. Learning this nonstandard English may prove to be of benefit in teaching students from varied cultural backgrounds.

Finding a workable compromise between students using colloquial or nonstandard English at all times, and a teacher insisting on only standard English, may prove to be challenging. Often students fail to realize that more opportunities will be available to them if they are able to use standard English in appropriate situations. On the other hand, teachers sometimes criticize colloquial English in all situations without realizing that this may antagonize their students unnecessarily.

Most psychologists estimate that approximately 7 percent of communication is totally verbal. The other 93 percent is a combination of nonverbal and verbal. Attitudes, actions and words all combine to form communication between teacher and student. Students from special populations are sensitive to this "total" communication. If there is a discrepancy between a teacher's words and nonverbal communication, the students will probably become distrustful of the words.

Educators must better understand the role that language plays in a student's life. Language is an integral part of one's personality. If it is rejected, the individual feels rejected. Teachers should also remember that a student's language is his or her medium of learning. In other words, the student uses that language to organize experiences, think, talk over needs, react to the world, express emotions. When teachers undermine a student's language, they undermine the student's ability to learn.

THE ROOTS OF THE PROBLEM

Many vocational teachers are disappointed when they find they cannot establish rapport with minority students or overcome cultural barriers that sabotage the learning process. They may resort to punitive techniques that are only temporarily inhibiting. Some teachers quickly give up. Others continue to try, but to no avail. Fortunately, there are always some vocational educators who can motivate students and create a good learning atmosphere.

Working With Minority Students

Some causes of difficulties in working with minority students are:

1. *Expectation patterns.* It has been documented that student growth is positively correlated with teacher expectations. Teachers call forth adequate behaviors when they expect their students to be adquate. Teacher expectations develop out of the teacher's background. His or her assets and defects enter into all interactions with students. If you clinically analyze a student to find out why he or she is not learning without also clinically analyzing the teacher, only half of the work is done.

2. *Routines.* Some teachers may fail to establish or even recognize the importance of routines in the classroom.

3. *Fears.* Teachers often experience personal fears when entering a cultural framework alien to their own backgrounds.

Overcoming Prejudices

Perhaps the simplest rule of thumb for "starting on the right foot" when teaching minorities is to begin with a positive attitude. In this way, a teacher can overcome two major problems mentioned previously: stereotypic attitudes and lack of knowledge about the students' cultural backgrounds. By addressing these two problems simultaneously, it may be possible to solve both. Stereotypes are often difficult to shake. Perhaps one of the most effective ways to rid oneself of harmful stereotypes is to learn about the cultural backgrounds of others. Becoming familiar with and sensitive to the cultural characteristics of the community in which students live is homework a teacher can do as learning activities are planned (Sheppard, 1974). As a teacher studies cultural backgrounds and accepts students as individuals, the old stereotypes seem less and less appropriate.

It is important to distinguish among various ethnic groups to determine how to meet their needs. For example, middle-class Italian students experience different needs than do poor Puerto Rican inner-city students. These differences can influence behavior and learning. Students who have to worry about bare necessities usually cannot learn as well as those who are well fed or clothed.

Minority group students suffer more than others from rejection in society as well as in school. They believe that the dominant group is responsible for their past and present segregation, limitations and restrictions. They are aware and resentful that society has not offered them equal opportunities, and that there is serious interference with the exercise of the human and civil rights to which they are entitled. The classroom teacher must recognize the reality of these experiences and, being sensitive to the injustices of the past and present, make every effort to assure students that he or she does in truth want them in the program and will do everything possible to make sure they learn.

Achieving Success

All students have a need to achieve success. Failure deprives them of the satisfaction of that need. Some students may fight back with patterns of violent aggression. Others withdraw, stop trying and become nonlearners. Some get physically sick.

Success to the student means, "I got it right!" Every student needs to get something right every day, to learn something and to know that the teacher is pleased. Success and praise are profoundly motivating to students. These events free the energy needed to make an effort and convince students they can learn.

Possibly one of the most difficult tasks the teacher must accomplish in working with minority students is confrontations with personal attitudes and values. Some may have to exchange long-held myths and superstitions for truths about people. Some may find that their thinking is clouded by stereotypes that require testing against the reality of individual differences. Prejudice, discrimination, rejection and exclusion on the basis of race, color, religion, creed, national origin, social class and mental ability have no place in the classroom.

INSTRUCTIONAL STRATEGIES

Suggested instructional strategies are as follow:

1. Reflect the cultural background of students in classroom situations. Educators should provide models with which ethnic minority students can identify. They should include on their bulletin boards pictures from magazines that represent students' cultural backgrounds. Another suggestion is to develop a class committee on multi-ethnic or multi-cultural education.

2. Don't allow "trying to identify with" get in the way of understanding. Some educators may assume that they have to exhibit the cultural characteristics of Blacks, Hispanics or Native Americans to work effectively with minority students. But many educators have had outstanding success with minority students without having much contact with the backgrounds or life styles of such individuals. These teachers placed themselves in the shoes of minority students and, with great compassion and empathy, tried to perceive the world through their students' eyes, experiences and cultural differences. While it is not necessarily wrong to try to identify with ethnic minority students, it is more important to understand.

3. Examine current instructional materials and method. Note whether they are being used to increase cultural understanding.

4. Read materials that will provide a better understanding of minority students.

5. Select and time your presentation of material carefully so that motivation and satisfaction are not thwarted.
6. Help the student learn by simplifying difficult tasks and presenting them in ways that will make them easier to grasp.
7. Consider the learning strategies of each student and adjust your teaching style accordingly.
8. Take advantage of student-initiated ideas to increase participation interest and learning. Make an effort to get everyone involved.
9. Involve parents of minority students. This will require encouragement, interesting school activities and problems that make sense. Most of all, it will require teachers who are energetic organizers and who can get along with people.
10. Help students assess their progress. Evaluate students' efforts, help them learn from their mistakes, and show them where and how they can improve their work.
11. Develop a community resource file of ethnic organizations and resources such as speakers, books and newspapers.
12. Don't try to "con" students from culturally different groups. "Tell-it like it is" includes an honest appraisal of problems. This can be one of the keys to overcoming many of the challenges a teacher faces at the outset of any program that involves students from different minority groups.
14. Make sure the instruction is practical and basic. Teachers must always be concerned with the "how" first and explain the "why" later (Hanna, 1967). Many educators believe that learning by doing is the best teaching method for students of all cultural and social backgrounds (Bobbitt and Letevin, 1971).
15. Provide rewards for success. Since failure may have been the most common classroom experience for many minority students, each success should be rewarded to assure repetition. It may be necessary to reward small steps to insure that the student will eventually reach the final goal. Vocational teachers have an advantage over other teachers in that their students are producing tangible goods as evidence of their achievements. Students can see that they have run a good bead or typed a neat letter. Self-sufficiency is needed to function as an adult and anything these students do that makes them feel self-sufficient is helpful.

Better Teacher Preparation Needed

Teacher education programs need to better prepare prospective teachers to function effectively with students from culturally different backgrounds. There is growing evidence that teacher education programs are beginning to produce teachers who can do their jobs more capably. Yung, Haynie

209

and Jennings (1978) point to the need for adequate teacher education programs:

> Vocational teachers with no special education background or comparable experiences are attempting to teach special needs students. This situation exists in public schools because there are virtually no teacher education programs which prepare teachers who will be or who are presently teaching special needs students. If such courses were included in teacher education programs, prospective teachers would have exposure to cultural backgrounds, to the strengths of these students, and optimally would have experience working with students from varied backgrounds.

Like most Americans, most teachers are not prepared for multi-cultural living. Teacher preparation is oriented mainly to the middle-income white student, the kind of student the teacher might have been just a few years earlier (Sheppard and Portinsky, 1976). The teachers of minorities have been less experienced than the teachers of the affluent. They are often less committed to careers in education, less knowledgeable about the philosophy and theories of education, and less involved with the overall purposes of education as they relate to equal opportunity.

In light of these conditions, a two-pronged attack on the problem must be made to: (1) reeducate the existing teaching force, and (2) completely overhaul teacher training programs. Through inservice education, teachers and administrators must be given an understanding of why such programs are needed. Most school systems currently make provisions for some inservice education, but it is generally misdirected. Sheppard, Conley and Leakes (1974) have proposed a teacher preparation model for working with minority students.

CONCLUDING COMMENTS

We are not nor shall we ever be the melting pot that textbooks have tried to make us. Our country consists of people with widely different needs, talents and backgrounds. We must recognize the need to extend the range of human variability and understand that being different does not mean being inferior.

Without doubt, the two important prerequisites for overcoming cultural barriers between teachers and minority students are understanding and what the "Queen of Soul" Aretha Franklin, calls R-E-S-P-E-C-T. The only choices are to modify the behavior of teachers, change the behavior of the students or change both to promote improved understanding.

In vocational education, the great challenge is to identify the special needs and to develop the unused talents of minority students. They will need support and encouragement, early success experiences and help in developing the skills to cope with frustration and despair. Innovative programs, teaching materials and techniques will have to be developed. New approaches to training teachers, administrators and counselors will be needed, along with greater community involvement.

REFERENCES

Bobbitt, F., and Letevin, L. *Techniques for teaching disadvantaged youth in vocational education.* East Lansing, Mich.: Michigan State University, Rural Manpower Center, 1971.

Hanna, L. *Reports on "teach" teacher education for advancing the culturally handicapped.* Columbus, Ohio: Ohio State University, 1967.

Lee, Arthur. *Learning a living across the nation: Project baseline (5th national report).* Flagstaff, Ariz.: Project Baseline, 1976.

Noar, G. *Sensitizing teachers to ethnic groups.* New York: Allyn and Bacon, 1972.

Sheppard, N. A. *Characteristics and myths: The disadvantaged learner.* Blacksburg, Va.: Virginia Polytechnic Institute and State University, College of Education, 1974.

Sheppard, N.A. *Identification of problems and competencies needed by vocational and technical education personnel teaching persons with special needs in Virginia.* Blacksburg, Va.: Virginia Polytechnic Institute and State University, Division of Vocational and Technical Education, 1975.

Sheppard, N. A., Portinsky, R. A., and Berry, M. (Eds.). *Teaching tips on cultural differences in vocational education: A guidebook of selected teaching activities.* Blacksburg, Va.: Virginia Polytechnic Institute and State University, Division of Vocational and Technical Education, 1977.

Sheppard, N. A., and Portinsky, Ruth. *Cultural diversity and the exceptional student in vocational education: Implications for teaching the culturally different black student.* Paper presented at the AVA Convention, Houston, Texas, 1976.

Sheppard, N. A., and Vaughn, D. L. *Guidelines for methods and techniques of teaching disadvantaged students.* Blacksburg, Va.: Virginia Polytechnic Institute and State University, Division of Vocational and Technical Education, 1977.

Sheppard, N. A., et al. Preparing inner city teachers. In Hunt and Silliman (Eds.). *The American School in its social setting.* Dubuque, Iowa: Kendall Hunt, 1974.

Yung, C. K., Haynie, R. C., and Jennings, J. E. *Preparing vocational teachers with competencies to effectively teach special needs students.* Pine Bluff, Ark.: University of Arkansas, Learning Resources Center, 1978.

FOR FURTHER READING

Banks, James A. (Ed.). *Teaching ethnic studies: Concepts and strategies.* Washington, D.C.: National Education Association, 1973.

Dawson, Elaine. *On the outskirts of hope: Educating youth from poverty areas.* New York: McGraw-Hill, 1968.

Vocational Instruction

Fantini, Mario D., and Weinstein, Gerald. *The disadvantaged: Challenge to education.* New York: Harper & Row, 1968.

The imperatives of ethnic education. *Phi Delta Kappan,* January 1972.

Maxwell, D. *Career education: Curriculum materials for the disadvantaged.* Columbus, Ohio: Ohio State University, Center for Vocational and Technical Education, 1973.

McGough, R., and Wright, P. L. (Eds.). *Proceedings of national workshop on vocational education leadership for special populations.* Blacksburg, Va.: Virginia Polytechnic Institute and State University, Division of Vocational Education, 1978.

Moody, Ferman B., and Sheppard, N. Alan. The status of blacks in vocational education: Reflections and perspectives. *Vocational education for special groups.* Washington, D.C.: American Vocational Association, 1976.

Passow, A. Harry. *Urban education in the 1970's.* New York: Teachers College Press, 1971.

V

STUDENT ORGANIZATIONS: AN INTEGRAL PART OF INSTRUCTION

1.
STUDENT ORGANIZATIONS . . . VOCATIONAL EDUCATION IN ACTION

Mildred Reel

The classroom comes alive when vocational student organizations are used as part of the instructional program. They open up practical opportunities for students and extend classroom learning into the community, the business world and the home. Members not only learn the skills of an occupation but experience what it means to carry out responsibilities, make their own decisions and understand the importance of ethics on and off the job. As one young man put it, "It's the kind of education you can't get from a book."

There are eight student organizations that operate within the framework of the school curriculum: Future Farmers of America, Future Homemakers of America, Distributive Education Clubs of America, Future Business Leaders of America-Phi Beta Lambda, Vocational Industrial Clubs of America, Office Education Association, Health Occupations Students of America and American Industrial Arts Students Association. Through each organization has its own unique style and identity, all have the common goals of leadership, citizenship and career preparation.

Several million dues-paying members benefit directly from the vocational student organizations each year. And because these groups operate within the school system, many lives are touched over and above what the records might indicate. Yet some vocational educators, bound by the dollar squeeze and overloaded schedules, question the value of vocational student organizations. What, in fact, do they contribute to vocational education?

"LIFE" TO LEARNING

Vocational student organizations capitalize on the skills learned in class. They give "life" to learning. For instance, a popular chapter project for home economics students enrolled in a food service course is to run a mini-restaurant and experience all aspects of the business from bottle-washer to boss. They choose a restaurant name and theme, plan menus, order and prepare food, divide up duties and, of course, meet and greet the customers. A part of the preparation is discussing sanitation, safety, customer relations, and time and motion management. The money they raise might support a new chapter project or go towards a community cause.

Another example is the Future Business Leaders of America, which is coordinating a special management training project co-sponsored by the Hilton Hotels. Students chosen as part of this pilot project will plan and develop their own hypothetical hotel for Hilton to review and judge.

Food for America is a service project activity of the Future Farmers of America designed to help elementary teachers tell students about food preparation. These are just a few of the many innovative projects taking place throughout the country that help enliven the vocational education curriculum.

Student organizations also take projects that might seem rather routine, such as car washes and bake sales, and turn them into tremendous learning experiences. For one thing, such activities give students a chance to run their own show. They provide a forum for young people to practice management skills in an informal setting. And they challenge young creative minds to give ordinary "done-before" events a new twist.

These projects also reinforce the value of working with others to meet a common goal. For example, a bake sale can turn into a teen-operated health food boutique and a car wash can become an intergenerational project when students invite senior citizens and young children to be a part of the event.

Tackling the Tough Issues

Student organizations aren't afraid to tackle the tough issues either. Projects taking place within curricula across the country deal with societal concerns such as alcohol use and abuse, cheating, teen parenting and on-the-job stress.

Energy is another hot topic. Last year six of the vocational student groups in Oklahoma cooperated in a statewide energy conservation campaign conducted with the Oklahoma State Commission on Energy.

Many of the student organizations' projects—such as career fairs and topical film festivals—benefit the whole school. A school in Columbia, Maryland, sees its vocational student organizations as an educational force because they sponsor speakers and general assemblies that are pertinent to all teens.

Beautification and conservation projects are popular student organization activities. Working with community members, students put pride back into the community. These projects include refurbishing an historical village lighthouse, converting an old school house into a museum and transforming a vacant lot into a mini-park for toddlers. Thousands of other activities taking place each year meet the needs of the elderly, the handicapped, children and dropouts.

What does all this have to do with vocational education? It has to do with helping students develop skills to be full-fledged citizens—to become aware of social problems and how they can make a contribution to humanity as well as to their pocketbooks. Through participating in student organization activities, youths learn to work and get along with all kinds of people outside their peer group—an essential skill to take with them to the world of work. They find out that learning can be fun and that it can go on throughout their lives.

Attitudes Toward Work and Life

Vocational student organizations help young people develop a professional attitude toward work and a positive attitude toward life. They involve young people in action that has meaning for them today. Students also acquire the skills to be members and leaders of the organizations of tomorrow—whatever form these may take. Not to be overlooked is the important role organizations play in fulfilling the human need to belong, particularly during the difficult adolescent years.

The clientele served by vocational student organizations includes young men and women, urban and rural students and all ethnic groups. Leadership opportunities are open and can be experienced by all.

Chapter members learn how to function within a group. They lead and participate in group discussions, preside at meetings and work effectively within committees. The students plan their own projects and see them through to completion. They also have the great leadership opportunity of serving as officers at the local, state and national levels.

State and national leadership meetings held by each organization give students a chance to receive recognition for their special skills and talents. For some, traveling to meetings like these is their first time away from home and their first overnight stay in a hotel. They meet students from all over the state or nation and rub elbows with adults who can be invaluable role models as career, community and family leaders. Youth and adults learn from each other as they focus on issues of common concern.

A listing of potential dropouts finding their places through a student vocational organization might read like the script of a soap opera. Complete turn-arounds in attitudes toward education are common. It's heartwarming, for instance, to watch a national officer who once said, "I'd be on the street if it were not for the organization," preside before an audience of thousands or meet the President of the United States so graciously that it brings tears to your eyes.

Products of vocational student organizations have gone on to become a Deputy Commissioner in the Bureau of Occupational and Adult Education, state directors of vocational education, legislators, college deans, presidents of companies, even the President of the United States.

The influence of vocational groups has rubbed off on community leaders, teachers, parents and whole families who have become a part of the action. They, too, have reached new heights in their opportunities for involvement.

A Public Relations Tool

Student organizations are an important public relations tool for vocational education as well as a vehicle for helping vocational students learn to function within an organizational structure. Invitations for community participation seep into the school system through the student groups and parents find it easier to participate in their children's education through this informal setup.

Student leaders at all levels carry the benefits of vocational education to legislators, the White House, to business and industry, and to other organizations and agencies. State and national staffs of the vocational student organizations give visibilty to vocational education through publications, programs and public information campaigns. A few of the student groups have international exchange programs, which help spread the word about vocational education into other corners of the world. From what other source would vocational education reap such benefits?

Any organization, of course, is merely a structure. To be effective, vocational student organizations must have adults who understand their value and who help young people understand that what you get out of an organization is what you put into it. It also takes adults who know how to use student organizations as a way of teaching and have the skill and knowledge to integrate organization activities into the curriculum. Teaching through an organization where there are youth officers and members and where projects relate directly to subject matter is energizing for all involved: the teachers, students, school and community.

The Challenge of Change

Change is imminent and it behooves the vocational student organizations to constantly reassess their philosophy, their goals and objectives, and their way of working. Are we headed into the future with realistic expectations? Are we relinquishing that which is outdated and keeping pace with the needs of today's youth?

A big challenge is tying more closely with the national goals set by the Bureau of Occupational and Adult goals which are evaluated annually. Other areas of concern include reaching the "non-joiner" and the dropout and expanding programs within the inner city and isolated rural areas. National leaders are also seeking ways to finance the student organizations at all levels so that opportunities can be extended to all students enrolled in vocational education programs.

Urgent Needs

In order for vocational student organizations to reach their full potential and be of maximum benefit to vocational education, there is an urgent need for:

- the support of state directors of vocational education so that adequate state leadership is provided and the vocational student organizations can be written into the state plan as a functional part of vocational education.
- teacher training institutions to prepare advisers who see the student organizations as an essential method of teaching in vocational education and to provide for continuous training at the state and national levels.
- legislation that recognizes the vocational student organizations as a part of vocational education and provides for funding at the state and local levels.
- professional vocational educators to recognize and promote vocational student organizations as a way of teaching vocational education goals.
- the inclusion of vocational student organization members in setting and evaluating vocational education goals at all levels of operation.

CONCLUSION

Vocational student organizations are the heart and soul of vocational education. They are vocational education's most effective resource for dealing with the challenges facing the profession. They are vehicles for:

1. Encouraging students to enroll in vocational education.
2. Providing an informal teaching/learning atmosphere.
3. Expanding experiences and opportunities for vocational education students in the marketplace.
4. Enriching the instructional program with hands-on experience.
5. Motivating students to develop positive self-concepts.
6. Developing attitudes about social and civil responsibilities.
7. Providing leadership experiences and the opportunities to work effectively with peers and with adults.
8. Meeting and associating with vocational educators—which paves the way for refueling the profession with dedicated, ethical professionals.
9. Providing easy access to and involvement of parents.
10. Publicizing vocational programs and linking schools with communities.

Vocational student organizations help young people prepare and cope with many aspects of life. Members see the value of work, experience the handling of resources, make decisions, set goals, work together and experience relationships outside their own age and peer groups.

Student organizations put the ACTION in vocational education.

STUDENT ORGANIZATIONS: AN INTEGRAL PART OF INSTRUCTION

2.
FFA AS AN INTEGRAL PART OF INSTRUCTION

Ira A. Dickerson

Some may question whether or not the Future Farmers of America (FFA) is or should be an integral part of instruction. When one considers the benefits to be derived from the FFA as a teaching tool, however, the logical conclusion is that it fits naturally into the program of vocational agriculture and helps it function properly.

The vocational agriculture program has made great progress during the 60 years of its existence. Its teachers have been singled out for special recognition for the quality of their instructional programs. In order for vocational agriculture to continue to grow, the elements responsible for success of the instructional program should be analyzed and emphasized.

Elements of the Vocational Agriculture Program

There are two basic causes for the success of vocational agriculture programs. First and most fundamental has been the acceptance of the supervised occupational experience program as the basis for a highly functional instructional program. This acceptance has permitted unlimited development of the program from the very beginning. The supervised occupational experience program has withstood the test of time and has been used as a curriculum development model in other areas of vocational education.

The second cause was the creation of the Future Farmers of America. As Backarich (1971) notes, "Born in the Depression and nurtured in adversity, no more effective teaching tool has ever been devised."

The FFA provided nourishment for the tremendous growth of the entire vocational agriculture program. Although the FFA was conceived originally as an extracurricular or supplementary form of instruction, good teachers actually made it a part of the agriculture curriculum. Through their vision and effort, the FFA became an integral part of instructional programs, making them richer, more practical, more meaningful and more challenging to thousands of vocational agriculture students. In short, the FFA built a strong program on the foundation provided by the supervised occupational experience program.

The *FFA Advisor's Handbook* (1975) states that the vocational agriculture program consists of three elements: organized instruction, supervised occupational experience and the FFA. Each category is enriched through planned activities offering students opportunities to use knowledge and skills acquired in each of the other categories.

Vocational agriculture programs are based on an educational philosophy holding that all instruction must grow out of student needs and desire to learn. With this aim in mind, teachers have developed instructional programs based on the students' own problems. The FFA has provided an opportunity to add zest and enthusiasm to what was formerly a factual approach to learning.

DEVELOPING PERSONAL VALUES

The FFA helps students to develop needed competencies that would be difficult to acquire in regular classroom settings. These competencies are required in social relationships, cooperative undertakings, leisure activities and group leadership situations. Employers say desirable personal characteristics are essential for success in employment. Through the FFA, teachers have a means of helping students develop the employability skills so vital on the job.

Pride of Identity

The FFA gives students a special pride of identity with agriculture/agribusiness. Through this organization. they learn to deal with ordinary agricultural problems and develop confidence in their ability to perform.

By creating links to the community, the FFA has opened up new fields of endeavor for students. Many individuals, organizations, businesses and agencies contribute to the advancement of students in vocational agriculture by providing awards for accomplishments in the FFA program. These awards have served to expand and promote improved practices in the student's supervised occupational experience program.

Incentives to Learn

The desire to excel gives students inspiration and motivation to learn new ways of doing things. The FFA has provided a tremendous incentive to students to learn and apply the latest and best practices to their supervised occupational experience programs. The recognition available through degree advancement is dependent in part upon successful participation in the supervised occupational experience program. In an effort to qualify themselves for advanced degrees, many students have exerted greater effort in their vocational agriculture classes than they might have otherwise. This incentive to advance keeps students involved in continuous study and application over an extended period of time. What better learning situation can be envisioned than that of a student who has a real problem and is determined to solve that problem because he or she has a deep-seated, sincere urge to reap the benefits awaiting that solution?

CRITICISMS OF THE FFA

The integration of the FFA into the instructional program has been criticized in some quarters. An examination of these criticisms reveals that certain practices have evolved that are not educationally sound. These include the following:

1. In some cases, too much time is devoted to certain FFA activities at the expense of instructional time dealing with agricultural problems. This tendency creates an imbalance between the two parts of the curriculum. No teacher wants to turn out students well versed in parliamentary procedure but entirely lacking in vocational proficiency.
2. Some teachers have placed an unhealthy emphasis on winning contests. No student should be indoctrinated in the belief that winning first prize is more important than doing an economical, profitable job with a project.
3. In some cases, undue emphasis on contests has caused students to overemphasize production at the expense of other factors that contribute to efficiency. The student who learns to produce maximum yields without due consideration of the costs involved is not being fitted for a successful career in agriculture.

Regardless of these needs for improvement, the many opportunities for enriching instruction through the FFA program far outweigh the weaknesses. Most vocational agriculture teachers would be reluctant to teach without having the FFA to augment their efforts.

INTEGRATING THE FFA INTO THE CURRICULUM

Some of the ways FFA activities have been employed to strengthen the total instructional program follow.

The FFA Program of Work

The careful planning and execution of a chapter program of work can be a useful teaching device. A program of work must be planned by students and centered on the needs of the individual members, the school and the community.

Sound criteria must be followed if chapter activities are to make a maximum contribution to the education of the members. These activities should:

1. Follow the provisions of the local, state and national FFA constitutions and purposes.
2. Provide for participation by a maximum number of the members.
3. Challenge members to perform to the maximum.
4. Provide desirable learning experiences for members.
5. Stimulate interest and motivate action by the individual member.
6. Be realistic in scope and attainable as a result of member effort.
7. Comply with sound business principles when economic undertakings are involved.
8. Emphasize the value of community responsibility and citizenship.
9. Provide opportunities for leadership training.
10. Provide cooperative experiences in group coordination and action.
11. Meet individual needs.
12. Contribute to the overall objectives of the school and community.
13. Emphasize moral responsibility in individual and group action.
14. Provide opportunities for developing desirable social and personality traits.
15. Pertain to agriculture/agribusiness.
16. Be possible to evaluate.

FFA Degree Requirements

The various FFA degrees require that students show consistent progress in their supervised occupational experience program. In planning the program with students, the teacher should emphasize the importance of measurable progress for advancement in the FFA. The desire to excel is a natural tendency and the FFA gives the teacher an opportunity to couple a sound learning program with this natural urge.

Individual FFA goals should be set for each student at the beginning of the course of study. Whenever such goals are built around good supervised occupational experience programs, the outcomes prove to be beneficial and satisfying to both teacher and student.

FFA Awards and Contests

Too often awards programs and contests are planned and then students are encouraged to enter them. Good teachers, on the other hand, plan appropriate supervised occupational experience programs and leadership activities with students and then encourage them to gain recognition for doing excellent work. Students should participate in planning supervised occupational experience programs and FFA activities based upon their individual interests and career goals. They should then be urged to make the best showing possible in activities that grow out of their planned programs.

Cooperative Undertakings

Through the FFA, students can carry out cooperatively many decisions reached in their regular studies. For instance, while studying the job of "procuring containers" in an ornamental horticulture class, students may decide to use containers of a specific type and size. They may then discover the containers are not sold locally or that they are expensive in small quantities.

The FFA could deal with this situation on a cooperative basis. The students could agree in their FFA chapter meeting to pool their resources and buy the containers cooperatively. The job could be delegated to a committee and dealt with in an effective and efficient manner. More importantly, students would learn how to cooperate with one another, and those who actually supervised the undertaking would receive valuable business experience. Why try to teach cooperation as a cold and uninteresting subject when it can be dealt with as a very real problem? An excellent learning situation is missed when teachers fail to employ FFA activities to help students solve problems cooperatively.

FFA Activities and Courses of Study

Courses of study should be planned to include instructional units growing out of the supervised occupational experience programs and FFA activities. Attending a cattle show or livestock day at the county or state fair is not just an extra activity tossed in for good measure. Rather, this and similar activities can be important parts of a student's growth in the field of agriculture. Since they are important, they should not be sandwiched into the program, but should be planned as an integral part of the activities for the year.

The activities of the supervised occupational experience program and the FFA program of work should be complementary parts of a single instructional program. This means employing the FFA not only as a means for teaching jobs that grow out of the supervised occupational experience program, but also devoting regular classroom time to teaching certain leadership phases of the FFA program.

There is no reason to "bootleg" FFA activities into the classroom. If they are worth doing at all, they are worth being incorporated into the instructional program so they can be done right. Students should be taught wherever and whenever they can learn most readily.

Advancement toward Agricultural Proficiency

Qualifications for advancement in the FFA should be established in terms of proficiency in vocations in agriculture/agribusiness. Students who progress toward proficiency should be recognized and encouraged. Those who make little progress may not be seriously interested in a career in agriculture. Good teachers should hold to the basic need for students to work toward vocational proficiency. Coordinating FFA opportunities with student needs will aid materially in this matter.

Field Trips, Tours and Visits

Field trips, tours and visits conducted through the FFA may be used to expand teaching opportunities. Nothing helps more to broaden students' vision and sharpen their interests than seeing problems dealt with successfully by others. Sometimes this can be seen in nearby agricultural businesses, on farms in the community, on the other side of the county, or in another state or region. Wherever it is, students learn when they observe people actually solving agricultural problems.

A tremendous benefit of the FFA trip is the motivation established when a student sees things firsthand that before had been just topics of conversation. How many students first feel the urge to try a new idea when they see innovations in agriculture from the windows of their advisor's automobile or a school bus? This idea should be developed to the farthest limits, but teachers must always remember that observation alone does not assure learning. Observation coupled with teaching does promote learning.

To these seven major ways in which FFA can strengthen an instructional program may be added many day-to-day benefits. Through the medium of the FFA, skillful teachers can get more teaching done than ever before and yet deal with students on an informal basis. School becomes a pleasure to students and the teacher becomes an older, respected consultant.

REFERENCES

Backarich, Page. The FFA as a teaching resource. *The agricultural education magazine*. September 1971.

Future Farmers of America. *FFA advisor's handbook*. Alexandria, Va.: National FFA Center, 1975.

STUDENT ORGANIZATIONS: AN INTEGRAL PART OF INSTRUCTION

3.
INTEGRATING THE FUTURE HOMEMAKERS OF AMERICA INTO THE CLASSROOM

Lucille Frick

The Future Homemakers of America was created as an integral part of home economics in 1945. The founders envisioned the organization as an informal structure for learning; that vision has not been totally fulfilled. In this chapter, we will consider the steps necessary to fully integrate Future Homemakers into the home economics classroom.

NATIONAL GOALS

As a national vocational student organization, the goal of the Future Homemakers of America is to help youths assume their roles in society through home economics education in personal growth, family life, vocational preparation and community involvement. The following eight statements summarize its purposes: (1) to provide opportunities for self-development and preparation for family and community living and for employment, (2) to strengthen the function of the family as the basic unit of society, (3) to encourage democracy through cooperative action in the home and community, (4) to encourage individual and group involvement in helping to achieve worldwide brotherhood, (5) to institute programs promoting greater understanding between youths and adults, (6) to provide opportunities for decision making and for assuming responsibility, (7) to become aware of the multiple roles of men and women in today's society, and (8) to develop an interest in home economics, home economics careers and related occupations.

Whether a project is completed individually or cooperatively with members of a chapter, these objectives are reached in a variety of ways. Students learn as they plan and carry out activities. Relationships with peers, family and community members are fostered through chapter activities. Participation in the decision-making process enables youth to explore their values. Opportunities for leadership are available. The Future Homemakers of America provides a climate for youth to grow, be creative, plan, assume responsibilities and develop life skills.

Two Types of Chapters

There are two types of chapters. FHA chapters place major emphasis on projects involving consumer education, homemaking and family life education. They also explore jobs and careers related to home economics, with the realization that homemakers fill multiple roles as community leaders and wage earners.

HERO (Home Economics Related Occupations) chapters place major emphasis on preparation for jobs and careers, recognizing that workers also fill multiple roles as homemakers. In order to be eligible for membership through Grade 12, a student must be taking or have taken a course in home economics.

INTEGRATING CHAPTER ACTIVITIES INTO THE CLASSROOM

By using the organizational structure as an informal teaching base and using the resources described here, the teacher can integrate chapter activities into the classroom.

Program Action Impact

A key to integrating Future Homemakers of America activities into the classroom is to use methods that involve students. Program Action Impact (PAI) is a basic resource that teaches youth a process for planning. It utilizes a problem-solving technique with the following basic steps:

1. Brainstorm to identify concerns and issues related to individual, family, job/career and community.
2. Narrow identified concerns and issues by exploring resources that can help develop them into a project.
3. Determine what project to accomplish.
4. Decide what needs to be done.
5. Form a plan.
6. Act on the plan.
7. Analyze what happened.

PAI is so logical that it enables teachers, advisors and preservice teachers to teach a process. Secondary students and FHA/HERO members learn to plan for themselves with ease and much enthusiasm. PAI has been used successfully in preservice methods classes, inservice workshops and state FHA/HERO meetings. In all cases, the participants carried out the process with little assistance.

The steps in the technique can be adjusted if necessary as a project develops. For example, it might be necessary to brainstorm before deciding what needs to be done or to analyze what happened at various steps.

Encounter

A major purpose of Future Homemakers of America is to provide opportunities for self-development. *Encounter* is a method for developing personal growth experiences through class or chapter activities, while encouraging and guiding individuals in setting individual goals for self-improvement.

Encounter's goal-setting process correlates well with home economics curricular areas, especially interpersonal and family relations. Students choose an area in which they feel they need to grow. The teacher and others assist the student, as needed, in setting up a plan of action. By incorporating PAI experience into planning, the student can usually develop an individual *Encounter* project.

Teen Times

The use of *Teen Times,* the magazine of the Future Homemakers of America is another valuable method for integrating activities into the classroom. It ties youth concerns into the curriculum. Using feature stories and clippings from the magazine, students can hold discussions, do projects, and develop displays, bulletin boards, mobiles, banners, buttons, posters and collages.

ADVANTAGES TO INTEGRATION

By integrating Future Homemakers of America activities into the classroom, a skillful teacher can strengthen the total home economics curriculum. Through the use of PAI, the students identify concerns that are important to them, thereby creating a curriculum that can provide meaningful learning experiences. Similarly, using *Encounter,* students can choose activities that will help them reach a personal goal.

What better way is there to develop decision-making skills, responsibility, an improved self-concept and leadership qualities than to allow young people to determine goals, formulate a plan for carrying out activities, take action and evaluate results? Additional leadership opportunities await students at district, state and national levels. One has only to attend a Future Homemakers of America meeting for a short time to be impressed by the abilities and the leadership qualities displayed by FHA/HERO youth.

An additional advantage for the advisor of integrating organizational activities into the classroom is that all home economics teachers can share the advisor responsibilities. Also, students who are actively involved in FHA/HERO activities are more motivated to complete activities. In using PAI, the students develop and carry out many of the learning experiences such as locating and making arrangements for resources, field trips and resource persons.

SUGGESTED GUIDELINES

To help FHA/HERO advisors integrate chapter activities into the classroom, a series of four workshops was conducted at Purdue University in

Indiana. Participants included FHA/HERO members, chapter and district advisors, state and national FHA/HERO consultants, teacher educators and graduate students.

The approaches to integration identified during this meeting can be categorized as organizational, structural, philosophical and curricular. These can be used in meetings of teacher advisors and students as a starting point for generating additional ideas.

Organizational Approaches

1. How can teachers not designated as FHA/HERO advisors be interested, trained, updated and actively involved in the integration process? Develop inservice workshops to acquaint potential advisors with the processes. Use resources developed at state and national levels.

2. How can the advantages of integrating Future Homemakers of America into the classroom be given widespread publicity? Sell administrators, advisory boards, teachers and students on the value of Future Homemakers by use of a worthwhile program.

3. How can chapters be encouraged to coordinate activities of both FHA and HERO members? Use one advisory board for home economics, FHA chapters and HERO chapters.

4. How can all activities be conducted during school time when some FHA/HERO members are not enrolled currently in a home economics class? Establish an FHA/HERO activity corner in the home economics department or use a display case, bulletin board postings, newsletter or school announcements.

5. How can the cooperation of the school administration be gained? Inform administrators of the advantages of integrating chapter activities into the classroom. Include an administrator on your advisory committee. Invite administrators to an FHA/HERO chapter or state meeting. Share *Teen Times* with them.

Structural Approaches

1. How can the Future Homemakers of America maintain its identity within a classroom structure? Plan an orientation session to interpret the goals of the Future Homemakers of America and how it functions through classroom activity to expand the knowledge and develop the leadership potential of members.

2. How do you get class members to join FHA-HERO and pay dues if they can reap the same benefits without belonging? Discuss what roles organizations play in society and why we pay dues to organizations. Point out the opportunities dues-paying members have to hold office, vote, participate in social activities and take part in district, state or national meetings.

3. In what ways can potential leaders be helped to run for district, state or national office when funds are not readily available? Collect home economic dues from everyone and designate a portion as FHA/HERO chapter dues. Initiate money-raising projects to defray dues expenses.

4. What structure can be used for a large home economics department with many students? Have students formulate an appropriate structure for electing officers within the class that fits their specific situation in the school.

Philosophical Approaches

1. Why is Future Homemakers of America important? It expands home economics and vocational education, giving youth opportunities for decision making and leadership development. To provide continuity conduct training sessions for new officers, using older members as leaders.

2. What does an FHA/HERO chapter do for youth? It encourages students to accept challenges and responsibility and to learn cooperation. They also experience the important role of organizations in society.

Curricular Approaches

1. How can FHA/HERO activities be incorporated into the curriculum? Become familiar with and use PAI, *Encounter,* and *Teen Times* in teaching.

2. In what ways can home economics help youth in the area of personal growth? Use *Encounter* to individualize instruction in personal and family life.

USING THE ORGANIZATION TO AID INSTRUCTION

First, become familiar with Future Homemakers of America. Valuable resources are available at the national, state and local levels. Discuss approaches with other teachers and split up or rotate responsibilities.

Contact school administrators to keep them informed of your plans. Consider the administrative limitations of school policies and scheduling, as well as student interests, concerns and goals. Consult your advisory committee.

Discuss various chapter structures with students and have them select a plan that will be effective. With their help, select an appropriate organizational structure, types of activities, and meeting times and locations. Formulate a plan to accommodate those members who are not enrolled currently in a home economics class.

Identify procedures for selecting leaders, establish a dues system for members, and identify privileges and responsibilities of dues-paying members. Establish budget needs and determine ways of financing chapter activities. At the beginning of the semester or year, hold an orientation session in each class to identify the relationship of the Future Home-makers of America to vocational education and to specific instructional activities.

Additional Aids

Many home economics teachers have indicated that their preservice training did not prepare them for the role of FHA/HERO advisor. Some aids for FHA/HERO advisors and teacher educators are available. At the recommendation of the Teacher Education Development Committee of the Future Homemakers of America, I developed a module on the organi-zation called *Working with FHA/HERO Youth* for use by preservice and inservice home economics teachers. The module fosters the development of basic competencies that relate to the structure and function of Future Homemakers of America, the relationship of the organization to the home economics program, resources for FHA/HERO members and advisors, and responsibilities of the advisor. A new resource to be used with the module is a sound tape and filmstrip—"Getting It All Together." It consists of two parts: (1) Integrating FHA/HERO into the classroom, and (2) Integrating FHA/HERO into the classroom through *Program Action Impact.*

Inservice training workshops are especially beneficial because they provide an explanation and demonstration of methods as well as sugges-tions from more experienced advisors and FHA/HERO members. State and national FHA/HERO meetings are another good source for ideas. To assist in the presentation of workshops, state or national meetings, the Future Homemakers of America has developed a Field Consultant Pro-gram consisting of a group of specially trained chapter advisors and teacher educators. Upon request, they help design and lead workshops or meetings focusing on concerns of participants. The national office also publishes a special newsletter for teacher educators and will begin a new adult leader periodical in 1979.

V

STUDENT ORGANIZATIONS: AN INTEGRAL PART OF INSTRUCTION

4.
DECA AS A VITAL COMPONENT OF INSTRUCTION

Thomas Hephner

The history of the Distributive Education Clubs of America (DECA) parallels closely that of distributive education. Incorporated October 17, 1946, DECA was initiated officially as a national organization in 1948 in St. Louis, Missouri, when 17 charter member states approved the first constitution and adopted the name Distributors Club of America. In January 1950, the name was changed to the Distributive Education Clubs of America.

The distributive education program received its first official recognition and federal funding with the passage of the George Dean Act in 1936. Several local organizations had been established earlier as supplementary clubs to distributive education programs. The existence of these clubs, which held regional and later statewide meetings, led eventually to the development of the national organization.

DECA'S BROAD GOALS

The framers of the first DECA constitution listed among their purposes several items that had a direct relationship to the distributive education curriculum.

1. To develop leadership in the field of distribution.
2. To provide opportunities for intelligent career choices in distribution.
3. To allow practical application of distributive education through competition.
4. To create and nurture an understanding of our free, competitive. enterprise system.

The original founders believed from the beginning, then, that DECA was to play an important role in moving the student from theory to practice.

This curriculum relationship was spelled out even more clearly in a conference sponsored by the U.S. Office of Education (USOE) in 1959. A group of distributive educators, the director of DECA and representatives from the distribution and marketing community established principles to aid in establishing new DECA chapters. The implications for curriculum are clear in several of these principles:

1. DECA is an integral part of the distributive education program.
2. The local chapter's activities should be directed primarily to educational activities that are concerned with distribution.
3. The local chapter's activities should complement, supplement and strengthen the instructional program.
4. Each activity undertaken should have some relationship to the needed competencies of the students who are seeking careers in the field of distribution.

Additional principles generated at this meeting were directed to the need for group participation, individual and student-centered activities and the necessity for continuing student involvement in program management.

A National Rationale for the Curriculum

The first noteworthy attempt at establishing a national rationale for the distributive education curriculum occurred at the 1963 USOE Distributive Education National Conference. Scheduled in anticipation of the 1963 legislation, this conference sought answers to critical questions held by distributive educators at that time. The policy statements formulated in the 1963 conference molded the philosophical base of the discipline for years to come. One of the major goals of the 1963 conference was to examine the nature and scope of instructional content in distributive education.

Edward Nelson presented a paper supporting the concept that distributive education represented an instructional discipline. This paper, "Bases for Curriculum Development in Distribution," continues as the foundation of distributive education curriculum philosophy today. According to Nelson, "Occupational acquisition, adjustment, and advancement in the field of distribution are accompanied by a set of specific competencies exercised in the form of judgments and decisions . . . standards for employment are found in four distinct areas."

These four areas consist of social competency, basic skills competency, technology competency and marketing competency. Nelson stated further that all four competencies were "best achieved when they were taught in reference to the components of the free, competitive enterprise system." A fifth major area was later identified as economics and the free enterprise system. Attention was focused on the marketing competency area as the discipline for which distributive education assumed primary instructional responsibility.

232

DECA as a Vital Component of Instruction

The second major outcome of the 1963 conference was the development of a national classification system of the occupational areas served by distributive education. Thus, two landmark models for distributive education were established. Distributive educators created an enduring curriculum philosophy and identified the occupational areas for which distributive education was responsible.

Linking Occupations with the Curriculum

The occupations could now be linked with the curriculum. One could examine the curriculum to see if it was meeting the student's occupational objectives. It was also possible now to determine which competencies students working in different distributive occupations might have in common and which needs were unique to a student working in a specialized occupation.

Nelson's identification of the four broad competency areas and the subsequent Crawford study (1967) led to a listing of 10 content areas to be taught in the distributive education curriculum: math, communications, sales, display, advertising, human relations, management, operations, merchandising, and product and service technology. The curriculum was content-oriented and continued to be so for some time. Most learning experiences were built around the general merchandising occupational area.

DECA activities followed this content approach closely. However, group and individual activities were still stressed, in keeping with the earlier commitment to the individual student. The competitive events held at the district, regional, state and national levels may best illustrate the relationship DECA had with the curriculum. It should be emphasized, however, that many local and district DECA chapters were developing programs of work that included group activities and objectives not related directly to the competitive events. DECA members learned valuable skills through participating in community fund-raising projects, carrying out market research projects for the local business community, speaking at service club functions, and planning and participating in various school-wide functions.

To understand the close coordination between DECA competitive activities and the distributive education curriculum that existed, one has only to look at a state association DECA manual outlining the competitive activities for high school students.

I. Individual Research Manuals
   A. Careers in Distribution Manual
   B. Merchandise Sales Manual
   C. Areas of Distribution Manual
   D. Studies in Marketing
      1. Automotive and Petroleum Industry

2. Food Industry
3. Service Industry
4. Home Furnishings Industry
5. Variety Store Merchandising
6. Specialty Store Merchandising
7. Department Store Merchandising

II. Individual Participation Experiences
   A. Selecting and Training Judges
   B. Competitive Events
      1. Advertising
      2. Display
      3. Job Interview
      4. Parliamentary Procedure
      5. Public Speaking
      6. Sales Demonstration
      7. Student of the Year

III. Group Activity and Chapter Projects
   A. Chapter Program of Work (Chapter of the Year)
   B. Creative Marketing Project

DECA recognized the specialized occupational areas and gave students opportunities to prepare in-depth studies in their specialty. To be sure, DECA at all levels has had a tendency to emphasize those competency areas that seem to be a more natural part of the program. For example, the development of leadership skills is a major and natural activity for DECA members. The development of social skills is also a natural competency area for DECA to emphasize. The attention to human relations skills through local activities and competitive events is also a major contribution of DECA.

Both distributive education and DECA needed to take a closer look at objectives, Though the word *competency* appeared early in the history of both organizations, the impact of a competency-based curriculum was yet to come.

THE NEW SHAPE OF DECA

As the distributive education curriculum has changed, so has DECA. In recent years, DECA has moved toward a competency-based competitive event system. Through this approach, DECA has related its activities more closely to the distributive education curriculum.

Corbin (1971) researched the role of DECA in the distributive education curriculum. In a unique study, he identified 12 goals and 72 objectives for the high school division of DECA, based on the assumption that

DECA as a Vital Component of Instruction

"DECA is a co-curricular activity that complements, supplements, and strengthens the distributive education instructional program." One can see the implications for curriculum in the top four DECA goals identified by Corbin's panel of experts. They are:

1. Develop leadership characteristics,
2. Develop self-confidence and/or self-acceptance,
3. Develop a greater understanding of our free enterprise system.
4. Develop occupational competencies needed for careers in marketing, merchandising and management.

The New Competency-Based Competitive Events

DECA has initiated a completely new program of individual competitive events. The new events are competency based, using the Crawford competencies as well as competencies identified by other studies.

In a related change, two levels of competence are identified: master employee and manager/owner (or supervisor). Eight major occupational clusters serve presently as areas of competition. If a beginning distributive education student enters a DECA competitive event, he or she would probably enter as a master employee. If that same student had an occupational objective such as becoming a supermarket manager. then he or she would enter the food marketing event at the manager/owner level.

The third major change evident in the new competitive event structure is the evaluation of students in multiple content areas within an occupational cluster. As the event is scheduled, learning experiences from a selected number of the 10 content areas in the curriculum become the basis for competition. The guidelines for each competitive event are written carefully, outlining the competencies to be demonstrated, the behavioral objectives to be met and the evaluative instrument to be used. Students must demonstrate their skills in a number of instructional areas rather than just one. The involvement with the business community has increased as a result of the new competitive event format.

The significance of the new competitive events and DECA's new competency-based rationale is that DECA is now more closely related to the curriculum. The competitive events offer an attractive choice of learning experiences for distributive education teacher-coordinators and students. The relationships to classroom learning experiences and on-the-job learning experiences scheduled from a competency-based training plan are direct. The teacher and student need only decide the most appropriate experiences to help the students master the desired competency.

FUTURE OPPORTUNITIES FOR DECA

DECA will remain a preferred choice for learning experiences in the areas of leadership development, decision-making skills, human relations interaction and similar affective competency areas. Also, DECA will continue to help teacher-coordinators reinforce competencies already mastered. Competitive events will provide a means of assessing how well the students have mastered competencies.

As distributive educators continue to develop learning experiences designed to help students master competencies, the need for experiences that involve *multiple* competencies will be greater. In the working world, a given experience, i.e., a sales transaction, will involve perhaps a dozen or more related competencies rather than just one or two.

DECA has made a commitment to develop competitive events for new occupational clusters based on increased student enrollment in an occupational cluster area, DECA membership in a cluster area, and occupational trends in a given cluster area.

For DECA to be considered as a source of competency-based learning experiences for students—all DECA activities should identify the competencies that are mastered as a result of completing the activity. This concept should not only apply to competitive events, but also to the student chairperson of a local DECA chapter who coordinates the construction of a DECA float for the homecoming parade.

DECA has the opportunity and the structure to help distributive educators solve a long-standing instructional problem—a strategy to teach the mastery of a skill and the consequent appreciation of the mastered skill. This blending of the cognitive and affective domains has not always been achieved. Competency-based learning experiences have shown some promise in solving this problem.

DECA is in a better position today to contribute to the learning experiences of distributive education students than ever before in its history. The decision to move to a competency-based curriculum and the matching of competencies with occupational objectives have made DECA an integral and important part of the distributive education curriculum.

REFERENCES

Corbin, Steven B. Integrating DECA goals into the DE program. *Business education forum,* January 1977.

Crawford, Lucy C. *A competency pattern approach to curriculum construction in distributive education* (vol. 1). Blacksburg, Va.: Virginia Polytechnic Institute and State University, 1967.

Crawford, Lucy C., and Meyer, Warren G. *Organization and administration of distributive education.* Columbus, Ohio: Charles E. Merrill, 1972.

Nelson, Edwin L. *Bases for curriculum development in distribution.* Paper presented at the USOE National Conference for Distributive Education, 1963.

VI

THE APPRAISAL OF INSTRUCTION

1.
THE ASSESSMENT OF LEARNING: A BASE FOR INSTRUCTIONAL EVALUATION

Tim L. Wentling

Instruction of vocational education programs is a lot like sales of cure-all medicine by a huckster. He swears by the product, has many cases of success to cite and can produce a testimonial from someone in the audience. However, one must wonder how widely the product has been used, what percentage of users the success cases represent, and in some cases, how honest the salesperson is.

Similarly, all vocational educators have confidence that their instruction is relevant, reliable and effective. They can produce a successful former student and many can produce follow-up or placement statistics. In very few cases, however, can vocational educators (or any educators, for that matter) produce solid evidence as to the success of individual courses and programs—true evidence in the form of learning assessments.

Advancement in the use of assessments can facilitate communication of program successes to appropriate audiences such as school boards, administrators, other instructors, potential students, current students and others with a stake in vocational education.

In addition, the use of student learning assessments in the evaluation of instruction is given impetus by several recent laws. The Education of All Handicapped Children Act (PL 94-142) mandates that annual assessments of educational progress be made for all handicapped students. The Education Amendments of 1976, Title II (PL 94-482), specify that states must evaluate all vocational programs at least once every five years. According to the rules and regulations for PL 94-482, programs must be evaluated by assessing planning and operational processes, the success of program graduates and *student achievement*.

These mandates, coupled with the "Age of Accountability" within public schools, provide sufficient motivation for vocation educators to undertake the assessment of student learning as a base for evaluating instruction. This chapter has the goals of: (1) presenting the pros and cons of learning assessment in an attempt to spark dialogue among professionals, (2) pointing out some general concerns and techniques in the assessment of learning, (3) suggesting ways of using learning assessments in the evaluation of instruction, and (4) making recommendations for advancing the state of the art in the use of learning assessments.

THE PROS AND CONS OF LEARNING ASSESSMENTS

The use of student learning assessments to evaluate instruction can be argued from many points of view. The most obvious argument is based on the idea that the purpose of all instruction is student learning. If this is true, the primary base of instructional evaluation should be student assessment. If students fail to learn, in most cases instruction is weak.

A second advantage of student learning assessments is that they provide feedback to teachers about areas of instruction that need further emphasis. That is, a review of test results or other measures can provide an indication of specific course content with which students had difficulty. This type of input (formative evaluation) can provide a base for remedial activities.

Thirdly, student assessment can enhance instruction. The results of student assessments can be used to demonstrate to students that their learning is progressing. For those students who are not progressing well, the knowledge of assessment results can spur them on to further study.

Another advantage of using student learning assessments is that they can help to insure quality control of instruction over a period of time. If standardized achievement measures or criterion-referenced examinations are used year after year by an instructor, the results of such instruments can be used to compare groups or classes to determine if instruction is consistent. Of course, classes or groups may vary upon entrance and this would require consideration in the post comparisons.

Shortcomings of Assessments

The use of student learning assessments in instructional evaluation also has many shortcomings. First, by using assessments, instructors may limit their teaching to testable content or do the proverbial "teaching to the test." If the test is based upon the right content, however, teaching to the test may not be so terrible.

Another disadvantage of assessments is related to the underdevelopment of measurement technology. Compared to measurement in the physical sciences, the measurement of learning is in its infancy, lacking preciseness. The technology in the assessment of cognitive learning (thinking skills) is further advanced than the assessment of affective (feeling) and performance (doing) behaviors. Many standardized cognitive achievement tests that have undergone extensive tryout, analysis and revision, however, have a known error of four to eight points on a one hundred point scale.

An additional drawback is the time that assessment can consume. Most learning assessments require student time that may displace instructional time. In addition, instructor time is usually required to prepare or write the measuring instrument, administer it and score student responses.

A final disadvantage of assessment is related to its limited focus. It indicates only levels of learning rather than focusing on the processes of instruction. In other words, it fails to point out what is wrong with the instruction. For example, if student assessment results in an auto mechanics program indicate low achievement, the instructor or supervisor does not know the reasons for the problem. Other types of evaluation may be needed to augment student learning information.

The pros of using learning assessment results in the evaluation of instruction outweigh the cons. Recognition of the shortcomings can, however, provide the impetus for devising ways of minimizing their effects in the evaluation of instruction.

THE FOCUS OF LEARNING ASSESSMENT

The term *student learning* is almost as broad as terms such as *athletic performance* or *financial success*. Therefore, it is important to define the term carefully so it can be addressed in a practical way.

Vocational programs consist of many types of learning with many sub-categories. A number of formal approaches for classifying behavior have been formulated. Cognition or thinking has been identified as a major domain of student learning (Bloom et al., 1956). The cognitive domain includes the most basic level of thinking, the recall of facts, as well as more complex levels such as analysis, synthesis and evaluation.

Another major type of student learning exists within the interest/attitudinal or affective area. The affective domain (Krathwohl, 1964) encompasses behavior such as "being totally involved." For example, in determining a student's interest in a vocational course, an instructor might find that the student first was aware of the course, then obtained more information, then told someone about the course and finally enrolled in the course. Each step indicates increased interest.

The performance domain is an area of student learning that has special importance to vocational education. It is made up of two subdomains, the psychomotor domain (Simpson, 1966) and the perceptual domain (Moore, 1970). This combination includes student learning and relates to doing physical tasks through the use of muscles for movement (psychomotor) and the senses for input (perception).

The three domains of student learning provide a way of breaking down job tasks as well as classifying measures of learning. Although the domains help us look at learning, it should be emphasied that they are interdependent. For example, most performance skills require knowledge and an affective component for their successful completion. A welder must know the proper temperatures and possess good safety attitudes to perform adequately.

Another Perspective on Assessment

Assessment can also be considered from a "point of reference," i.e., a norm-referenced or a criterion-referenced point. When a student's learning (in the form of test scores, ratings, etc.) is compared to that of other students, it is norm referenced. Traditional schemes of grading, standardized testing and performance competition are examples of norm-referenced assessments. Norm referencing is useful if selection of the most qualified student is important or if there is a need to determine how an individual or group compares to others in a particular type of behavior.

Criterion referencing attempts to compare an individual's learning not with that of other students, but with a standard or continuum of performance. That is, a student's evaluation has nothing to do with the performance of other students—it is related only to a predetermined behavior. For example, each person in a group of dental hygiene students could be assessed in terms of how well he or she removes 95 percent (the criterion) of calculus in the oral cavity of a patient. In this case, the performance of one student means nothing in comparison to the group.

TECHNIQUES FOR LEARNING ASSESSMENT

There are many ways to assess learning within vocational programs. A thorough coverage of techniques and instruments for assessment is beyond the scope of this chapter. A brief overview is presented and the reader is referred to Erickson and Wentling (1976), Cross (1973), and Bloom, Hastings and Madaus (1971) for detailed coverage.

Assessment of Performance

The assessment of performance is an activity in which all vocational educators have participated. Even before formal education existed, the performance of apprentices was assessed by master craftsmen. Vocational instructors assess student performance through many means—sometimes intertwining assessment with instruction. In almost all cases, performance is assessed by observing and evaluating the process or product of the act being performed.

For example, typing students can be observed and rated according to how well they exhibit desired behaviors such as sitting straight, holding wrists up, keeping eyes on the copy rather than on the keyboard, etc. This is a process assessment. An alternative approach would be to examine the product of the same typing students. That is, the typed copy or output could be reviewed for correct margins, spacing and incidence of errors. Obviously, both types of assessments have utility in judging the learning of vocational students. The ultimate assessment of learning within the performance domain usually includes both process and product assessment.

Three types of techniques can be used in assessing performance: (1) the identification test, (2) the simulator or work sample test, and (3) the employer survey. The employer survey is not addressed here because it is covered in the chapter by Erickson in this volume.

The identification test is the most basic type of performance test. It measures an individual's capability, using both knowledge and sensory input, to identify materials, tools, equipment components and other job-related items. An identification test can be as basic as asking students to identify wood samples and as complex as asking students to identify auto parts, their wear or deficiency, the cause of the deficiency and recommendations for remedy of the cause (Comer, 1970).

The second major type of performance test includes the simulation and work sample test. The work sample test is a controlled test that is administered using the actual conditions of the work situation. The examinee is required to use the same procedures that would be employed in an actual job situation. Simulation tests, on the other hand, are designed to replicate the work situation by using specialized equipment or making modifications in existing equipment.

The project method of instruction in many vocational education laboratories uses a form of work sample test. However, within a measurement or assessment context, the work sample test is administered in a more highly controlled situation. Usually, a one-on-one relationship between examiner and student exists. The content of work sample and simulation tests can vary from simple drawing or sketching tasks to complex tasks such as those used in the medical laboratory.

Assessment of Affective Learning

Tyler (1973) has identified four categories of affective objectives and focal points for affective learning assessment: interests, attitudes, values and appreciations. The assessment of these four categories of learning is difficult for several reasons. First, the technology of measurement is primitive in the affective domain (at least from an instructor's point of view) when compared to the performance and cognitive domains. Also, it is very difficult to measure the effects of instruction on affective behavior because, in many cases, the effect is long term, possibly not being exhibited for months or years after instruction. For example, the teaching of pride in one's work by a vocational instructor may not be measured or observed until students have entered the work world and have had the opportunity to perform and exhibit the pride that was taught. These difficulties, however, should not be used as excuses for failing to assess affective learning. Instead, they should provide a challenge and a goal for the advancement of learning assessment within the affective domain. The content area of safety is a good example of affective learning within vocational programs. It can provide a model for further development.

Alternate ways of assessing affective learning include direct observation, interviews, questionnaires and inventories, projective techniques, and unobstrusive measures. Direct observation involves viewing and recording a student's behavior following a stimulus and making inferences about the underlying affective causes of the behavior. For example, a nursing student's reaction to patient criticism might be observed and judged in the assessment of interpersonal skills.

The interview technique involves asking predetermined questions regarding a student's attitude toward a particular object or person. Interview information can be used to determine an individual's attitude toward course content, job activities, authority figures, co-workers and so on.

Questionnaires and inventories are a written form of the interview. Students are presented with questions or items which they must respond to or select. Questionnaires can contain open ended as well as the selection type of items.

Projective techniques involve asking students to respond or react to a task or object without being aware of the reason. For example, students might be asked to write a short essay on the important features of a job. The essay would reveal the values held by students related to a job.

The fifth technique for assessing affective learning is the unobtrusive measure. Unobtrusive measurement involves the observation of individuals or artifacts without the awareness of students. For example, the review of textbooks at the end of a school term to determine the extent of their use (as determined by wear) is an example of an unobtrusive measure.

The assessment of affective behavior is important to the evaluation of instruction. In particular, affective learning has been a priority in many human service fields, but it is important in any career field where people are involved.

Assessment of Cognitive Achievement

Assessment within the cognitive domain in vocational programs has received much more attention and has been used more extensively than assessment within the performance and affective domains. This is primarily due to the fact that student performance objectives and test items for cognitive skills are easier to prepare than those for other domains. Consequently, procedures and techniques for assessing cognitive skills are the most highly developed and most emphasized. If student learning assessment provides a base for instructional evaluation, however, vocational educators will surely wish to have their instruction evaluated on more than the cognitive achievement of their students.

Paper and pencil tests are the primary means for assessing cognitive achievement. Two basic categories of items are typically included in these tests: recognition items and constructed response items. Recognition items present the student with a stimulus and a series of choices from which he or she can select the most plausible alternative. These include multiple choice, true-false, and matching items.

Constructed response items, on the other hand, require the student to construct or write out his or her response to the item. Examples of constructed response items are definition, short answer and essay.

USING THE RESULTS OF LEARNER ASSESSMENTS

The results of learner assessments in vocational programs have traditionally been used to evaluate students and to assign grades. Composites or ranges of test scores have also provided instructors with general indications of how their students are doing. However, the use of student learning assessments can be advanced and expanded.

The reference made in PL 94-482 to the use of student achievement results in the evaluation of vocational programs provides one impetus. However, it is important to maintain a certain amount of caution in meeting this mandate. If the results are used improperly, the result could be mandated curricula and other effects that might limit vocational education's sensitivity to individual and community needs. This caution is especially relevant to statewide testing efforts. Locally conducted assessments have less chance of producing negative effects. Therefore, this section emphasizes the use of student learning results in evaluating instruction at the local level by local personnel. It is at this level that real improvements in instruction can be made.

Bloom et al. (1971) point out that quizzes, progress tests and other evaluation techniques have been used by instructors to cover brief periods of learning. They point out, however, that the results are used primarily to motivate students and to mark their work. Only rarely does an instructor use the results to modify instruction. In vocational education, teachers do use learning assessments to aid in evaluating instruction, but often in an informal and cursory way. The following paragraphs provide suggestions for further use of student learning information.

Informal Feedback

The informal use of assessment results occurs in many ways, such as: 1) general review of test scores, 2) review of individual tests, 3) scoring of tests in class, and 4) discussion of tests after scoring.

The general review of assessment scores is done by almost all vocational instructors. If a norm-referenced approach is used, the instructor usually displays student scores in a range from the lowest score to the highest. Of course, this facilitates the determination of grades, but it also has utility in evaluating instruction. A general review of the range of scores exhibits how well the class has done overall in achieving the course or program objectives. If the highest score in a group is 70 out of a possible total of 100, a potential problem exists. The problem may lie in the assessment instrument, which may have been unrealistic or too difficult. An alternative explanation is that the group experienced difficulty with at least part of the instruction. This may highlight a shortcoming and need for improvement in the instruction.

The informal review of test scores can be extended if the scores are less than expected or indicate an instructional deficiency. The further study can be accomplished through the review of individual tests, rating scales or interview schedules. This specific review can focus on identifying the parts of the instrument in which students had the most difficulty or experienced the greatest failure. For example, a test in a food management program may include several groups of items that focus on nutrition, proportion planning and recipe conversion. By reviewing the individual tests, an instructor might identify one of the three areas of the test that contains a large portion of the missed items. This signals to the instructor that a weakness in the instruction may be causing problems for students in a particular content area. A further extension of this process might involve asking a small group of students to explain the instructional difficulty from their point of view.

Another informal approach to the use of assessment results can benefit students as well as instructors. This approach involves the tallying of assessment scores in class. That is, if a paper and pencil test is used, students can either score their own test or that of another student. Once scoring is complete, the instructor can identify groups of items that relate to a particular topic and ask students to raise their hands if an item was responded to incorrectly as its number is called out. This provides a general indication of areas that are weak (or test items that were defective). This process can provide feedback similar to that obtained in the previously mentioned approach (review of individual tests) without requiring an inordinate amount of instructor time.

The fourth informal approach, discussion of assessment results with students, may be a culminating step for one or more of the three other approaches. It can provide both summary input as well as suggestions for improving instruction. The discussion of assessment results can aid students in identifying their strengths and weaknesses. In addition, students can learn from their mistakes. For example, as students go over their tests, they can identify their errors and learn the correct responses to the items missed. Further, they may be able to discuss a point they might have misinterpreted previously. Thus, learning can be enhanced through assessment.

Of equal import, class discussion can be used to elicit reasons for low levels of performance within specific areas of the test. For example, if the nutrition portion of a food management test was answered poorly, the instructor could ask students why their performance was low. Furthermore, students can provide valuable suggestions for improving the instruction.

Formal Approaches

Some of the informal techniques presented in the previous section can be formalized to enhance their credibility and utility. These include item analysis and subscore analysis. In addition, the use of individual and group profiles and graphs can provide a means for using student assessment information in the evaluation of instruction.

Item analysis is a technique used frequently for evaluating test items. It has great potential for facilitating the evaluation of instruction. One way of doing an item analysis to meet this purpose is to graphically display item responses for each student in the class. Table 1 presents such a display. Here a plus ($+$) sign indicates a correct response and a minus ($-$) sign indicates an incorrect response. The chart can be used to identify items that were responded to incorrectly by a majority of the class. This

Table 1
A DISPLAY OF TEST ITEM RESPONSES

Objective	Terminology—Fire Science													
Content Area	Fire Types			Flammable Liquids				Flammable Solids				Fighting Agents		
Items	1	2	3	4	5	6	7	8	9	10	11	12	13	14
Students:														
Jake Gabe	+	+	+	−	−	+	−	+	+	−	+	−	−	+
Jack Walter	+	+	+	+	−	+	+	+	+	+	−	−	+	+
Jack Daniels	+	−	+	−	−	+	+	−	−	+	+	+	−	−
Hiram Walker	+	+	+	−	−	+	+	+	+	+	+	−	+	−
Jill Smith	+	+	+	+	−	−	+	−	−	−	+	+	−	−
Frida White	−	−	−	−	−	+	+	+	+	+	+	+	+	−
Carol Music	+	+	+	+	+	+	−	−	−	−	+	−	+	−
Leroy Brown	+	+	+	+	−	+	−	−	+	+	−	+	−	+

can aid the instructor in identifying areas of instructional weakness. This type of display can also aid in recognizing individual students who might be having difficulty with a particular part of a course or program. This could provide a good base for the planning of remedial instruction.

Another approach to the use of student assessment results in instructional evaluation is subtest or subscore analysis. This approach involves the calculation of means or percentiles for total test and subtest scores. Subtests are sections within a test that pertain to a particular part of the total content being assessed. The simplest way to analyze subscores is to calculate and display them in a grid or matrix, with student names or numbers on one axis and subscore titles on the other axis. Table 2 presents a subscore review grid for a group of dental hygiene students. Assuming that the scales or possible totals of each subtest are equal, an instructor can review Table 2 and determine that the areas of pharmacology and radiology need remediation. Of course, the instructor may have to use other evaluative techniques to determine the cause of low scores within these two areas.

Another approach to observing subscale performance of students involves comparison of programs. For example, the subscores of the National Board Dental Hygiene Examination are reported to all dental hygiene programs in the United States that had students participating in a particular examining session. Table 3 presents part of the National Board results, with subscores presented in the form of decile ranks (e.g., 90%-100% = decile 10).

Table 2
SUBSCORE REVIEW GRID FOR DENTAL HYGIENE STUDENTS

	Student Number													
Subtest	1	2	3	4	5	6	7	8	9	10	11	12	13	14
Anatomy	10	12	13	11	11	11	10	9	11	10	12	12	11	10
Pharmacology	4	3	3	4	5	9	4	3	2	3	1	1	4	4
Periodontal Disease	11	11	12	13	14	13	13	10	10	9	10	11	12	12
Histology	16	16	17	17	18	16	16	15	14	17	17	20	19	15
Radiology	4	4	4	5	3	3	3	2	8	5	5	4	2	2
Dental Materials	12	12	14	14	14	16	15	14	16	16	21	16	15	20

Table 3
NATIONAL SUBSCORES FOR DENTAL HYGIENE STUDENTS

Group Rank	School Code	A	B	C	D	E	F	G	H	J	K	L	M	N
1	38	10	10	5	10	10	3	10	10	7	9	10	9	10
2	46	9	9	10	9	10	10	10	4	10	10	7	7	9
3	51	10	9	10	10	10	8	7	10	9	9	9	3	7
4	54	10	6	10	9	7	10	6	7	8	10	10	7	10
5	63	7	8	9	10	9	6	7	9	6	4	9	10	6
6	69	6	8	5	7	5	4	9	9	10	10	8	9	9
7	72	8	9	8	6	6	7	9	10	5	7	5	10	7
8	78	9	7	4	9	9	9	9	7	10	6	2	8	4
9	80	10	6	8	7	7	8	4	9	9	6	6	7	4

This type of table allows instructors and administrators to see the areas of strength and weakness in a program as evidenced by student performance. Further evaluation can then be done, using other techniques such as an advisory committee, facility evaluation and evaluation of instructional materials. In addition, a ranking chart such as the one in Table 3 can also indicate how a program is doing in comparison with similar programs in other institutions. This can provide impetus to improvement.

Another way of using subscores is to display them for the same program over time. Table 4 presents two subscores over a period of five years. By observing this graph, an instructor or administrator can observe changes in achievement that may be occurring. For example, achievement on subscale 2 dropped between testing times in 1976 and 1977. There may

246

be many reasons for this drop. By being aware that a drop occurred, instructional personnel can look for reasons and identify ways to increase student learning within this content area.

Table 4
CHANGES IN TWO SUBSCORES OVER FIVE YEARS

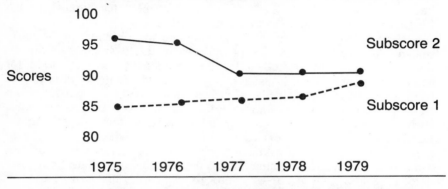

THE FUTURE: CAUTIONS AND RECOMMENDATIONS

This chapter has pointed out the pros and cons of using student assessment data in instructional evaluation, presented a review of bases upon which learning assessment is built and outlined several practical approaches for using assessment information to improve instruction. This section will suggest several activities that could improve current practices in using the assessment of learning as a primary base for the evaluation of instruction.

First, caution must be taken in the wide-scale use of learning assessment information. That is, if national or even state standards are established for student performance, two negative side effects may result. First, standards may be interpreted as ultimate goals and not minimal standards. This may result in instructors striving for attainment of the standards, with little concern for helping individual students go beyond the standards. A second negative effect may be the standardization of curricula. This may not sound negative, and it is not if a minimum curriculum is defined. If carried to an extreme, however, standardization of curricula could adversely affect vocational instruction's sensitivity to the needs and interests of individuals and the specific training needs of community employers. It is highly recommended that learning assessments be used primarily at the local level to improve instruction. Uses such as reporting and accountability should assume secondary roles.

It is recommended that systematic attempts be made to advance the technology of measurement in vocational programs. It is hoped that local, state and national commitments by funding agencies and experts will be made to improve upon the techniques and instruments used to assess learning in vocational programs. The development of performance tests, attitude scales and other instruments will facilitate the use of student learning assessments.

It is further recommended that the use of student learning assessments in vocational programs be extended beyond the assessment of cognitive learning. This means that vocational instructors may need to expand their knowledge of performance and affective assessment techniques through formal and informal staff development activities.

A final recommendation, and probably the most significant one presented here, emphasizes the use of other evaluative techniques to supplement the assessment of student learning. Although there is a need for student assessment, there is also a strong need to insure the work relevance of measures by using evaluative techniques such as the student follow-up study, the employer survey and advisory committees as evaluation teams. Also, process evaluation results should be used to facilitate the understanding of program deficiencies by instructors and administrators. Techniques such as personnel evaluation, evaluation of community resources, evaluation of facilities, evaluation of instructional materials and cost/ outcome analysis are examples of process techniques that can be used to explain student learning effects and to facilitate planning improvement.

The implementation of these recommendations will no doubt increase the utility of student learning assessments and aid in accomplishing the major goal of all evaluation—the improvement of programs for vocational students.

REFERENCES

Bloom, B. S., et al. *A taxonomy of educational objectives: The cognitive domain* (Handbook 1). New York: David McKay, 1956.

Bloom, B. S., Hastings, J. T., and Madaus, G. F. *Handbook on formative and summative evaluation of student learning.* New York: McGraw-Hill, 1971.

Comer, J. C. A diagnostic work sample instrument for assessing automotive trade competence. Doctoral dissertation, Wayne State University, 1970.

Cross, A. A. *Home economics evaluation.* Columbus, Ohio: Charles E. Merrill, 1973.

Erickson, R. C. and Wentling, T. L. *Measuring student growth: Techniques and procedures for occupational education.* Boston: Allyn and Bacon, Inc., 1976.

Krathwohl, D. R., Bloom, B. S. and Masia, B. A. *Taxonomy of educational objectives: The affective domain* (Handbook 2). New York: David McKay, 1964.

Moore, M. R. The perceptual-motor domain and a proposed taxonomy of perception. *AV Communication Review,* 1970.

Simpson, E. J. The classification of educational objectives: Psychomotor domain. *Illinois Teacher of Home Economics,* 1966.

Tyler, R. W. Assessing educational achievement in the affective domain. East Lansing, Mich.: The National Council on Measurement in Education, Spring 1973.

THE APPRAISAL OF INSTRUCTION

2.
TECHNIQUES FOR APPRAISING VOCATIONAL INSTRUCTION

Richard C. Erickson

If vocational educators are going to be accountable for the instruction that occurs in their classes, then it is imperative that they devote some of their working day to appraising that instruction. Being accountable means knowing the real as well as the intended outcome of instruction. The purpose of this chapter is to present some techniques that vocational educators should find useful in appraising their instruction. The rationale underlying each technique is presented to assist those who wish to adapt any of these techniques for use in a local vocational program.

GIVING A FOCUS TO THE APPRAISAL PROCESS

The primary purpose for appraising vocational instruction is to improve the learning environment. There is little to be gained if the data gathered focus on facets of the instructional program that are irrelevant to how well students develop the intended skills.

Concerns such as the type, level and geographic location of the school or the age, weight, sex or personality type of the teacher are generally irrelevant to the success of the instructional program. Consequently, such irrelevant areas of concern should not be the focus of attempts to assess instruction.

The same is true for relevant aspects of instruction that are uncontrollable. Considerations such as students' general mental ability, eye-hand coordination and perceptual skills are relevant to success in the instructional program, but they are not really teacher controllable. To focus on them in assessing vocational instruction is to gather data and information in areas of concern that have little or nothing to suggest for improving instruction.

For example, students seem to learn more quickly when (1) they understand and accept the objectives of the instruction they receive and (2) the instruction is presented in a manner that is to them both clear and concise. These factors are appropriate areas of concern for the appraisal process because they are relevant to success in the instructional program and can be controlled by the teacher to some extent. Moreover, these are aspects of the program that the teacher can improve, if necessary. It is the relevant and uncontrollable aspects of the instruction that should be the focus of any attempt to assess instruction.

AREAS OF CONCERN

All relevant and uncontrollable areas of concern can be classified into two broad categories: process or product. Process areas of concern cause one to focus the appraisal of instruction on the instructional processes— that is, the manner in which the instruction is prepared and delivered. Product areas of concern, on the other hand, cause one to focus the appraisal of instruction on the product or end result of the instruction— that is, the students who received the instruction and the skills they have acquired as a direct result of the instruction. Examples of process and product areas of concern follow:

Process Areas of Concern
1. Instructional Objectives
2. Lesson Plans
3. Instructional Media
4. Assessment and Feedback
5. Student/Teacher Rapport
6. Instructional Facilities

Product Areas of Concern
1. Skills Learned
2. Knowledge Developed
3. Problem Solving Abilities
4. Safety Habits
5. Work Attitudes
6. Employability

Each of these areas of concern is relevant and controllable. The two listings are mutually exclusive. As vocational teachers begin to formulate plans for assessing their instruction, they should first decide whether the focus will be on process or product, and then select specific areas of concern. The third step is to develop the key questions to be answered by the assessment.

KEY QUESTIONS

Key questions are utilized to sharpen or narrow the focus of the assessment to the point where the only data and information obtained in assessing the instruction are those that will be of value in making improvements in the vocational program. In this third step, one or more key questions are formed for each area of concern. Sample questions that might be associated with each of the foregoing process and product areas of concern follow:

Process Areas of Concern

1. Instructional Objectives
    a. Have instructional objectives been prepared for each unit of instruction?
    b. Are the objectives specified in measurable terms?
    c. Are the objectives made known to the students at the start of each lesson?

2. Lesson Plans
   a. Are lesson plans developed for each unit of instruction?
   b. Are the lesson plans prepared in a proper and useful format?
   c. Does the teacher follow the lesson plan in presenting the instruction?

3. Instructional Media
   a. To what extent does the teacher use effective teaching aids?
   b. In what ways are various media used to increase the efficiency or the effectiveness of the instruction?

4. Assessment and Feedback
   a. Are quizzes and examinations based upon the instructional objectives?
   b. Do students receive timely feedback about their performance on quizzes and examinations?
   c. Are the examinations both valid and reliable?
   d. Does the teacher return quizzes and examinations to the students and review their performance on them?

5. Student/Teacher Rapport
   a. Is the teacher always firm and fair in his or her relations with students?
   b. How often is the instructional process disrupted by discipline problems?
   c. How well does the teacher handle discipline problems?
   d. How much respect do students have for the teacher and vice versa?

6. Instructional Facilities
   a. To what degree is the laboratory equipment equivalent to that found in the world of work?
   b. Is a replacement schedule used for all laboratory equipment?
   c. To what degree is the laboratory equipment maintained at a level equivalent to or better than that found in the world of work?
   d. Is all equipment set up in compliance with acceptable safety standards?
   e. Does the amount of laboratory space available per student meet accreditation guidelines?

Product Areas of Concern

1. Skills Learned
   a. To what degree are the skills learned (those that are important for securing employment as a _____)?
   b. How adequately can program completers and leavers perform on the job each of those skills learned in the instructional program?

251

2. Knowledge Developed
   a. Do graduates know those things that are necessary to become successful workers?

3. Problem Solving Skills
   a. Can those who complete the instruction diagnose and solve problems that are common to the trade?

4. Safety Habits
   a. Do program graduates have a higher rate of lost-time accidents than others on the job?
   b. Do program graduates exhibit concern for their safety and the safety of others while on the job?

5. Work Attitudes
   a. Does the work produced show that the student feels a sense of pride in doing a job right?
   b. Do program completers show a high regard for starting and ending the workday on time?
   c. Do graduates work in harmony with their fellow workers and supervisors on the job?
   d. Do the actions of program graduates show a high degree of loyalty to the employer?

6. Employability
   a. What percentage of program graduates and leavers are employed or pursuing advanced instruction in the occupational area in which they received their vocational instruction?
   b. How many graduates and leavers have been dismissed from their initial employment as a result of not being able to (1) perform the necessary job tasks, (2) follow established company personnel policies, or (3) get along with others on the job?

Information Sources

Data and information to provide answers to key questions like the foregoing must be gathered from a variety of sources such as: vocational teachers, current students, parents, dropouts, advisory council members, school administrators, graduates and employers.

When the areas of concern, key questions and information sources have been established, the appraisal can be targeted to provide precisely the data and information needed to point up the strengths and weaknesses in the instruction being assessed. Then and only then would one begin to select the techniques for collecting the data and information needed to assess and to improve the vocational instruction. As with the areas of concern and key questions for the appraisal process, the actual techniques or instruments for appraising vocational instruction are of two types: process centered and product centered.

PROCESS-CENTERED TECHNIQUES

Process-centered techniques are designed to assist in gathering assessment data and information that are important for answering key questions associated with selected process-oriented areas of concern. They vary somewhat in format, depending upon the information sources they are designed to tap.

Student-Oriented Techniques

Considerable research and development has been focused on student evaluation of instruction. It has become clear that students are in a unique position to assess certain aspects of the instruction they receive. When students are approached in the proper manner, they can provide some information and data that otherwise might be unobtainable. Popular approaches currently in use usually employ instruments like rating scales, checklists and questionnaires. Detailed guidelines for developing these instruments have been offered by Wentling and Lawson, who indicate that ". . . the greatest advantage of such instruments may actually be to the instructors in helping them to identify how the learners perceive their teacher's instructional abilities, techniques, and activities" (1975). Brief descriptions and sample items based upon a process-centered area of concern and related key questions will be presented here.

Teacher Ratings Scales. Guilford (1954) classified rating scales into some rather general categories, including graphic, numerical and cumulative point. Remmers (1963) added another category: multiple choice. Sample items for these general classifications follow. Each flows from the area of concern "Instructional Objectives" and its related key questions, which were presented earlier.

Graphic Rating Scale

Instructional objectives are made known to students at the start of each lesson.

Always   Usually   Sometimes   Seldom   Never

Numerical Rating Scale

The objectives for this course are ones that can be measured.

    __1. Strongly agree
    __2. Agree
    __3. Uncertain or don't know
    __4. Disagree
    __5. Strongly disagree

Cumulative Point Scale

The teacher has prepared objectives for each lesson in this course.

    __Yes   __No

These objectives are presented to the class at the start of each lesson.
   __Yes   __No

Multiple Choice Rating Forms

To what degree are the objectives of this class made clear to you?
   __a. I never have problems understanding them.
   __b. Generally they are clear to me.
   __c. Sometimes they are not too clear.
   __d. I have difficulty understanding them.

Checklists. These are listings of behaviors or activities that can be checked by students to provide a description of what they see occurring in class. The following checklist flows from the area of concern "Assessment and Feedback" and its related key questions.

Checklist of Teacher Activities

In this class does your teacher:

	Always	Usually	Never
1. Use lesson objectives as the basis for test questions?	_____	_____	_____
2. Review tests with the class shortly after they are graded?	_____	_____	_____
3. Post or report tests scores shortly after tests are taken?	_____	_____	_____
4. Give tests that focus equally on all the instruction you are being tested over?	_____	_____	_____

Peer-Oriented and Supervisor-Oriented Techniques

The principal process-oriented technique for assessing instruction in education and training programs has been supervisor ratings. Recently, observation and rating of instruction by peers or fellow teachers has become a popular technique as well. Both supervisory and peer-oriented techniques follow essentially the same format. When used in conjunction, they can provide a more balanced and therefore more accurate assessment of the processes associated with the instruction being assessed. Whether supervisory or peer-oriented, the techniques for obtaining data and information for assessing instruction can be classified as employing either direct observation or unobtrusive procedures.

Direct Observation Techniques. Wentling and Lawson (1975) present Odinre's two "effects," which may be operant in procedures for assessing instruction. They rely heavily on direct observation of the teacher's performance in the classroom or laboratory.

The "halo effect" is the tendency for ratings to be too high because of:
  1. Past record—good past work tends to carry over into the present.
  2. Compatibility—those we like, we rate higher.

3. Timing—a good job yesterday is valued higher than a good job last week.
4. Blind spot—I don't see defects that are similar to my own.

The "horn effect" is the tendency for ratings to be too low because of:

1. Perfectionism—our expectations may be too high. Consequently, we are disappointed.
2. Conflicts—an individual may disagree too often.
3. Lack of empathy—the student may be a maverick or nonconformist.
4. Guilt by association—the student has something in common with a known poor performer.
5. Dramatic incident—a recent goof can wipe out a year's work.

These and other factors show the necessity of preparing good instrumentation (checklists, rating scales, and the like) to (1) direct the observer's attention to the specific aspects of the instructional process to be assessed and (2) reduce the degree to which ratings are either inflated or reduced by the various extraneous factors that can creep into the observations made by supervisors or peers.

The types of instruments that might be developed for use by supervisors and peers in appraising vocational instruction are the same as those used by students. The content of the instruments, however, could be quite different.

For example, the following checklist items would be more appropriate for peer and supervisor assessment of instruction than student assessment of instruction. They flow from the area of concern "Lesson Plans" and its related key questions.

Checklist of Teacher Activities

Are lesson plans for the instruction in this course:

	YES	NO
1. Developed for each unit of instruction and filed in the Department Office?	_____	_____
2. Prepared in a proper and useful format?	_____	_____
3. Followed by the teacher when presenting the instruction?	_____	_____

The appropriateness of the items to be included in any checklist for assessing vocational instruction is determined by (1) the key questions to be answered by the assessment and (2) who will be responding to the items. Because students, supervisors and peers, for example, will vary somewhat in their capabilities for responding to certain areas of concern, each checklist should be custom designed.

Unobtrusive Techniques. Unobtrusive techniques for assessing vocational instruction employ procedures to insure that students or teachers are not aware that any assessment is taking place. Direct observation can be an unobtrusive technique if the person being observed is not aware of it.

Unobtrusive assessments focusing on the area of concern "Student/ Teacher Rapport" and its related key questions might include the following techniques:

1. Noting the numbers of students sent to "the office" (for disciplinary action) by the vocational teacher.
2. Noting the numbers of small tools that are broken, lost or otherwise unaccounted for in the laboratory area(s).
3. Noting the frequency with which the course name or number or the name of the teacher appears on restroom walls and other locations around the school.

The data obtained from unobtrusive observations such as these would provide some assistance in assessing student/teacher rapport as an area of concern in the overall assessment of vocational instruction. Likewise, data reflecting the number of accidents that occur in a vocational course could reflect positively or negatively on the safety instruction in that course. For those who wish to use unobtrusive measures to assess vocational instruction, two points are to be kept in mind. Every attempt must be made (1) to gather and record such information in a systematic manner, and (2) to interpret it in light of other evidence when possible.

Teacher Self-Evaluation Techniques

Since improving instruction is the primary reason for assessing vocational instruction, teacher self-evaluation techniques are among the most effective of those presented in this chapter.

Performance Recordings. The simplest form of self-evaluation for vocational teachers is to record and review the recordings of themselves "in action." The nature of the recording process can range from a simple audio tape recording to the more complex color videotape recording.

Reviewing the Recording. The review process can be as simple as sitting down with a cup of coffee and leisurely playing back the recording. The teacher could also complete a checklist or rating scale that focuses on process-related key questions immediately after viewing or listening to the recording. A more precise evaluation can be achieved by incorporating into the review process an objective analysis of the recorded interaction between the students and their teacher.

The most common system for systematically categorizing teacher and student behavior is Flander's interaction analysis (1970). Others who have developed observation systems for use in research and teacher self-evaluation include: Hughes (1959), Smith (1962), and Amidon (1966). Resources that provide detailed discussion for those interested in adopting, modifying or developing a systematic approach to reviewing and recording teacher behavior for self-evaluation purposes include books by Gordon (1966), Amidon and Hough (1967), and Ober, Bently and Miller (1971).

The complexity of the review process for teacher self-evaluation is not directly proportional to its value in assessing and improving vocational instruction. Process-related aspects of instruction can be improved considerably if vocational teachers would do nothing more than listen with a critical ear to a tape recording of themselves teaching a class.

PRODUCT-CENTERED TECHNIQUES

Product-centered techniques are designed to assist in gathering assessment data and information that are important to answering key questions associated with selected product-oriented areas of concern. The product of the instruction to be assessed is the student. The assessment procedures are of two types. Each varies in format depending upon the information source(s) it is designed to probe: teachers, employers or supervisors.

Teacher Appraisal of Critical Competencies

Vocational teachers who conduct competency-based programs (Evans, Holter and Stern, 1976) are in a good position to appraise their instruction by focusing on its products. The competencies to be developed by the instruction are those that are requisite to successful employment. Moreover, each competency has been captured in a measurable student performance objective. Answers to many of the key questions in product areas of concern like "Skills Learned" and "Knowledge Developed" can be obtained by vocational teachers who test their students to determine if they indeed can demonstrate that they have the skills and knowledge necessary to perform successfully on the job. This can be accomplished with traditional testing procedures.

Michaels and Karnes (1950) and Erickson and Wentling (1976) present a variety of techniques for directly assessing student attainment of performance objectives or critical competencies in vocational programs. These range from paper and pencil tests to assess the attainment of key knowledge and understanding to performance tests to assess students' ability in using specific job skills.

In most cases, performance testing is necessary to assess a student's mastery of a given job skill. Very often, indirect methods such as essay, true-false and multiple choice examinations do not provide complete assurance that students can perform specific job skills. Carefully developed and validated performance tests must be used in these instances if vocational teachers are going to assess these critical competencies with a high degree of certainty. One alternative, of course, is to rely on feedback from employers or supervisors of program graduates in appraising vocational instruction.

Employer/Supervisor Appraisal

Perhaps the ultimate measure of the value of vocational instruction is the degree to which those who have received the instruction are employed successfully in an occupation that requires them to use the instruction on the job. If former vocational students are successfully employed and drawing substantially upon the knowledge, understanding, skills and attitudes learned in their vocational program, the instruction in that program should, on the whole, receive high marks.

Data and information obtained from employers or supervisors of former vocational students are product centered and should focus on any or all of the previously listed product-related areas of concern. They can be particularly useful, however, in answering key questions in areas of concern like "Safety Habits," "Work Attitudes" and "Employability."

Wentling and Lawson (1975) offer a variety of techniques for obtaining follow-up data and information from employers and supervisors. The types of instruments that might be developed for use with employers and supervisors are the same as many of those presented earlier in this chapter (e.g., rating scales, questionnaires, checklists). The actual content of the instruments would, of course, differ considerably in focus. For example, the employer/supervisor rating scale might be used to assess vocational instruction for the area of concern "Work Attitudes."

Employer/Supervisor Rating Scale

While working on the job, to what degree does _____:

(name here)

1. Exhibit a sense of pride in his or her work?
   Always   Usually   Sometimes   Seldom   Never
2. Start and end the workday on time?
   Always   Usually   Sometimes   Seldom   Never
3. Work in harmony with other workers?
   Always   Usually   Sometimes   Seldom   Never

If employers and/or supervisors give high ratings on such scales or on other instruments that focus on key questions from product-related areas of concern, then the relevant vocational instruction received by the program graduates working under their supervision should also receive high ratings.

PROCESS-CENTERED OR PRODUCT-CENTERED APPRAISAL—WHICH WAY?

The purpose of this chapter is to review for vocational teachers and administrators some basic considerations that are important in appraising vocational instruction. The importance of developing a focus for the appraisal and the role that areas of concern, related key questions and sources of information can play in developing an adequate focus have been emphasized. This discussion was followed by a presentation of both process- and product-centered techniques for appraising vocational instruction. At this point, you may be asking, "Which way should one go— process or product?"

The answer to this question, of course, depends upon the primary purpose for appraising the instruction. If one is searching for *specific aspects* of the instruction that need to be improved to raise overall levels of efficiency and effectiveness, then process-oriented areas of concern and key questions are the way to go. If one is interested in obtaining an assessment of the *general efficiency and effectiveness* of all the vocational instruction included in a particular program, then product-oriented areas of concern and key questions are the way to go. In practice, however, it is almost imperative that both process- and product-centered assessments be employed.

During the initial years of either a new vocational program or a new vocational instructor, the emphasis very definitely should be upon assessment of instruction that focuses on process-oriented areas of concern (i.e., instructional objectives, lesson plans, student/teacher rapport, and the like) and their associated key questions. The intent here would be to obtain "early on" diagnostic data and information that would point up specific facets of the instruction that need improvement before more students are exposed to it. To rely solely upon process-centered assessment of vocational instruction, however, could lead to instruction that appears to be functional, but doesn't really provide students with salable skills. The presence of good instructional objectives, lesson plans and student/teacher rapport does not guarantee that all program graduates will be employable. For example, a program could include all these instructional components, but fail because outdated technical processes and equipment were used.

In order to assure that this does not happen, a product-centered assessment of instruction must be conducted. Graduates and even program dropouts must be followed up and answers to key questions (such as "What percentage of program graduates are employed in or are pursuing advanced instruction in the occupational area for which they were prepared?") must be found if one is to be assured that the vocational instruction does indeed achieve its intended objectives. It must be demonstrated that program graduates do find and hold jobs for which they were prepared and that they do so with a higher percentage of success than others.

But product-centered assessment of vocational instruction alone is not the answer, either. In general, it provides little data and information that are useful for diagnostic purposes. To know that graduates of an instructional program are not working out to the satisfaction of their employer tells us that something is wrong with the instructional program. But who knows precisely where the instruction is strong and where it is weak? No one will know until an adequate process-centered assessment has been conducted.

Clearly, both process- and product-centered assessments of vocational instruction are needed. The former can provide diagnostic data and information related to specific process-centered areas of concern and key questions. The latter can provide overall data and information that are useful in validating the instruction with regard to its ultimate impact upon program completers. The question, then, is not which way, but how much *diagnostic* versus *validation* data and information are needed to assess adequately this instruction at this stage in its development and use? The answer to this question can be given only by the vocational teacher and then only for that instruction for which he or she is responsible.

REFERENCES

Amidon, E. J., and Hough, J. *Interaction analysis: Theory, research, and application.* Reading, Mass.: Addison-Wesley, 1967.

Amidon, E. J., and Hunter, E. *Improving teaching.* New York: Holt, Rinehart and Winston, 1966.

Erickson, Richard C., and Wentling, Tim L. *Measuring student growth: Techniques and procedures for occupational education.* Boston: Allyn and Bacon, 1976.

Evans, Rupert N., Holter, Arnie, and Stern, Mary. Criteria for determining whether competency should be taught on-the-job or in a formal technical course. *The Journal of Vocational Education Research,* Spring 1976.

Flanders, N. A. *Analyzing teaching behavior.* Reading, Mass.: Addison-Wesley, 1970.

Gordon, Ira J. *Studying the child in school.* New York: John Wiley, 1966.

Guilford, J. P. *Psychometric methods* (2nd ed.). New York: McGraw-Hill, 1954.

Hughes, Marie, et al. *The assessment of the quality of teaching: A research report.* USOE Cooperative Research Project, No. 353. Salt Lake City, Utah: University of Utah, 1959.

Michaels, William J., and Karnes, M. Ray. *Measuring educational achievement.* New York: McGraw-Hill, 1950.

Ober, Richard L., Bently, Ernest L., and Miller, Edith. *Systematic observation of teaching.* Englewood Cliffs, N.J.: Prentice-Hall, 1971.

Remmers, H. H. Rating Methods in research on teaching. In Gage, N. L. (Ed.), *Handbook of research on teaching.* Chicago: Rand McNally, 1963.

Smith, B. O., et al. *A study of the logic of teaching.* USOE Cooperative Research Project, No. 258. Urbana, Ill.: University of Illinois, 1962.

Wentling, Tim L., and Lawson, Tom E. *Evaluating occupational education and training programs.* Boston: Allyn and Bacon, 1975.

YEARBOOK AUTHORS

Camille G. Bell, chairperson and professor of home economics education in the College of Home Economics at Texas Tech University, has conducted statewide workshops for first and second year vocational home economics teachers of the handicapped. She was the investigator for a project funded by the Research Coordinating Unit of Occupational and Technical Education at the Texas Education Agency and developed a handbook for vocational education for the handicapped. She is a past vice president of the American Vocational Association.

Paul V. Braden is senior economist and acting chief, Division of Economic Research, U.S. Department of Commerce. He has also served as principal investigator for the Occupational Training Information System in Oklahoma and as director of management systems for the National Center for Research in Vocational Education.

Herbert H. Bruce, Jr., director of the Curriculum Development Center in Kentucky, has worked in this leadership role since 1969 and has been involved in developing curriculum materials in vocational education since 1960.

Morrell J. Clute, professor in administrative and organizational studies at Wayne State University, has been teaching graduate students, writing and presenting papers on human uniqueness for the past 12 years.

Ira A. Dickerson, assistant professor and acting head of the Department of Agricultural Education in the Division of Vocational Education, University of Georgia, has served as a teacher of vocational agriculture and as director of the Georgia FFA-FHA Camp.

Richard C. Erickson, professor and chairman of the Department of Practical Arts and Vocational-Technical Education, University of Missouri–

Columbia, conducts research and teaches graduate courses that focus on measurement and evaluation in vocational education. He is coauthor of *Measuring Student Growth—Techniques and Procedures for Occupational Education.* He served as a vice president of the American Vocational Association and as editor of the *Journal of Industrial Teacher Education.*

Lucille Frick, assistant professor of home economics education at Purdue University, has conducted workshops on integrating activities of the Future Homemakers of America into the classroom and is a member of the Future Homemakers of America Teacher Educator Task Force.

Thomas Hephner, program coordinator for vocational and technical education at Virginia Commonwealth University, has written several articles and lectured widely on curriculum, competency-based instruction and individualized instruction for distributive education.

Edwin L. Herr is professor and head of the Division of Counseling and Educational Psychology and director of the Addictions Prevention Laboratory at Pennsylvania State University. He has written some 200 articles and 15 books, including *Foundations of Vocational Education* (with Rupert Evans), *Career Guidance Through the Life Span: Systematic Approaches, Vocational Guidance and Human Development* and *The Emerging History of Career Education.* Dr. Herr is currently president of the National Vocational Guidance Association.

Gordon F. Law, editor of the first AVA yearbook in 1971, is university chair of Undergraduate Teacher Education at Rutgers University. He has been employed as a journeyman brick mason, teacher and administrator of area vocational schools.

Helen A. Loftis, professor and chairman of the Department of Home Economics Education at Winthrop College, was director of the five projects she describes in her chapter on an exemplary model for change.

Thomas E. Long, associate professor of vocational education at Pennsylvania State University, has published widely on vocational education and guidance topics and has given special attention to women in nontraditional occupations, record keeping, mathematics requirements in vocational education and vocational development. He formerly served as Research Coordinating Unit director for the Pennsylvania Department of Education.

Sally Mathews has been with the Indiana Curriculum Materials Center since 1975. As media and curriculum coordinator, she selects, collects, develops and produces instructional media, and conducts teacher inservice programs. In addition to her background in health occupations, she has worked in commercial television and radio and in instructional television.

Gary E. Moore, assistant professor of agricultural education at Purdue University, has published numerous articles with direct applications to the classroom setting.

L. H. Newcomb, associate professor of agricultural education at Ohio State University, has published widely in professional journals, is a co-author of the book *The FFA and You,* and is author of the third edition of the *Review and Synthesis of Research in Agricultural Education.*

Krishan K. Paul is project director at the Urban Observatory of Metropolitan Nashville–University Centers. He has extensive experience in developing information systems for vocational education planning, follow-up of graduates and manpower surveys. Dr. Paul worked previously as staff director at the Tennessee Department of Economic and Community Development and as research and development specialist at the National Center for Vocational Education, Ohio State University. Among his recent publications are a book on occupational analysis and a paper on the role of vocational education in the nation's economic development.

L. Allen Phelps, assistant professor of vocational and technical education at the University of Illinois, is director of a project entitled "Leadership Training Institute/Vocational and Special Education," which is funded by the Bureau of Education for the Handicapped. He teaches graduate courses and conducts research related to special needs learners in vocational education.

Ronald L. Redick, associate professor, Curriculum and Instruction, West Virginia University, has conducted workshops, served as curriculum consultant for publications and funded projects, and presented speeches on curriculum and instructional modification in mainstreaming.

Sharon S. Redick, associate professor of home economics education at West Virginia University, blends academic preparation, research and practical experience in teaching handicapped students as a background for publications and consultation on mainstreaming in home economics. She has written three curriculum guides on mainstreaming, conducted workshops, directed funded projects, presented speeches and served as consultant on mainstreaming and independent living skills.

Mildred Reel, executive director, Future Homemakers of America, has been a vocational home economics teacher, state advisor of Future Homemakers of America in Illinois and assistant national advisor for Future Homemakers of America. She has served as executive director of the Future Homemakers of America for the past 16 years.

William B. Richardson, associate professor and chairman of the Agricultural Education Section at Purdue University, has directed research projects and published widely on topics related to the jobs of local teachers.

Carl J. Schaefer, professor of education at Rutgers State University, has been active in curriculum development, program evaluation and occupational competency testing. In 1976 he received the Outstanding Service Award from the American Vocational Association.

Paul Scott, assistant professor of vocational education and director of the Vocational Education Materials Center at the University of Georgia, has conducted curriculum projects that have resulted in ten totally individualized vocational programs. He has also conducted research and made presentations on the topic of individualized instruction in vocational education.

N. Alan Sheppard, associate professor of vocational education at the Virginia Polytechnic Institute and State University, is currently on leave serving as staff director for the Federal Council on Aging at the Department of Health, Education and Welfare. He has had wide experience as a teacher educator, researcher, author and consultant in the area of special needs in vocational education. He has conducted numerous state, regional and national conferences to focus attention on the needs of individuals from special populations. He is the past president and founder of the National Association for the Advancement of Black Americans in Vocational Education.

Daniel E. Skutack, assistant professor, Georgia State University, is involved in the development of the local evaluation and external validation component of the vocational evaluation system now in use in Georgia.

Robert E. Spillman, deputy superintendent for occupational education in Kentucky, has provided leadership in curriculum development since 1968 and has been a member of the board of directors of the Vocational-Technical Education Consortium of States for five years.

Hazel Taylor Spitze is professor and chairperson of home economics education at the University of Illinois at Urbana–Champaign and editor of *Illinois Teacher of Home Economics.* She has been director of workshops in curriculum development and of projects in development of curriculum materials. She is author of *Choosing Techniques for Teaching and Learning* and coauthor with Mildred Griggs of *Choosing Evaluating Techniques.*

Merle E. Strong is director of the Wisconsin Vocational Studies Center and professor of the Departments of Educational Administration and Continuing and Vocational Education. He began as a staff member in the U.S. Office of Education in the Vocational Education Division, where he worked with a national committee of vocational education curriculum materials specialists and an ad hoc intergovernmental committee. Dr. Strong has served on several national committees named to address the use of military curriculum materials. He was the editor of the fifth AVA yearbook.

Yearbook Authors

Lloyd W. Tindall is director of projects for the vocational education of handicapped students at the Wisconsin Vocational Studies Center, University of Wisconsin-Madison. He has conducted state and national projects in the area of vocational education of handicapped students, provided inservice training for teachers, and developed, collected and disseminated vocational materials through a free loan system for Wisconsin educators.

Gail Trapnell, assistant professor of distributive education at Virginia Polytechnic Institute and State University, has given presentations to state, regional and national conferences, conducted workshops in eight states and served as a consultant to various national research projects. She is a past vice president of the American Vocational Association.

Ralph W. Tyler is director emeritus of the Center for Advanced Study for the Behavioral Sciences. He has been actively engaged in assisting and consulting in the development of curricula and instructional programs, including the Eight-Year Study, the Cooperative Study in General Education, the National Curriculum Study of Social Work Education, the Curriculum for the Preparation of Physicians, Nurses, Area Cultural Specialists.

D. Lynette Vaughn, research associate and graduate student at New Mexico State University, formerly taught vocational home economics. She has given various presentations, seminars and workshops on teaching special needs students and coauthored a set of guidelines for vocational teachers of disadvantaged students.

Grant Venn, Callaway Professor of Education, Georgia State University prior to his death in 1979. He was a former U.S. associate commissioner of education for Adult, Vocational, and Manpower in the U.S. Department of Health, Education, and Welfare. He was a former vocational agriculture teacher and served as principal, superintendent of schools, college president and director of field training for the Peace Corps.

Ralph C. Wenrich, professor emeritus of vocational education and practical arts at the University of Michigan, has been interested in leadership in vocational education since 1964, when the University of Michigan Leadership Development Program in Administration of Vocational and Technical Education was first launched. He now takes the view that effective leadership behavior in administrative and supervisory roles is also applicable to the teacher's role. He has published several books and articles on administration in vocational education.

Tim L. Wentling, associate professor and director, Office of Vocational Education Research, University of Illinois at Urbana–Champaign, has conducted research, courses and workshops on student assessment and evaluation. He has also written or coauthored more than 40 articles and two textbooks on the subject.

INDEX

267

Index